Sanctified by the Spirit

Sanctified by the Spirit

*John Owen, Habits of Grace,
and Biblical Counseling*

Colin R. McCulloch

Foreword by Jeremy Pierre

Reformation Heritage Books
Grand Rapids, Michigan

Reformation Heritage Books
3070 29th St. SE
Grand Rapids, MI 49512
616-977-0889
orders@heritagebooks.org
www.heritagebooks.org

Printed in the United States of America
24 25 26 27 28 29/10 9 8 7 6 5 4 3 2 1

Library of Congress Cataloging-in-Publication Data

Names: McCulloch, Colin R., author.
Title: Sanctified by the spirit : John Owen, habits of grace, and biblical
    counseling / Colin R. McCulloch ; foreword by Jeremy Pierre.
Description: Grand Rapids, Michigan : Reformation Heritage Books,
    [2024] | Includes bibliographical references and index.
Identifiers: LCCN 2024003938 (print) | LCCN 2024003939 (ebook) |
    ISBN 9798886861051 (paperback) | ISBN 9798886861068 (epub)
Subjects: LCSH: Counseling—Religious aspects—Christianity. |
    Owen, John, 1616-1683.
Classification: LCC BR115.C69 M34 2024 (print) | LCC BR115.C69
    (ebook) | DDC 259—dc23/eng/20240226
LC record available at https://lccn.loc.gov/2024003938
LC ebook record available at https://lccn.loc.gov/2024003939

For Kari

*Witnessing the Spirit's work of grace in you is one
of the greatest joys and privileges of my life.*

Contents

Foreword

Good historic theology is like a tap on the shoulder. A nice firm tap makes you look up from what you're doing, reminding you that, whatever the given task may be, it's only part of the picture. Whatever problem you're trying to solve and whatever tools you're using to solve it are only part of what you ought to consider. Such a shoulder tap is a friendly reminder to look up and see more broadly.

In this book, Colin McCulloch dares to summon the great John Owen to give us all a nice firm tap, firm enough to make us look up and see that the way we talk about habit may be narrower than we realize.

This is understandable, in a sense. Like any field of study, biblical counseling responds to the concerns of the surrounding culture. The specific cultural concern in this case is how to understand and fix problems in human behavior. And habit is a core phenomenon that is widely observed in our culture, from formal research to common sense observation. In short, our culture understands this basic truth: *People's behaviors and habits somehow show who they are.* Biblical counselors have sought to make sure that their explanation for this truth is based on a biblical understanding of the human heart—namely, that our hearts are corrupted by sin and in need of redemption in Christ.

But exactly *how* that works out in counseling is a living conversation. In this book, Colin traces how Jay Adams began a unique conversation, carried on by David Powlison and others, about how redemption works itself out in human habit. In a word, *sanctification* is at the center of this conversation—how God's character is formed in the human soul.

John Owen wrote a lot about sanctification. A firm tap on the shoulder from a man centuries removed from our time will do us a world of good, not only for our theoretical understanding of sanctification but also for our practice of soul care. Owen was thinking through the same practical questions in his own time as we are now: How does a person's conduct relate to his identity, and how does an embodied soul make in-the-moment choices? Why do people live with distressed and disordered minds, and why do they seem enslaved to unbreakable patterns of behavior? But Owen doesn't simply give us more insight into the mechanics of human behavior.

Rather, Owen has us look up at the broad horizon of the triune God's work in the human soul. The Spirit conveying the benefits of the Son's work, which the Son accomplished in happy reliance on the Father. Grace as a force not merely to forgive but to train—in fact, to *infuse*—a habit of grace that shapes the soul of a believer. It's big and broad and wonderful. And it will make us consider *habit* with a good deal more dimension than we did before.

This book will broaden your wonder at the work of God in the souls of people. And that is the best way to be truly *theological* in our understanding of habit in human behavior and in our practice of caring for souls. Though sanctification is certainly about human activity in the change process, it is first and foremost about God's activity—his *ongoing* activity—in changing the human heart.

I know some shoulder taps can be annoying, if they distract you from what you're doing. But this one won't be. It will actually make you far better at what you're doing by reminding you of the broader and deeper things.

—Jeremy Pierre

Preface

This book represents my life coming full circle. Upon graduating from college, I encountered John Owen's famous work *The Mortification of Sin*, which had a life-changing effect on me. I never could have imagined that, years later, I would publish a work largely focused on John Owen.

I could not have completed this book without the help of many brothers and sisters. My doctoral supervisor, Jeremy Pierre, is the primary reason I ended up choosing the field of study for the research that produced this work, and his thinking has positively influenced me in more ways than I'm sure I even realize. Michael Haykin and Kyle Claunch sat on my dissertation committee and made this work stronger through their helpful comments and critiques.

The members of Farmdale Baptist Church consistently encouraged me and prayed for me throughout my studies, and my fellow elders graciously allowed me time to study and write. Will McCartney showed me how to faithfully manage the demands of caring for a family, pastoring a church, and writing a dissertation. Drew Sparks was a faithful friend in the trenches of doctoral work who spurred me on in my research and challenged me intellectually, even as he worked on his own dissertation.

My parents, Bob and Ruth Ann McCulloch, raised me in Christ and exposed me to the means of grace, which is why I am who I am today. They also generously supported my education and calling. My in-laws, Tim and Sharon Beougher, encouraged me, offered babysitting, and allowed my family to live with them at least twice over the course of my work on this project.

My children—Andrew, Emma, James, and Samuel—provided the laughter I needed to not take myself too seriously. May God use the truth that He has imparted to me through this study of John Owen to shape them into faithful followers of Christ. My wife, Kari, is every bit as worthy as I am of whatever honor comes from the completion of this work, as I could not have done it without her. Her continual interest, support, encouragement, and feedback kept me going. Walking together with her on the road of sanctification is one of the greatest privileges of my life.

Most of all I thank God, who, in His infinite wisdom, has taken a dull, undeserving man like me and called me to teach His truth for His glory. I look forward to the day when He will complete the work that He has begun in me, the day when I will go to enjoy His presence forever.

—Colin R. McCulloch

Introduction

In 1970, Jay Adams (1929–2020) lit the spark that ignited a decades-long debate among Christians over the relationship between Christianity and secular psychologies and psychotherapies.[1] In his first book, *Competent to Counsel*,[2] he challenged Bible-believing Christians to critically engage with the largely secular understanding of the human person and of human change that had come to pervade the church throughout the nineteenth century and into the mid-twentieth century.[3] Adams became the driving force behind a growing movement

---

1. By "psychologies" and "psychotherapies" I refer to two different aspects of understanding human personhood. Specifically, psychologies are descriptive and theoretical assertions regarding the nature and function of human beings, and psychotherapies are proposed methods for bringing about human change. A psychotherapy is always based upon some underlying psychology. As David Powlison has explained, Christianity is itself a psychology because the Bible provides a comprehensive and coherent understanding of human nature and functioning, and Christian ministry is itself a psychotherapy because the Bible provides a clear methodology by which to bring about human change, one that is based upon its own assertions regarding human nature. Thus, the biblical counseling movement has resulted from a collision between competing psychologies and psychotherapies. See David Powlison, "A Biblical Counseling View," in *Psychology & Christianity: Five Views*, ed. Eric L. Johnson, 2nd ed. (Downers Grove, Ill.: IVP Academic, 2010), 245–73.

2. Jay E. Adams, *Competent to Counsel: Introduction to Nouthetic Counseling* (Grand Rapids: Zondervan, 1970).

3. E. Brooks Holifield traces pastoral care in America from the colonial period to the mid-1960s and notes the role of Protestant pastoral care in the creation of America's "therapeutic culture." He argues that "changing attitudes toward the 'self' in American religion" are central to this development. Summarizing his work, he writes, "The story proceeds from an ideal of self-denial to one of self-love, from self-love to self-culture, from self-culture to self-mastery, from self-mastery to self-realization within a trustworthy culture, and finally to a later form of self-realization counterposed against cultural mores and cultural institutions." Holifield's summary represents well the prevailing cultural context

that sought to bring the Bible back to counseling and counseling back to the church, a movement that became known as biblical counseling.

Adams is widely acknowledged as the founding father of the biblical counseling movement—yet, even among those who appreciate his foundational work, many have been critical of certain aspects of his theology and methodology. Perhaps the most fundamental aspect of Adams's work with which his critics have engaged is his understanding of motivation and behavior.[4] Behavior refers to *what* people do, while motivation refers to *why* they do it—but the specifics of why people do what they do were of little concern to Adams. Knowing that they are sinners was enough to explain the motivation behind their behavior. Rather than emphasizing the need to discern one's motivation, Adams emphasized the need to observe one's behavior.[5] He read the "put off, put on" language of the New Testament as a two-factor process of dehabituation and rehabituation.[6] The task of the counselor is to help the counselee to put off sinful habits and to put on righteous habits.

In response to this, the generation of biblical counselors that followed Adams[7] argued that he capitulated to secular psychotherapies

---

against which Adams reacted in his work. See E. Brooks Holifield, *A History of Pastoral Care in America: From Salvation to Self-Realization* (Nashville: Abingdon Press, 1983), 12.

4. Heath Lambert notes that the "issue of motivation has received more attention than any other in biblical counseling theory." See *The Biblical Counseling Movement after Adams* (Wheaton, Ill.: Crossway, 2012), 67.

5. Adams famously wrote, "Usual counseling methods recommend frequent long excursions back into the intricacies of the whys and wherefores of behavior. Instead, nouthetic counseling is largely committed to a discussion of the what. All the why that a counselee needs to know can clearly be demonstrated in the what. *What* was done? *What* must be done to rectify it? *What* should future responses be? In nouthetic counseling the stress falls upon the 'what' rather than the 'why' because the 'why' is already known before counseling begins. The reason why people get into trouble in their relationships to God and others is because of their sinful natures. Men are born sinners." See Adams, *Competent to Counsel*, 48, italics original.

6. Jay E. Adams, *The Christian Counselor's Manual: The Practice of Nouthetic Counseling* (Grand Rapids: Zondervan, 1973), 176–90.

7. Heath Lambert has helpfully distinguished between two generations of biblical counselors. The "first generation" refers to Jay Adams and those who followed his approach to counseling. The "second generation" refers to David Powlison and those who followed his approach. Although biblical counselors are certainly not a monolithic group, it is safe

by letting behaviorism creep into his understanding of sanctification. They suggested that Adams failed to recognize the importance of the motivations of the heart in sanctification and thereby missed one of the central scriptural emphases regarding human nature and functioning.[8] Adams believed that only God can know the heart of a person—thus, he focused only on what can be observed about the person from the outside.[9] Offering what he described as an update to Adams's view, however, David Powlison (1949–2019) argued that "We depart from the Bible if we ignore motives and drift towards an externalistic view of man."[10] Powlison believed that the biblical counseling movement needed to emphasize internal motivation in order to approach a more thoroughly biblical understanding of human change. Although Powlison described Adams's view as a "first approximation of a biblical view" with a "wealth of detail to fill in," the new emphasis on internal motivation did more than simply advance Adams's work.[11] Two divergent views of sanctification arose within the movement, each with its own distinct methodological target in the task of counseling. The first view, represented by Adams, targeted observable, habituated behaviors in seeking to bring about change. In contrast, the second view, represented by Powlison and the large majority of biblical counselors who are still active today, targeted the motivations of the heart.

---

to say that the modern biblical counseling movement is most closely associated with the thought of the second generation. In this work, I will assume Lambert's distinctions by referring to Adams and his associates as the first generation and to those who came after Adams, such as Powlison and those whom he influenced, as the second generation. See Lambert, *The Biblical Counseling Movement after Adams*, 47.

8. See Edward Welch, "How Theology Shapes Ministry: Jay Adams' View of the Flesh and an Alternative," *Journal of Biblical Counseling* 20, no. 3 (Spring 2002): 16–25; George M. Schwab, "Critique of 'Habituation' as a Biblical Model of Change," *Journal of Biblical Counseling* 21, no. 2 (Winter 2003): 67–83.

9. Jay Adams, "The Heart of the Matter," *Institute for Nouthetic Studies* (blog), May 7, 2012, https://nouthetic.org/the-heart-of-the-matter/; Jay Adams, "Heart Idols?," *Institute for Nouthetic Studies* (blog), August 6, 2014, https://nouthetic.org/heart-idols/. See also J. Cameron Fraser, *Developments in Biblical Counseling* (Grand Rapids: Reformation Heritage Books, 2015), 112.

10. David Powlison, "Crucial Issues in Contemporary Biblical Counseling," *Journal of Biblical Counseling* 9, no. 3 (1988): 56.

11. Powlison, "Crucial Issues in Contemporary Biblical Counseling," 57.

In one of the most significant critiques of Adams from the second generation of biblical counselors, Edward Welch explains that one's counseling methodology is grounded in the distinctives of one's theology. In fact, as Welch notes, one of the fundamental aims of biblical counseling is "to make an explicit connection between theology and practice."[12] The first and second generations of biblical counselors diverge in their approaches to counseling not merely because of differences in their personalities or preferences. Rather, their divergence arises from the different theological conclusions that each stream draws from Scripture. Indeed, the divergent emphases on habituation and heart motivation emerge from two distinct models of sanctification, and, although the two share a number of features, the differences are great enough to cause significant variation in each generation's approach to helping people change.

In recent years, multiple authors have noted the need to reassess these divergent streams and determine how the emphases of each should be appropriated in advancing the biblical counseling movement.[13] I suggest that these streams should not be assessed simply to determine how they can be synthesized into one framework that incorporates the best aspects of both. Such work could produce helpful results—however, I submit that the most fruitful approach is to assess these divergent models of sanctification in light of the Reformed tradition out of which each has arisen.[14] Specifically, we

---

12. Welch, "How Theology Shapes Ministry," 16.

13. See Lambert, *The Biblical Counseling Movement after Adams*; Fraser, *Developments in Biblical Counseling*; Greg E. Gifford, "The Role of Habits in Spiritual Maturity from the Perspective of the English Puritans" (PhD diss., Southwestern Baptist Theological Seminary, 2018); Greg E. Gifford, "Jay Adams' Teaching of Habituation: Critiqued, Revisited, and Supported," in *Whole Counsel: The Public and Private Ministries of the Word: Essays in Honor of Jay E. Adams*, ed. Donn R. Arms and Dave Swavely (Memphis: Institute for Nouthetic Studies, 2020), 129–46; Brian A. Mesimer, "Habits and the Heart: Reclaiming Habituation's Place in Biblical Counseling" (MA thesis, Reformed Theological Seminary, 2018); Brian A. Mesimer, "Rehabilitating Habituation," *Journal of Biblical Counseling* 34, no. 2 (2020): 53–79.

14. The movement has been associated with Reformed institutions—particularly Westminster Theological Seminary—since its inception, and both Adams and Powlison publicly stated the connection between the biblical counseling movement and the Reformed tradition. See Jay E. Adams, "Biblical Counseling and Practical Calvinism," in

can best assess these two models against Puritanism, the stream of the Reformed tradition that is most noted for its ability to integrate deep theological reflection and practical Christian piety.[15]

Although numerous works by Puritan authors could be consulted in order to assess these divergent models of sanctification, I limit my focus in this book to the writings of John Owen (1616–1683). His works provide a rich collection of resources for the care of souls. However, Owen's doctrine of sanctification is particularly relevant because he thoroughly explained the internal work of the Holy Spirit in making believers holy, as well as how this work manifests both in the internal functions of the heart and in external acts of righteousness. Thus, Owen emphasized the importance of internal motivation and external behavior, but he grounded both in the work of the Spirit. He explained the Spirit's internal operations in sanctification as an infusion and increase of habitual grace, and it is through this concept that Owen's work offers its greatest correction to the doctrine of sanctification within the modern biblical counseling movement.

The Practical Calvinist: An Introduction to the Presbyterian and Reformed Heritage, ed. Peter A. Lillback (Fearn, Scotland: Christian Focus, 2002), 484–94; David Powlison, "Calvinism and Contemporary Christian Counseling," in *The Practical Calvinist: An Introduction to the Presbyterian and Reformed Heritage*, ed. Peter A. Lillback (Fearn, Scotland: Christian Focus, 2002), 495–503. Another institution central to the biblical counseling movement has been The Master's University and Seminary (formerly The Master's College). Pastor John MacArthur and his colleagues published *Introduction to Biblical Counseling: A Basic Guide to the Principles and Practice of Counseling* (Dallas: Word Books, 1994)—as well as the updated *Counseling: How to Counsel Biblically* (Nashville: Thomas Nelson, 2005)—in an effort to promote the principles of biblical counseling. Although MacArthur and The Master's University and Seminary do not hold to the wider tenets of the Reformed faith, they do hold to its Calvinistic soteriology, which is central to a Reformed understanding of sanctification.

15. Multiple works from within the biblical counseling movement have noted the rich resources provided by the Puritans for personal ministry. See Timothy Keller, "Puritan Resources for Biblical Counseling," *Journal of Pastoral Practice* 9, no. 3 (1988): 11–44; Ken L. Sarles, "The English Puritans: A Historical Paradigm of Biblical Counseling," in *Introduction to Biblical Counseling: A Basic Guide to the Principles and Practice of Counseling*, ed. John MacArthur (Dallas: Word Books, 1994), 23–37; Mark A. Deckard, *Helpful Truth in Past Places: The Puritan Practice of Biblical Counseling* (Fearn, Scotland: Mentor, 2010); Lambert, *The Biblical Counseling Movement after Adams*, 25–26; Fraser, *Developments in Biblical Counseling*, 106–7.

In this work I will argue that John Owen's conception of Spirit-infused habitual grace appropriately corrects and develops two divergent frameworks for understanding sanctification within the biblical counseling movement. Owen portrayed Spirit-infused habitual grace as the internal, metaphysical work whereby God sanctifies His people and conforms them to the image of Christ.[16] He demonstrated that the Holy Spirit produces sanctification by 1) infusing a habit—or principle—of grace in the soul of believers at regeneration, which inclines them away from sin and toward righteousness; 2) increasing the operations of that habit of grace upon the faculties of the soul; and 3) bringing forth the effects of that habit of grace through the actual fruit of righteousness borne by believers.[17]

Owen's understanding of sanctification corrects and reconciles two divergent conceptions of sanctification that have developed among the first and second generations of biblical counselors, respectively. The first, represented by Jay Adams and his followers, regards habituation as primary in bringing about human change, while the

---

16. For a helpful discussion of the importance of the concept of infused habits for a metaphysical understanding of regeneration and sanctification, see J. V. Fesko, "Aquinas's Doctrine of Justification and Infused Habits in Reformed Soteriology," in *Aquinas among the Protestants*, ed. Manfred Svensson and David VanDrunen (Hoboken, N.J.: Wiley-Blackwell, 2017), 249–65. Aaron Prelock has also provided a thorough treatment of Owen's understanding of habit in relation to the thought of Thomas Aquinas and the Reformed Scholastics in "Disposition: An Approachable Ontology," *New Blackfriars* 103, no. 1108 (November 2022): 761–78. See also his relation of Owen's understanding of habit to pastoral theology in "The Pastoral Disposition in the Thought of John Owen" (PhD diss., VID Specialized University, 2020).

17. Because infused grace is not a common concept in modern evangelical discourse, it is necessary to briefly explain how the word "infusion" here differs from its use in Roman Catholic theology. Roman Catholics locate infused grace within the doctrine of justification. In doing this, they conflate justification and sanctification and, thus, hold to a doctrine of justification that depends in part on the work of believers. In contrast, Reformed Protestants distinguished infusion from imputation. Justification occurs by the imputation of Christ's righteousness to believers. They are reckoned righteous by virtue of a righteousness that is not their own. Sanctification occurs by the infusion of righteousness—or grace—and, although such righteousness is wholly wrought in us by a work of the Holy Spirit, it is a righteousness that can be called our own. Thus, infusion, rightly located, is a thoroughly Reformed Protestant concept. I will treat this topic more fully in chapter 5 of this work.

second, represented by David Powlison and his followers, regards heart motivation as primary.

I will argue that, although both models contain certain appropriate emphases, both need correction or development and that Owen's theology of sanctification provides a wholistic framework that both affirms the models' strengths and corrects their weaknesses. My aim, therefore, is twofold. First, I seek to show that, while Jay Adams was right to emphasize the importance of habituation in sanctification, his explanation of habituation fell far short. Whereas Adams spoke of habituation in a strictly behavioral sense, Owen's explanation of habituation encompassed the whole salvific process (i.e., regeneration, sanctification, and glorification) and the whole of human functioning (i.e., internal heart motivation and outward action). Second, I will show that, although the second generation of biblical counselors have rightly emphasized the importance of heart motivation in human functioning, the movement has not adequately articulated the internal, metaphysical operations of the Spirit by which heart motivations are sanctified. As Owen demonstrated, believers are sanctified through the Holy Spirit's habitual infusion and increase of grace in their souls.

Chapters 1 and 2 of this work offer an overview of the divergent models of sanctification that have developed within the biblical counseling movement. Chapter 1 provides a detailed description of Adams's habituational model of sanctification, highlighting his foundational understanding of "the flesh" and tracing his exegesis of key texts that he used to support his argument. Chapter 2 examines Powlison's shift away from habituation and toward heart motivation. It discusses Edward Welch's and George M. Schwab's substantial critiques of Adams, as well as the subsequent lack of engagement with Adams as the movement has continued to develop its understanding of heart motivation. These two chapters lay the groundwork for introducing Owen's conception of Spirit-infused habitual grace as a means of assessing and correcting these two divergent models.

Owen's doctrine of sanctification was robust—to understand it, we must see how he grounded it in other major doctrines. Thus, chapters 3, 4, and 5 each focus on an aspect of Owen's overall theology that helps us understand his doctrine of sanctification. Chapter 3 explains Owen's understanding of trinitarian agency. Owen held to a classical understanding of trinitarian inseparable operations and appropriation of divine works. This aspect of his theology is important for the current study because it is within this framework that Owen asserted his view that the Holy Spirit is the "immediate operator of all divine works that outwardly are of God."[18] Thus, one cannot grasp Owen's understanding of sanctification apart from his conception of how the Spirit works in relation to the Father and the Son.

Chapter 4 serves as a bridge between my discussion of Owen's understanding of trinitarian agency and his understanding of Spirit-infused habits in sanctification. This chapter discusses Owen's Christology with regard to the Spirit's work upon the human nature of Christ. Owen understood that redemption requires that Christ have a human nature that is like ours in every way, yet without sin. Thus, although Christ's human nature was not marred by sin like ours, the Spirit worked upon his human nature in the same manner as ours, yet to an infinitely greater degree. Owen explained, "There is, moreover, required hereunto supernatural endowments of grace, superadded unto the natural faculties of our souls. If we live unto God, there must be a principle of spiritual life in us, as well [as] of the natural. This was the image of God in Adam, and was wrought in Christ by the Holy Spirit."[19] He later continued, after a long discussion of the work of the Spirit upon the human nature of Christ:

> And these are some of the principal instances of the operation of the Holy Spirit on the human nature of the Head of the church. The whole of them all, I confess, is a work that we can look little into; only what is plainly revealed we desire to receive and embrace, considering that if we are his, we are predestinated to be made conformable in all things unto him, and that by the powerful effectual operation of that Spirit which thus wrought all things in him, to the glory of God.[20]

---

18. John Owen, *A Discourse Concerning the Holy Spirit*, in *The Works of John Owen*, ed. William H. Goold (Edinburgh: Banner of Truth, 1967), 3:57.

19. Owen, *A Discourse Concerning the Holy Spirit*, in *Works*, 3:168–69.

20. Owen, *A Discourse Concerning the Holy Spirit*, in *Works*, 3:183.

Christ serves as the paradigmatic example of true sanctification—thus, if we are to understand the Spirit's work upon our own human nature, we must understand the Spirit's work upon His human nature.

After these chapters have established Owen's understanding of trinitarian agency and of Christ as the paradigmatic example of true sanctification, chapter 5 addresses how the Spirit works through the infusion and increase of habitual grace in the sanctification of believers. In this chapter I discuss nature and grace in Owen's anthropology, distinguish Owen's understanding of infusion from that of Roman Catholicism, and explain how the Spirit works through a person's dutiful use of means to infuse and increase grace in the soul such that the Spirit sanctifies and reorders the soul's faculties.

Chapters 6 and 7 propose specific theological and methodological developments and corrections for modern biblical counseling based upon my discussion of Owen's theology of sanctification. My hope is that this work will help to carry the biblical counseling movement forward with a pneumatologically grounded, historically informed theology of sanctification that incorporates the best of what the movement has offered thus far while also providing several important corrections. The work concludes with a summary of my argument and proposed areas for future study.

Chapter 1

The Habituational Model
of Sanctification

Jay Adams described sanctification as a process of putting off old habits and putting on new ones. This framework arose out of his understanding both of the Spirit's work in regeneration and sanctification and of the nature of man. Thus, in describing Adams's model of sanctification, I will begin with an overview of his pneumatology. I will then move to an overview of his anthropology, focusing specifically on his conception of "the flesh" in Paul's letters. I will conclude by explaining how his doctrine of sanctification relates to these two theological loci.

Adams's Pneumatology

Though Adams did not provide a robust pneumatology in his works, he often wrote about the work of the Spirit in counseling. Two themes regarding the Spirit and counseling come to the foreground when examining his work: the necessity of the Spirit's work and the Spirit's work through means.

The Spirit's Work Is Necessary

In his first—and, arguably, most important—published work, *Competent to Counsel*, Adams titled his second chapter "The Holy Spirit and Counseling."[1] He began the chapter with a clear statement: "Counseling is the work of the Holy Spirit."[2] His second major work, *The Christian Counselor's Manual*, begins similarly, with Adams arguing that the Holy Spirit is the principal person in the task of

---

1. Adams, *Competent to Counsel*, 20–25.
2. Adams, *Competent to Counsel*, 20.

counseling. Adams's confidence in the necessity of the Spirit's work in sanctification cannot be doubted: "The holiness of God's people that results from their sanctification by the Holy Spirit must be attributed entirely to Him as He works through His Word."[3]

Thus, in two of his most influential works, the founder of the biblical counseling movement set the task of counseling squarely within the realm of the work of the Holy Spirit. He argued that the goal of counseling is growth in holiness—namely, growth in those traits that only the Holy Spirit can supply. To deny the necessity of the Holy Spirit's work is to affirm the "innate goodness" and "autonomy" of man and, thus, to undercut the need for grace and the atoning work of Christ.[4] Without dependence upon the power of the Spirit, the task of counseling becomes a legalistic effort to achieve righteousness by our own works, which will only end in despair.[5]

Adams believed that both regeneration and sanctification are works of the Spirit. Regeneration occurs when "unregenerate persons are given life to believe by the Holy Spirit" and undergo an "instantaneous, unmerited change...of the whole inner life, disposing a sinner toward God for the first time in his life." Sanctification "consists of a gradual process...by which the Spirit enables the believer both to put off sinful patterns of life and replace them with holy ones."[6] Counseling, according to Adams, is an "application of the means of sanctification," and its prerequisite is "the Holy Spirit's presence in the life of the regenerate person."[7]

Adams believed so strongly in the necessity of the Spirit's regenerating and sanctifying work for the task of counseling that he refused to call a biblical counselor's work with an unbeliever "counseling." He explained,

---

3. Adams, *The Christian Counselor's Manual*, 6.

4. Adams, *Competent to Counsel*, 20.

5. Adams, *Competent to Counsel*, 20–21.

6. Jay E. Adams, *A Theology of Christian Counseling: More than Redemption* (Grand Rapids: Zondervan, 1979), 36.

7. Adams, *Competent to Counsel*, 73.

> You can't counsel an unbeliever if you mean by counseling what
> the Bible means by counseling—changing his heart; changing him
> at a level of depth. The man won't listen, because his heart is not
> oriented toward the Book, so he can't hear what it has to say, and
> he doesn't have the power to obey the Book, even if he wanted to.[8]

According to Adams, although unbelievers cannot be counseled, they can be "precounseled." Adams defined precounseling as "problem-oriented evangelism," whereby a counselor works to remove obstacles to the presentation of the gospel and hold out the hope of the gospel to those who are struggling.[9] Thus, Adams was so determined to ground the task of counseling in the Spirit's work that he would not even allow the word "counseling" to be used unless it was applied to believers who were indwelt by that Spirit.[10]

The Spirit Works through Means

Adams believed that the Holy Spirit works through the ordinary means of grace, such as "the ministry of the Word, the sacraments, prayer and the fellowship of believers."[11] The ministry of the Word through the task of counseling was the primary focus of Adams's work, the foundation of it all.[12] The Word of God reveals who we are to become in Christ, and the Spirit, working through the ministry of the Word, enables us to be thus transformed. Adams explained, "The Word has power, because the Spirit wrote and empowers it."[13] The relationship between the Spirit and the Word is such that "counseling

---

8. Adams, *A Theology of Christian Counseling*, 320.

9. Adams, *A Theology of Christian Counseling*, 320–22.

10. Today, biblical counselors have been more comfortable discussing biblical counseling as it pertains to unbelievers. See, for example, Robert D. Jones, "Biblical Counseling: An Opportunity for Problem-Based Evangelism," *Journal of Biblical Counseling* 31, no. 1 (2017): 75–92. The differences in approach are largely semantic—both those who are willing to use the term "counseling" and those who are not still believe that the Spirit's prior regenerating work is necessary in order for true, biblical change to come about.

11. Adams, *Competent to Counsel*, 21.

12. Jay Adams, "Change Them…Into What?," *Journal of Biblical Counseling* 13, no. 2 (Winter 1995): 17.

13. Adams, *A Theology of Christian Counseling*, 35.

without the Scriptures can only be expected to be counseling without the Holy Spirit."[14]

Adams was so confident in God's power to work by His Spirit through His Word in the lives of believers that he gave his book *A Theology of Christian Counseling* the subtitle *More than Redemption*. According to Adams, the salvation planned by the Father, accomplished by the Son, and applied by the Spirit through the means of the Word is to "elevate man *above* the state in which he was created."[15] Thus, for Adams, the Spirit's work through the Word is so powerful that it not only restores people to their natural condition but raises them above it, such that a Christian counselor "does not believe, *strictly* speaking, in a mere renewal, or restoration or redemption (of what was lost); biblically, he believes in *more* than redemption."[16] Christian counselors maintain a "super-redemptive stance" toward their Christian counselees due to their confidence in the abundantly gracious work of God in Christ that is applied by the Spirit.[17] Thus, Adams believed that the Spirit's work through the Word is the foundation of all truly Christian counseling, a foundation which promises heavenly results.[18]

---

14. Adams, *Competent to Counsel*, 24.

15. Adams, *A Theology of Christian Counseling*, 175 (italics original); cf. 177–78.

16. Adams, *A Theology of Christian Counseling*, 180 (italics original).

17. Adams, *A Theology of Christian Counseling*, 183.

18. Adams's conception of the relationship between nature and grace is somewhat out of step with the Reformed tradition, in that the Reformed often speak of grace as restoring nature rather than replacing or elevating nature. Owen often spoke of grace as "restoring," "repairing," and "renewing" that in our nature which was lost due to the fall. See Owen, *A Discourse Concerning the Holy Spirit*, in *Works*, 3:9, 102, 212, 244, 282, 285–86, 382, 418, 446, 455, 469, 580, 629. Such references to the relationship between nature and grace were also prevalent among the Reformed Orthodox, Owen's fellow Puritans, and later Reformed theologians. See, for example, Franciscus Junius, *The Mosaic Polity*, ed. Andrew M. McGinnis, trans. Todd M. Rester, Sources in Early Modern Economics, Ethics, and Law (Grand Rapids: CLP Academic, 2015), 38; Richard Sibbes, *The Bruised Reed and Smoking Flax* (Edinburgh: Maclaren and Macniven, 1878), 117; Herman Bavinck, *Reformed Dogmatics*, ed. John Bolt, trans. John Vriend (Grand Rapids: Baker Academic, 2006), 3:577; Herman Bavinck, *Essays on Religion, Science, and Society*, ed. John Bolt, trans. Harry Boonstra and Gerrit Sheeres (Grand Rapids: Baker Academic, 2008), 141; cf. Jan Veenhof, *Nature and Grace in Herman Bavinck*, trans. Albert M. Wolters (Sioux Center, Iowa: Dordt College Press, 2006); Dane C. Ortlund, "'Created Over a Second Time' or 'Grace Restoring Nature'?

Adams's Anthropology

The fundamental components of Adams's anthropology are his assertion of the centrality of the heart, his novel conception of the meaning of the term "flesh" (σαρξ) in Paul's writings, and his conception of human nature (φυσις).

The Heart

Although Adams focused methodologically on outward behavior, he believed that heart transformation was fundamental in order for true change to occur. He contrasted his view with B. F. Skinner's behaviorism, writing,

> This view is also concerned with change at a level of depth. It is not concerned about changing people on the surface alone; man and his actions and his attitudes must be changed at the inner core of his being so that his set of values and the springs of his motivation are affected. The Bible calls this inner power man's heart. It is from the heart that people's problems stem. This means that a new power from the outside is necessary for him to realize the goal of Christian counseling—to become more like Jesus Christ. In other words, Christian conversion is an essential element in this kind of counseling. If he is not a Christian, the counselee's relationship to God must be changed. He must come to the place where he recognizes that the Christian message about the cross is real. This old message from the Bible is that Christ died on the cross in the place of guilty sinners in order to transform their lives, beginning at the very heart of their being and then leading to needed outward transformation. Christian counseling has depth because it goes to the heart of human difficulty.[19]

Edwards and Bavinck on the Heart of Christian Salvation," *The Bavinck Review* 3 (2012): 9–29; John Bolt, "Herman Bavinck on Natural Law and Two Kingdoms: Some Further Reflections," *The Bavinck Review* 4 (2013): 64–93; Paul Helm, "Nature and Grace," in *Aquinas among the Protestants*, ed. Manfred Svensson and David VanDrunen (Hoboken, N.J.: Wiley-Blackwell, 2017), 229–47; Noah J. Weaver, "Grace Restores Nature: The Relationship of Nature and Grace in Christian Theology," *Puritan Reformed Journal* 9, no. 1 (January 2017): 65–83; Gregory W. Parker, "Reformation or Revolution? Herman Bavinck and Henri de Lubac on Nature and Grace," *Perichoresis* 15, no. 3 (October 2017): 81–95. See also my discussion of Owen's understanding of the relationship between nature and grace in chapter 5.

19. Adams, "Change Them…Into What?," 17.

For Adams, human nature could not be truly understood apart from the scriptural notion of the heart.[20] The heart encompasses the entirety of one's inner life and is the location of all rational human functioning. It is the "planning and motivation center" of one's being—the place where one "thinks with himself, reasons with himself, accuses and excuses himself."[21] It is most directly set against the visible, outer person.[22]

The hearts of all people are corrupted in their entirety due to the fall, resulting in a sickness of the soul that people cannot heal by their own power, such that everyone needs a new heart.[23] The heart, as the source of all sin, needs transformation:

> The only person who can really operate at a level of *depth* is the person who knows how to get to the *heart* of a man's problem. That's because the heart *is* the man's problem.... The murders, the adulteries, the evil thoughts, the sexual sins, the thefts, the false testimonies, the blasphemies (and all the rest) can be changed only in some superficial way, unless the heart out of which they come and by which they are generated is transformed by the Spirit of God using His Word.[24]

Despite the importance of the heart in human functioning, Adams asserted that one person cannot know another person's heart. Citing passages such as 2 Chronicles 6:30 and Jeremiah 17:9–10, he explained that our hearts are deceitful and that God is the only true Knower of hearts.[25] For this reason, Adams argued that the counselor's primary focus should not be to discern the motivations of the heart but rather to address the counselee's outward behavior. Discussing motivation in relation to counseling, he wrote,

> Motives are tricky. It is always wrong to make judgments about another's motives. The counselor, unlike God, can look only on

---

20. Adams, *A Theology of Christian Counseling*, 113.

21. Adams, *A Theology of Christian Counseling*, 312.

22. Adams, *A Theology of Christian Counseling*, 114–15, 311–12.

23. Adams, *A Theology of Christian Counseling*, 141–42.

24. Adams, *A Theology of Christian Counseling*, 310 (italics original).

25. Adams, *The Christian Counselor's Manual*, 21n2; Jay Adams, "Counseling and the Heart," *Institute for Nouthetic Studies* (blog), June 17, 2011, https://nouthetic.org/counseling -and-the-heart/; Adams, "The Heart of the Matter"; Adams, "Heart Idols?."

the outward appearance. But…he can discuss the counselee's motivational comments with him. He should listen carefully for such comments. Apart from motivation-revealing comments, he must confine his counsel to the counselee's outward behavior.

Adams explained further that, although counselors can ask their counselees about their motives, they should not necessarily trust the answers that they receive. "Since a man's heart is deceitful, the counselor cannot always be sure of the answers that he receives. How can he be certain that he, along with others involved, is not being 'used' or 'manipulated' to achieve some purpose high on the list of the counselee's hidden agenda? Well, the answer to that is simple: he can't!"[26]

Adams maintained that motivation was an important aspect of human functioning and change.[27] He even argued that counselors should inquire into the motivations of their counselees. However, in doing so, they should always remember that they are ultimately incapable of judging motives.[28] Having examined Adams's understanding of the heart, I now turn to his conception of "the flesh"—a concept that is closely related to his understanding of the heart yet somewhat difficult to reconcile with it.

The Flesh

Adams's conception of "the flesh" (σαρξ) in Paul's letters significantly influenced his understanding of sanctification. He argued that Paul

---

26. Jay E. Adams, *Lectures on Counseling* (Grand Rapids: Baker, 1978), 118; cf. 220. Although Adams instructed fellow counselors not to trust fully their counselees' statements about motives, he went on to argue after this quote that counselors should not treat their counselees with suspicion. Rather, they should carefully weigh their counselees' statements about motives against the counselees' outward behavior to discern if the two agree. This further supports Adams's claims that counselors should focus primarily on what can be observed outwardly about counselees' behavior because this is the only aspect of counselees' functioning of which they have direct knowledge.

27. Jay E. Adams, "What Alternative?," in *The Biblical Counseling Movement after Adams*, 168.

28. Adams, *Lectures on Counseling*, 220. It is important to note that Adams included a chapter on motivation in *The Christian Counselor's Manual*. However, this chapter was not focused on understanding the motivations of the counselee. Rather, it was focused on how counselors might motivate counselees to act upon their counsel. See Adams, *The Christian Counselor's Manual*, 161–70.

generally uses the word σαρξ to refer to the physical body and that Romans 6–8 and similar passages exhibit a specialized use of the word σαρξ, by which Paul refers to the physical body that has been "plunged into sinful practices and habits as the result of Adam's fall."[29] For Adams, the flesh of the regenerate man was equal to the sinfully habituated body that he carries over with him in conversion. Thus, the old man/new man struggle in the Christian life is literally a battle between the inner, nonmaterial man (i.e., the heart) and the outer, material man.[30]

Adams argued that, although there is a regular use of σαρξ in the writings of Paul and the other New Testament authors, several passages constitute a specialized use of the term. He provided Romans 6–8, Galatians 5:16–25, Ephesians 4:22–24, and Colossians 3:9–10 as examples of the specialized use.[31] For Adams, "flesh" (σαρξ) in Romans 6–8 and Galatians 5:16–25 is the same as the "old man" (παλαιος ανθρωπος) in Ephesians 4:22–24 and Colossians 3:9–10.

Adams saw in Romans 6–8 "an antithesis on the one hand, between the Spirit and the inner man that He is renewing, and on the other hand, the believer's body *as it is still wrongly habituated.*"[32] He interpreted Paul's use of "body" (σωμα) and "members" (μελος)

---

29. Adams, *A Theology of Christian Counseling*, 160n1; cf. Adams, "What Alternative?."

30. Adams consistently argued throughout his works that "body" and "flesh" in Romans 6–8 should be interpreted as the physical body. Interestingly, he specifically mentioned John Owen's figurative conception of "flesh" in these chapters as an invalid interpretation. See Jay E. Adams, *Sanctification and Counseling: Growing by Grace* (Memphis: Institute for Nouthetic Studies, 2020), 203n23.

31. Adams, *A Theology of Christian Counseling*, 160. I ought to note two things about this reference, in which Adams provides this list of passages. First, Adams only lists the book and chapter references for these passages. I have deduced the specific verses from other places in Adams's writings where he deals directly with these passages. Second, in this reference Adams also mentions Romans 12 as a supporting passage. However, Romans 12 contains no use of σαρξ, σαρκινος, or σαρκικος. On the one hand, Adams may have intended to refer to Romans 12:1, where Paul writes, "present your bodies a living sacrifice." However, the word for "body" in this verse is σωμα, not σαρξ. On the other hand, Adams may have intended to refer to Romans 13:14, where Paul writes, "Make no provision for the flesh (σαρκὸς)." Adams mentions this verse briefly in his discussion of the flesh in *Lectures on Counseling*, 232.

32. Adams, *Lectures on Counseling*, 232 (italics original).

throughout Romans 6–8 as evidence that Paul intends σαρξ to be understood in a physical sense:

> Of great significance in this discussion is the fact that, in spite of everything, *flesh* does have as its primary referent the corporeal. That fundamental feature cannot be removed so facilely. Look, for instance, at its synonyms and associations: the *body* [σωμα] of sin [6:6], the mortal *body* [σωμα, 6:12], the *members* [μελος, 6:13, 19; 7:5] of the *body* [this word is supplied by some translations], the deeds of the *body* [σωμα, 8:13], the *body* [σωμα] of this death [7:24], sin in the *members* [μελος, 7:23] (of the *body* [this word is supplied by some translations]), and so forth.[33]

Based on its association in Romans 6–8 with σωμα and μελος, then, Adams argued that Paul's use of the term σαρξ in this section of Romans must be primarily physical. He concluded, "Surely, in such company as it keeps, 'flesh,' even here, *must* be understood to refer to the corporeal unless there are stronger reasons, than to date have been forthcoming, to divest it of such content."[34]

Adams saw in Romans 7 a clear contrast between the flesh and the inner man, and from this contrast he drew further support for his position that the flesh refers to the physical body, for "what is the contrast to *inner man* if it is not the body?"[35] Thus, when Paul writes in Romans 7:25, "So then, with the mind I myself serve the law of God, but with the flesh the law of sin," Adams understood this battle between the mind and the flesh to be one between the regenerated inner man—who is empowered by the Spirit—and the outer, physical body—which is habituated to sin—respectively. Despite the fact that this seems to suggest some sort of dualism between the body (evil) and the soul (good), Adams strongly asserted that it does not.[36]

---

33. Adams, *Lectures on Counseling*, 233. The italicized English words are original to the quote. I have inserted the bracketed textual notes to clarify the underlying Greek words to which Adams refers. Note that some of the words to which he refers are not actually in the Greek text but are supplied by translators.

34. Adams, *Lectures on Counseling*, 233 (italics original).

35. Adams, *Lectures on Counseling*, 233 (italics original).

36. Adams, *Lectures on Counseling*, 232–33; Adams, *A Theology of Christian Counseling*, 160n1.

Thus, although Adams understood that σαρξ in Paul's writings can have multiple connotations, he believed that Paul's use of the term in Romans 6–8 represents a specialized, negative connotation of the word. "'Flesh' as Paul uses it in a negative sense, then means…a body habituated to the ways of the world rather than the ways of God."[37] Adams saw this same use of σαρξ in Galatians 5:16–25. He explained that when Christians think they are at war with themselves, "That is evidence of the Spirit at work within, challenging corrupt patterns of life habituated into your body by the sinful nature with which you were born."[38]

Furthermore, Adams clearly equated σαρξ in Romans 6–8 and Galatians 5:16–25 with παλαιος ανθρωπος in Ephesians 4:22–24 and Colossians 3:9–10, and he thought that both of these concepts in Paul's writings referred to the body that is habituated to sin:

> The idea of bodily habituation appears frequently in the pertinent contexts. The *flesh* is the 'former manner of life' or 'previous habits' also referred to as 'the old man' in Ephesians 4:22. It is 'the old man with his *practices*' in Colossians 3:9. It is the sinful ways that have been programmed and patterned into life by our sinful natures through continuous yielding of the 'members' of the body to sin (Rom. 6:13, 19). Before salvation, the Christian was a willing slave who offered the members of his body as instruments to carry out the wishes of his master, sin. Now, with the same willingness, he must learn to yield the members of his body to God. The power of habit is great. It is not easy to please God in a body that is still in part habituated to sin.[39]

Thus, for Adams, Paul's references to "the old man" and "the flesh" clearly refer to the physical body that a man's sinful nature has habituated to operate sinfully.

Adams's understanding of σαρξ led him to read Romans 7:7–25 as a reference to the experience of a Christian, and his examination of this passage provides one of the most revealing explanations of how

---

37. Adams, *Lectures on Counseling*, 233.

38. Jay E. Adams, *Galatians, Ephesians, Colossians, Philemon*, The Christian Counselor's Commentary (Hackettstown, N.J.: Timeless Texts, 1994), 53.

39. Adams, *Lectures on Counseling*, 233–34 (italics original).

he conceived of the relationship between sin and the flesh in the Christian life. His commentary on Romans 7:17 ("But now, it is no longer I who do [what I do not want], but sin that dwells in me") shows clearly his view of the distinction between the regenerated inner man and the sinfully habituated body: "It is no longer I (the new regenerate I) who produces sin, but the sinful practices of brain and body habituated in my members. The struggle is with the past carried over into the present by a habituated body."[40] Paul's use of the word "flesh" in verse 18 ("For I know that in me (that is, in my flesh [σαρκί]) nothing good dwells") clarifies that the "me" in which sin dwells in verse 17 is the sinfully habituated body.[41] The flesh as physical body, then, is the place where Adams believed sin continues to dwell in a regenerate person.

Regarding verse 20, where Paul writes, "Now if I do what I will not to do, it is no longer I who do it, but sin that dwells in me," Adams concluded,

> So, [Paul] repeats, it is not the new me that produces sin; it is the sin that dwells in me (in his bodily members: cf. v. 23). His sinful nature, with which he was born, programmed the parts (members) of his body to respond to various situations in life sinfully. So, in sanctification, the problem is to reprogram them in righteous ways, presenting the same members of the body to God for righteousness.[42]

Again, according to Adams, the "flesh" refers to the physical body that has been habitually programmed to sin. When people are converted, they carry their physical bodies with them into their new lives as Christians, and so they must work to dehabituate their bodies from sinning and rehabituate them to live righteously, which they can now do by the power of the Spirit.[43]

---

40. Jay E. Adams, *Romans, Philippians, I Thessalonians, II Thessalonians*, The Christian Counselor's Commentary (Hackettstown, N.J.: Timeless Texts, 1995), 61.

41. Adams, *Romans, Philippians, I Thessalonians, II Thessalonians*, 61.

42. Adams, *Romans, Philippians, I Thessalonians, II Thessalonians*, 62.

43. Adams explained the process of dehabituation and rehabituation in *The Christian Counselor's Manual*, 176–216. He wrote, "Breaking a habit is a two-sided enterprise that requires regular, structured, endurance in putting off and putting on. Dehabituation is *more* than that; it also involves rehabituation. When a counselee turns his back upon his old ways, at the same time he must turn to face God's new ones. If he does not, what he turns to face instead may be equally as bad or worse. If the new way is vague and indefinite, he

Adams saw an antithesis in Romans 6–8 between the flesh and the Spirit, one that is most evident in 8:1–17. He explained, "The Scriptures are unequivocal: it is the Spirit of God who, in opposition to the flesh, leads the believer into a new way of life."[44] Adams interpreted 8:1–2 to mean that regenerate persons are no longer slaves to sin, as they are now set free in Christ Jesus and are in Him. This means that, upon conversion, Christians immediately enter into a war between the flesh and the Spirit: "It is the Spirit Who opposes the habituated flesh (cf. Galatians 5:16–18) and enables us to win battles and gain ground."[45] If we walk according to the Spirit (8:4), we are enabled to do that which the law commands and, thereby, to work against the desires of "the wrongly-habituated body."[46]

For Adams, the war against the flesh is waged primarily in the mind, which, in Romans 8:5–7, refers to "the resultant thought of the mind. That is, what one determines to do."[47] Christians must set their minds on the Spirit rather than the flesh and, thereby, walk by the Spirit rather than the flesh (8:5–7).[48] Indeed, the mind is key to Adams's conception of sanctification in the Christian life. A much-debated passage from his first published work, *Competent to Counsel*, reveals his thinking on the battle between the mind and the flesh:

> Usual counseling methods recommend frequent long excursions back into the intricacies of the whys and wherefores of behavior. Instead, nouthetic counseling is largely committed to a discussion of the what. All the why that a counselee needs to know can clearly be demonstrated in the what. *What* was done? *What* must be done to rectify it? *What* should future responses be? In nouthetic

---

may vacillate from one thing to another, becoming confused and exasperated rather than developing new biblical ways of living. The process, then, should be clear both to the counselor and, through him, to the counselee," 188 (italics original). I should remind the reader that, although Adams described the process of dehabituation and rehabituation in a way that seems behavioristic, as I have written above, he does strongly emphasize the necessity of the Spirit in enabling this process. At worst, he can be accused of demystifying the work of the Spirit in sanctification (which he freely admits; see p. 186).

44. Adams, *Lectures on Counseling*, 234.

45. Adams, *Romans, Philippians, I Thessalonians, II Thessalonians*, 64.

46. Adams, *Romans, Philippians, I Thessalonians, II Thessalonians*, 65.

47. Adams, *Romans, Philippians, I Thessalonians, II Thessalonians*, 65.

48. Adams, *Romans, Philippians, I Thessalonians, II Thessalonians*, 65.

counseling the stress falls upon the "what" rather than the "why" because the "why" is already known before counseling begins. The reason why people get into trouble in their relationships to God and others is because of their sinful natures. Men are born sinners.[49]

The only "why" that Christians need to know regarding their sin is that they were born sinful, and though they have been regenerated, they retain a body that has been habituated to do evil. Thus, change involves learning what sinful patterns have been programmed into one's flesh and replacing those sinful patterns with godly patterns through a process of dehabituation and rehabituation.[50] The process of sanctification, then, is the exertion of mental effort upon the body, by the power of the Spirit, in order to make it stop sinning and start acting righteously.

Such a process is impossible for an unregenerate person because he is "in the flesh" (Rom. 8:8), but if someone has been regenerated, then he has the Spirit (8:9) and is enabled to work against the desires of the flesh. When you are regenerated, you receive the Spirit and are "enlightened in your inner person…even though you begin the Christian life with a body that is still dead to righteousness because it is programmed to sin…. The [inner man] wants to do good but is confronted with a body that wants to do evil. The body hasn't yet been raised to newness of life as the soul has (the soul, of course, still has much to relearn)."[51] Interestingly, Adams argued that 8:11 ("He who raised Christ from the dead will also give life to your mortal bodies [σώματα]") referred not to the resurrection and glorification but to progressive sanctification:

> Here the life imparted to the body by the Spirit is not the life it will receive at the coming of Christ. That will be its consummation. But the life envisioned in verse 11 is the ongoing work of the Spirit as

---

49. Adams, *Competent to Counsel*, 48 (italics original). Adams similarly advises against "why" questions in *The Christian Counselor's Manual*, 287.

50. This is the two-factor process of change (i.e., putting off and putting on) that Adams strongly emphasizes and that he draws from Ephesians 4:22–24 and Colossians 3:9–10, among other passages. See *The Christian Counselor's Manual*, 177–79; *Lectures on Counseling*, 236–38.

51. Adams, *Romans, Philippians, I Thessalonians, II Thessalonians*, 67.

He fights against the flesh (cf. Galatians 5:16–18). In other words, the Spirit will continue to enable the body to be habituated to the righteous ways of God. Even in this life He is in the process of reprogramming the members of this body that will die.[52]

This shows that Adams largely equated σαρξ with σωμα in Romans 6–8 and that, in his reading, both words refer to the physical body that is habituated to sin, which Christians carry with them after conversion and must fight by the Spirit.

Based on this analysis of Adams's interpretation of Romans 6–8, Galatians 5:16–25, Ephesians 4:22–24, and Colossians 3:9–10, I conclude this section by noting that, despite his explicit emphasis on the corporeal nature of the flesh, there is a sense in which Adams understood the flesh to have a redemptive-historical connotation. It seems that Adams saw Christians not as *being in* the flesh but as *having* a flesh. I take this from his reading of Romans 8:7–9, in which he argues that true Christians are not "in the flesh."[53] This is also consistent with his interpretation of Romans 7:5 and 7:14. Adams explained that Romans 7:5 ("For when we were in the flesh [σαρκί]") "refers to the pre-regenerate state of the Christian,"[54] and he interpreted Romans 7:14 ("For we know that the law is spiritual, but I am carnal [σάρκινός], sold under sin") to mean that, "though he is not in the flesh, the converted sinner is still bound up in fleshly ways."[55] Thus, I believe that the most accurate reading of Adams's view of the flesh is that regenerate persons are now *in* Christ and no longer *in* the flesh, yet they continue to *have* a flesh, which consists of a body (including a brain) that has been habitually programmed to sin.[56]

---

52. Adams, *Romans, Philippians, I Thessalonians, II Thessalonians*, 67.

53. Adams, *Romans, Philippians, I Thessalonians, II Thessalonians*, 65–66.

54. Adams, *Romans, Philippians, I Thessalonians, II Thessalonians*, 59.

55. Adams, *Romans, Philippians, I Thessalonians, II Thessalonians*, 61. Note that, though the NKJV renders σάρκινός as "carnal," Adams rendered it as "in the flesh." The latter rendering is common to several other modern translations as well.

56. For a similar defense of the position that Adams espoused, see John MacArthur, *Freedom from Sin*, John MacArthur's Bible Studies (Chicago: Moody Press, 1987). MacArthur writes, "In its ethical and moral sense, Scripture always speaks of the flesh as the believer's unredeemed body. Before we came to Christ we were engulfed in and captive to the flesh. Fortunately for the believer, however, that is history. Believers are not in the flesh.

Human Nature

In explaining human personality, Adams distinguished between a φυσις and acquired habits.[57] He explained, "At birth, God gave to each of us a basic deposit of inherited stuff which Scripture calls *phusis* [φυσις] (nature). This is a matter of gene makeup."[58] This is not the same as personality—rather, it is something akin to a person's unique instinctual drives.[59] Personality is a combination of φυσις and the acquired habit patterns that result from "how one uses the *phusis* [φυσις] in responding to life's problems and life's challenges."[60] Summarizing the relationship between the φυσις and acquired habits, he wrote,

> While the *phusis* [φυσις] is genetic and largely unchangeable, one may radically change the ways in which he uses his nature. Temperament, for instance, may be attributable to a given trait (there may well be in Tom inherited traits of persistence). But how this temperament develops and is used (on the one hand Tom may develop these traits as stubbornness, hardheadedness, etc., while on the other hand, the Spirit of God may develop them into patience and endurance) is his responsibility before God. So then, the counselee is responsible *in this way* even for the *phusis* [φυσις] (inherited nature).[61]

Adams used this distinction to emphasize his belief that change is, indeed, possible, because the negative or sinful aspects of one's personality are not attributable to one's inherited φυσις but to learned patterns of behavior that one has developed over time. Thus, if sinful patterns can be learned, then they can also be unlearned and replaced with righteous patterns through the Spirit.

But why is it that we continue to sin? The answer is that believers are not in the flesh, but the flesh is still in them! Although the flesh no longer makes you its slave, you still possess an unredeemed body, which remains susceptible to sin," 112.

　　57. Adams, *Competent to Counsel*, 75; Adams, *The Christian Counselor's Manual*, 172, 174; Adams, *A Theology of Christian Counseling*, 99, 236, 251.

　　58. Adams, *Competent to Counsel*, 74–75.

　　59. Adams, *Competent to Counsel*, 164n1.

　　60. Adams, *Competent to Counsel*, 75.

　　61. Adams, *The Christian Counselor's Manual*, 174 (italics original).

Adams thought that the φύσις was affected by one's fallen condition. He favored traducianism (the soul is passed from parent to child at conception) over creationism (each soul is newly created by God at the time of conception),[62] and he indicated that inheriting a φύσις from one's parents results in one's being born a sinner.[63] Although all people receive varying temperaments through their inherited φύσις, all sinful people will develop the capacities contained in their φύσις in a sinful direction unless and until they are converted by the Holy Spirit.[64] It seems, then, that the φύσις is a set of inherent capacities that an individual contains in his genetic makeup, which he has inherited from his parents. Apart from sin, such capacities would develop in righteous ways. Sinful people, however, cannot help but use their capacities in sinful ways.

Summary

Summarizing Adams's views on human nature, an unregenerate man has an inherited φύσις (i.e., genetic makeup or nature) and a corrupt heart. In his fallen state, his corrupt heart has used his φύσις to habituate his flesh (i.e., his body) to do evil. At conversion, a person receives the Spirit, and his inner man is regenerated such that he receives a new heart, while his outer, physical body remains habituated toward sin. His newly regenerated heart can now use his φύσις to dehabituate the sinful tendencies that remain in his body and rehabituate his body toward righteousness. As I will discuss below, sanctification is the process of the inner man yielding to the Spirit in order to use the φύσις to dehabituate the body from sinning and rehabituate it toward acting righteously. Through this process, the Spirit imparts life to the physical body (Rom. 8:11), a work that will ultimately be completed at the resurrection, when we receive our glorified bodies.[65]

---

62. Adams, *Competent to Counsel*, 75n1.

63. Adams, *Competent to Counsel*, 184.

64. Adams, *The Christian Counselor's Manual*, 369n2.

65. See Adams, *Romans, Philippians, I Thessalonians, II Thessalonians*, 70, commenting on Romans 8:23.

Adams's Theology of Sanctification

Because sanctification is, in essence, a process by which the believer grows in holiness through progressively putting to death indwelling sin and increasing in righteousness, one's theology of sanctification will necessarily be influenced by where one locates sin in the believer. Thus, in seeking to understand Adams's theology of sanctification, it is important to discern where he located indwelling sin.

As I have shown, Adams strongly asserted that sin remains in the habituated body of the regenerate person. However, he also maintained that sin originates in the heart. Some statements—e.g., "all sins are heart sins"—are difficult to reconcile with others—e.g., "It is no longer I (the new regenerate I) who produces sin, but the sinful practices of brain and body habituated in my members. The struggle is with the past carried over into the present by a habituated body."[66] Such statements make it difficult to ascertain the location from which Adams believed the regenerate person's sin arises.[67] However, his methodology of dehabituation and rehabituation demonstrates that the target of his counseling was the body habituated to sin. This suggests that Adams favored the body as the most apparent location of indwelling sin in the believer.[68]

---

66. See Adams, *A Theology of Christian Counseling*, 218; Adams, *Romans, Philippians, I Thessalonians, II Thessalonians*, 61.

67. A statement that is similarly difficult to reconcile comes in a discussion of habit based on Hebrews 5:13–14, in which Adams wrote, "It is in the innerspring of one's actions, in the heart of his personality that one must learn by consistent repetition to discern between good and evil." Here, undefined concepts are comingled and are used in a way that is seemingly inconsistent with their use in Adams's other writings. Elsewhere he consistently uses habit with reference to the body, but here he seems to use it with reference to the heart. See Adams, *Competent to Counsel*, 163. A statement that casts further confusion on Adams's position is "The heart is where the habit is. 'Heart,' in Scripture, includes the brain and the mind. The heart must be changed as the habit is; the habit will be changed as the heart is." See Adams, *Sanctification and Counseling*, 102. In the same work, on a single page (205), he locates the brain both in the body and in the heart, which blurs the line between the inner man and the outer man that Adams adamantly maintains elsewhere.

68. This is further supported by the stark contrast that Adams drew between idols of the heart and habits of the body in *Sanctification and Counseling*, 198–205. Adams believed that the search for heart idols lacks any warrant in Scripture. Fighting sin is not about locating and eradicating heart idols—rather, it is about putting off sinful habits and putting on righteous ones.

Habit

Adams defined habit as "the capacity to learn to respond unconsciously, automatically and comfortably."[69] Habit is a blessing that God has bestowed upon humanity, and it is primarily related to the body.[70] Humans cannot avoid habitual living because God has ingrained it into their design.[71] In unregenerate people, the body acquires sinful habits over time as the sinful heart trains the body in unrighteousness.[72] Adams explained, "It is the sinful inclination of the heart (the inner, unseen life) that causes the aggravating habituation of the material body."[73]

Central to Adams's understanding of habit is Jeremiah 13:23, in which the prophet states, "Can the Ethiopian change his skin or the leopard its spots? Then may you also do good who are accustomed to do evil." Following Calvin,[74] Adams argued that this passage refers not to the corrupt nature with which people are born but to the learned, deeply ingrained, sinful habits that they have acquired over time.[75] He

---

69. Adams, *A Theology of Christian Counseling*, 161; cf. Jay E. Adams, *Winning the War Within: A Biblical Strategy for Spiritual Warfare* (Woodruff, S.C.: Timeless Texts, 1994), 75.

70. Adams, *A Theology of Christian Counseling*, 161; Adams, *Romans, Philippians, I Thessalonians, II Thessalonians*, 61; Adams, *Winning the War Within*, 52.

71. Adams, *A Theology of Christian Counseling*, 232.

72. Adams, *A Theology of Christian Counseling*, 140–42.

73. Adams, *A Theology of Christian Counseling*, 108.

74. Calvin wrote of this text, "Learned men in our age do not wisely refer to this passage, when they seek to prove that there is no free-will in man; for it is not simply the nature of man that is spoken of here, but the habit that is contracted by long practice.... Jeremiah, then, does not here refer to man's nature as he is when he comes from the womb; but he condemns the Jews for contracting such a habit by long practice. As, then, they had hardened themselves in doing evil, he says that they could not repent, that wickedness had become inherent, or firmly fixed in their hearts, like the blackness which is inherent in the skin of the Ethiopians, or the spots which belong to the leopards or panthers. We may at the same time gather from this passage a useful doctrine—that men become so corrupt, by sinful habits and sinful indulgence, that the devil takes away from them every desire and care for acting rightly, so that, in a word, they become wholly irreclaimable." See John Calvin, *Commentaries on the Book of Jeremiah and Lamentations*, trans. John Owen, Calvin's Commentaries (Edinburgh: Calvin Translation Society, 1855), 2:191–92. Notice, however, that Calvin seems to indicate that the habit acquired through repetitive sinful practices becomes firmly fixed in the heart rather than in the body.

75. Adams, *The Christian Counselor's Manual*, 171; Adams, *A Theology of Christian Counseling*, 163, 235; Adams, *Sanctification and Counseling*, 205.

also relied upon Hebrews 5:13–14, which reads, "For everyone who partakes only of milk is unskilled in the word of righteousness, for he is a babe. But solid food belongs to those who are of full age, that is, those who by reason of use have their senses exercised to discern both good and evil." Commenting on this passage, he explained that the immature believers were unskilled in the word of righteousness because "they had failed to 'practice' and 'train' themselves in holiness." He concluded, "Holy living, then, involves habit. Patterns of holiness can be established only by regular, consistent practice."[76]

As I have discussed above, Adams also listed Romans 6–8, Galatians 5:16–25, Ephesians 4:22–24, and Colossians 3:9–10 as texts in which "Paul considers the problem of sinful habits (or behavior patterns) acquired by the response of our sinful natures to life situations, and the difficulties that these raise for regenerate persons who seek to serve God."[77] Habit is thus a central component of human functioning in general and of the Christian life in particular because the preregenerate sinful habits that remain in one's flesh are the central enemy in the Christian life and in Christian counseling.[78]

Dehabituation and Rehabituation

Adams believed in the power of the Scriptures to transform behavior, and he argued that this transformation has two aspects: one instantaneous and the other gradual.[79] The instantaneous aspect is conversion, which includes regeneration and justification.[80] The gradual aspect is sanctification. He described sanctification as a "process of

---

76. Adams, *Competent to Counsel*, 162.

77. Adams, *A Theology of Christian Counseling*, 160–61.

78. Adams noted that the real battle of the Christian life is between the Spirit and the flesh because the devil and his angels can do no more than tempt the flesh. See Adams, *Winning the War Within*, 52.

79. Adams, *A Theology of Christian Counseling*, 36.

80. Although Adams discussed justification as though it were a transformation, he clearly did not intend for it to be understood in a Roman Catholic sense. He described justification forensically as a declaration of innocence by God based on the active and passive obedience of Christ. Thus, he clearly intended justification to be understood in a Protestant sense. Nonetheless, his use of the word "transformation" to refer to it is confusing and out of step with historic Protestant terminology.

transformation by which a previously sinfully disposed and habituated life turns into one that pleases God more and more by conformity to His directive will (set forth in the Scriptures)."[81] Sanctification, then, is the reversal of the sinful habituation of the body by a redirection of the body toward righteousness.[82] It is the spiritual battle against "habits and patterns of thinking and doing developed before regeneration that are brought over into the postregenerate life."[83] This occurs through a process of dehabituation and rehabituation.[84]

For Adams, dehabituation and rehabituation constitute the two-factor process of change that Paul describes in Ephesians 4:22–24, in which he exhorts Christians to "put off, concerning your former conduct, the old man which grows corrupt according to the deceitful lusts, and be renewed in the spirit of your mind, and [to] put on the new man which was created according to God, in true righteousness and holiness." He explained that a liar does not stop being a liar simply because he has stopped lying. Rather, a liar stops being a liar when he has become something else: a truth-teller.[85] Adams described sanctification as a process of self-examination by which a person systematically identifies sinful habits and replaces them with righteous ones. He wrote,

> Since God has made counselees with the capacity for living according to habit, counselors must reckon with habit when seeking to help counselees change. They must help them consciously to take a hard look at their life styles. They must help them to become conscious of life patterns by carefully examining their unconscious responses. The unconscious must again become conscious. As they become aware of life patterns, they must evaluate them by the Word of God. What the counselee learned to do as a child he may be continuing

---

81. Adams, *A Theology of Christian Counseling*, 36.

82. Adams, *A Theology of Christian Counseling*, 161.

83. Adams, *Sanctification and Counseling*, 44n45.

84. Interestingly, Adams quoted John Owen to support his view of dehabituation and rehabituation: "Every lust is a depraved habit or disposition, continually inclining the heart to evil." See Adams, *Sanctification and Counseling*, 217n36, quoting Owen, *Of the Mortification of Sin in Believers*, in *Works*, 6:26. As I will demonstrate in subsequent chapters of this work, Owen's conception of habit significantly differed with that of Adams.

85. Adams, *The Christian Counselor's Manual*, 177–78.

to do as an adult. Pattern by pattern the counselor must help him to analyze and determine whether it has developed from practice in doing God's will or whether it has developed as a sinful response. There is only one way to become a godly person, to orient one's life toward godliness, and that means pattern by pattern. The old sinful ways, as they are discovered, must be replaced by new patterns from God's Word. That is the meaning of disciplined living. Discipline first requires self-examination, then it means crucifixion of the old sinful ways (saying "no" daily), and lastly, it entails practice in following Jesus Christ in new ways by the guidance and strength that the Holy Spirit provides through His Word. The biblical way to godliness is not easy or simple, but it is the solid way.[86]

As a resource for counseling, Adams provided a chart in which counselors and counselees would list in the left-hand column habits which must be dehabituated and in the right-hand column habits which must be rehabituated.[87] The process must occur by the Word and the Spirit, and it must stress one's whole relationship to Christ in conjunction with practical steps, such as enlisting help from others and restructuring certain aspects of one's life in order to break the old habits and practice the new ones.[88]

A counselor should have great hope in this process when counseling a truly regenerate person.[89] Because the person has a new heart granted by the Spirit, because the Spirit works through the Word, and because the Word provides a process of dehabituation and rehabituation that helps Christians change, the counselor should maintain great confidence. Practically, Adams believed that it ordinarily takes about six weeks of consistent effort to replace a habit.[90] Thus, he employed

---

86. Adams, *The Christian Counselor's Manual*, 182–83.

87. Adams, *The Christian Counselor's Manual*, 189 (figure 2).

88. Adams, *The Christian Counselor's Manual*, 190–211.

89. Adams, *Sanctification and Counseling*, 240. The great hope that Adams believed a counselor should have in the process of counseling was also the basis of the title for his book *A Theology of Christian Counseling: More Than Redemption*.

90. Adams, *Sanctification and Counseling*, 78. Adams's confidence in this process is further demonstrated by the average number of counseling sessions per counselee during his tenure at the Christian Counseling and Educational Foundation (CCEF). Powlison noted that, in 1970, when Adams was still at CCEF, the average number of sessions was 4.7. Adams left in the mid-1970s, and, by 1980, the average number of sessions had risen to 7.1. By 1990, it had risen to 12.4 sessions. See David Powlison, *The Biblical Counseling*

a somewhat brisk approach to counseling, one which used directness and the authority of the Word to coach a regenerate person through change by a process of dehabituation and rehabituation.[91]

Adams's Habituational Model: Summary and Conclusion

Adams believed that the Holy Spirit is necessary to effect change and that the primary means of this change is the Word of God. He also believed in the centrality of the heart in human functioning, such that, in order for people to truly change, they must receive new hearts. However, these foundational tenets of the Reformed faith were muddled in Adams's theology by his conception of the flesh as the sinfully habituated physical body, which led him to focus methodologically not on the progressive renewal of the soul but, rather, on the dehabituation and rehabituation of the physical body. This focus on habituation was largely abandoned by the generation of counselors that succeeded Adams. This generation focused instead on the motivations of the heart, motivations that Adams believed could not be known and should not be pursued. Further, the two streams within the biblical counseling movement differed not merely in their methodological emphases but also in their theological emphases. Adams believed that the heart could not be known and was not the source of indwelling sin in the life of a believer. David Powlison and his followers believed that the heart is the source of indwelling sin in the life of a believer and that the motivations of man's heart can be drawn out, examined, and progressively changed by the work of the Spirit through the Word. Thus, their methodological target shifted from the external to the internal.

Movement: History and Context (Greensboro, N.C.: New Growth Press, 2010), 213–14. This increase displays the clear theological and methodological shifts that occurred within the biblical counseling movement between Adams and Powlison and their respective followers.

 91. Powlison, *The Biblical Counseling Movement*, 213.

Chapter 2

The Heart-Motivational Model
of Sanctification

In a 1988 article, "Crucial Issues in Contemporary Biblical Counseling," David Powlison urged the biblical counseling movement to develop a greater understanding of human motivation.[1] He did this without directly citing any divergence with Adams or his understanding of habituation. Rather, he pointed to "a lack of emphasis and articulation" regarding motivation. According to Powlison, Adams had already provided "a basic structure in biblical fashion," but counselors needed to fill in more details. He concluded, "Filling in that detail will make us realize that motivational issues play a far more prominent role than we have realized, both conceptually and in counseling practice."[2]

What followed as the movement progressed, however, was not a simple filling in of details. In 1995 Powlison published his seminal article, "Idols of the Heart and 'Vanity Fair,'" which marked a significant turning point in the way biblical counselors talked about human change, firmly centering the discussion on motivation rather than habituation.[3] Again, Powlison did not directly set his framework against that of Adams, but a clear divergence was evident.[4] Since the publication of Powlison's article, two articles in the *Journal of Biblical Counseling*—one by Edward Welch and another by George

---

1. Powlison, "Crucial Issues in Contemporary Biblical Counseling," 53–78.

2. Powlison, "Crucial Issues in Contemporary Biblical Counseling," 57.

3. David Powlison, "Idols of the Heart and 'Vanity Fair,'" *Journal of Biblical Counseling* 13, no. 2 (Winter 1995): 35–50.

4. It was also evident that Adams himself noticed this shift, as he published multiple attacks against the "idols of the heart" approach to counseling. See Adams, *Sanctification and Counseling*, 198–200; Adams, "Counseling and the Heart"; Adams, "The Heart of the Matter"; Adams, "Heart Idols?."

M. Schwab—have directly attacked Adams's view of habituation.[5] Outside of these two articles, direct engagement with Adams or his view of habituation was for many years almost nonexistent, and the widely assumed approach to biblical counseling across the movement has been centered on heart motivation, an approach for which counselors have proposed several models.[6] However, some recent works have sought both to defend Adams's approach to habituation and to recover an understanding of habituation for biblical counseling that differs from that of Adams.[7]

In this chapter I will first discuss Powlison's shift in focus from habituation to heart motivation. Second, I will examine Welch's and Schwab's critiques of Adams's understanding of habituation. Third, I will outline the major heart-motivational models that biblical counselors have proposed. Finally, I will conclude by discussing the attempts from within the movement to recover habituation in sanctification.

Powlison's Shift toward Heart Motivation

A number of authors have noted that Powlison prompted a shift in emphasis within the biblical counseling movement from outward,

---

5. Welch, "How Theology Shapes Ministry"; Schwab, "Critique of 'Habituation' as a Biblical Model of Change."

6. The most important of these models are proposed in Michael R. Emlet, "Understanding the Influences on the Human Heart," *Journal of Biblical Counseling* 20, no. 2 (Winter 2002): 47–52; Elyse Fitzpatrick, *Idols of the Heart: Learning to Long for God Alone* (Phillipsburg, N.J.: P&R, 2001); Timothy S. Lane and Paul David Tripp, *How People Change* (Greensboro, N.C.: New Growth Press, 2008); Jeremy Pierre, *The Dynamic Heart in Daily Life: Connecting Christ to Human Experience* (Greensboro, N.C.: New Growth Press, 2016).

7. See Gifford, "The Role of Habits in Spiritual Maturity from the Perspective of the English Puritans"; Gifford, "Jay Adams' Teaching of Habituation"; Greg E. Gifford, *Heart and Habits: How We Change for Good* (The Woodlands, Tex.: Kress Biblical Resources, 2021); Mesimer, "Habits and the Heart"; Mesimer, "Rehabilitating Habituation"; Michael R. Emlet, "Practice Makes Perfect? Exploring the Relationship between Knowledge, Desire, and Habit," *Journal of Biblical Counseling* 27, no. 1 (2013): 26–48. Gifford attempts to validate Adams's understanding of habituation by comparing it to that of the Puritans, while Mesimer uses both contemporary and historical sources to critique Adams in order to bring a renewed emphasis on habituation to the biblical counseling movement today. Emlet relies on contemporary discussions of habit from outside of the biblical counseling movement.

observable, habituated behavior to inward heart motivation.[8] In 1988, Powlison himself argued that it is dangerous to underemphasize the motivations of the heart:

> We depart from the Bible if we ignore motives and drift towards an externalistic view of man. The caricature that [biblical counselors] are "behavioristic" indeed may be true more often than we would like to admit. The Bible itself tells us behavior has "reasons." Behavior flows "from within, out of men's hearts" (Mark 7:21), as we all know and affirm. But both our theory and practice have not given this area the attention it needs. We must become as familiar with the practical, everyday details of "faith and idolatry" as we are with the details of those acts of sin and righteousness which flow from our hearts. The changes for which biblical counseling must aim are both internal and external.[9]

Such a statement paved the way for a later article in which he would more fully develop the concept of "heart idolatry."

In "Idols of the Heart and 'Vanity Fair,'" Powlison developed two concepts. The first concept, "idols of the heart," refers to his assertion that the "characteristic and summary" words with which Scripture describes our sin are "idolatry" in the Old Testament and "desire" in the New Testament. "Both are shorthand for *the* problem of human beings," he argued.[10] The second concept, "vanity fair," deals with the context in which humans live. Drawing on Bunyan's portrayal of Vanity Fair in *The Pilgrim's Progress*, Powlison noted that "idolatries are both generated from within and insinuated from without."[11] Counselors must be aware not only of the temptations that might arise from within a person's heart but also of the societal idolatries in which he might be tempted to participate. Powlison used these two concepts to promote a more holistic view of how a person becomes

---

8. Eric L. Johnson, *Foundations for Soul Care: A Christian Psychology Proposal* (Downers Grove, Ill.: InterVarsity Press, 2007), 109–10, 596; Lambert, *The Biblical Counseling Movement after Adams*, 70–80; Fraser, *Developments in Biblical Counseling*, 76–89; Jeremy Lelek, *Biblical Counseling Basics: Roots, Beliefs, and Future* (Greensboro, N.C.: New Growth Press, 2018), 30.

9. Powlison, "Crucial Issues in Contemporary Biblical Counseling," 56–57.

10. Powlison, "Idols of the Heart and 'Vanity Fair,'" 36 (italics original).

11. Powlison, "Idols of the Heart and 'Vanity Fair,'" 36.

drawn into sin. He also used these concepts to both commend and confront the tendency of psychology-oriented Christians to spend a great deal of time seeking to discern motivations. He commended their recognition that inner motivation is, indeed, important. However, he also confronted their tendency to discern motivations simply for the purpose of meeting felt needs. He did this by explaining the moral component of motivation. Humans are not merely motivated by inner desires; their desires are sinful, or idolatrous, if they are set on anything other than God.[12]

Almost twenty years after the publication of "Idols of the Heart and 'Vanity Fair,'" Powlison republished the article with an introduction that cautioned against what had come to be known as "idol hunts."[13] In this introduction, he stressed that the intention of the original article was not to encourage deep and unhelpful introspection but, rather, to make clear that sin is more than behavior. He explained that he did not write the article to teach a counseling methodology but to clarify why people do what they do.[14] Powlison's introduction indicates that theological emphases drive methodological practices and that one's perceived theological imbalance will often be the target of one's critics. Adams believed that motivation was important, but he emphasized the remaining habits of the flesh, which drove him to focus methodologically on dehabituation and rehabituation. This led to the accusation that he was a behaviorist. Powlison began to emphasize motivation, which drove him to focus methodologically on discerning the "why" of human behavior.[15] This led to the accusation that he was an idol-hunter who oversimplified the scriptural portrayal of sin.

---

12. Powlison, "Idols of the Heart and 'Vanity Fair,'" 48–49.

13. David Powlison, "Revisiting Idols of the Heart and Vanity Fair," *Journal of Biblical Counseling* 27, no. 3 (2013): 37–42.

14. Powlison, "Revisiting Idols of the Heart and Vanity Fair," 38.

15. See, for example, David Powlison, "X-ray Questions: Drawing Out the Whys and Wherefores of Human Behavior," *Journal of Biblical Counseling* 18, no. 1 (Fall 1999): 2–9. Although Powlison does not mention Adams in this article, the phrase "Whys and Wherefores" clearly recalls Adams's quote in *Competent to Counsel* in which he brushes off the "whys" and "wherefores" as unimportant (48).

Powlison recognized that "idols of the heart" was only one metaphor among several in Scripture that connect inward motivation and outward behavior.[16] Thus, he should not be accused of simplistically distilling Scripture's entire portrait of human functioning into one metaphor. However, his emphasis on heart motivation, which was represented by his discussion of idolatry, did constitute a significant shift in the theological and methodological emphasis of biblical counseling.[17]

Two Critiques of Adams on Habituation

In 2002 and 2003, two articles that critique Adams's view of habituation appeared in the *Journal of Biblical Counseling*. The first, by Edward Welch, deals with a particular aspect of Adams's theology, while the second, by George Schwab, deals with his exegesis. Welch's article is titled "How Theology Shapes Ministry: Jay Adams' View of the Flesh and an Alternative." In this article, Welch provides a basic outline of Adams's view of the flesh as the body habitually programmed to sin, which I have examined in more detail above. He then critiques Adams's view, claiming that it is unreliable and anomalous when compared with the variety of views on the meaning of "flesh."[18] The main intent of Welch's article is to display how Adams's faulty theological conclusion led him to faulty methodological practices. He provides twenty bullet points that he asserts would be the negative results of such a faulty theology, most of which center on an overemphasis on behavior and habit and an underemphasis on motivation.[19] The alternative view provided by Welch is that "flesh" actually refers to a group of Judaizers within the New Testament church who sought to compel others to continue living under the stipulations of the Old Covenant.[20]

---

16. Powlison, "Idols of the Heart and 'Vanity Fair,'" 36.

17. See also Howard Eyrich and Elyse Fitzpatrick, "The Diagnosis and Treatment of Idols of the Heart," in *Christ-Centered Biblical Counseling: Changing Lives with God's Changeless Truth*, ed. James MacDonald, Bob Kellemen, and Steve Viars (Eugene, Ore.: Harvest House, 2013), 339–50.

18. Welch, "How Theology Shapes Ministry," 18.

19. Welch, "How Theology Shapes Ministry," 22–23.

20. Welch, "How Theology Shapes Ministry," 24–25. He cites Walter Russell, *The*

Schwab's article, titled "Critique of 'Habituation' as a Biblical Model of Change," treats a number of texts used by Adams to support his understanding of habituation.[21] He concludes that Adams's theory of habituation "is not actually substantiated in any of his citations."[22] Schwab suggests that Adams's theory of habituation is more influenced by secular psychologist O. Hobart Mowrer than by Scripture, even going so far as to say that Adams must have assumed Mowrer's theory in order to draw the conclusions from Scripture that he did.[23] According to Schwab, this does not necessarily mean that Adams's theory of habituation is false—he merely argues that the theory is not taught by the texts that Adams used to support it.[24] Now that Adams's view has been shown to be inconsistent with the Scriptures, Schwab concludes, future work needs to return to the Scriptures in order to discern a properly biblical understanding of habit.[25] Few counselors heeded Schwab's suggestion for more than a decade following his article. In the meantime, though, many worked to develop the relationship between counseling, the motivations of the heart, and sanctification.

Flesh/Spirit Conflict in Galatians (Lanham, Md.: University Press of America, 1997) and Herman Ridderbos, *Paul: An Outline of His Theology* (Grand Rapids: Eerdmans, 1975) as those who have influenced his view on this matter. Adams responded to Welch's article, disavowing many of the implications Welch asserts regarding his view and maintaining that Paul used the word "flesh" to explain how "sin gains control of the believer's body as a result of programming by the sinful spirit of man in his unregenerate state, and then through habitual practice takes over, bringing these habits into the new regenerate life." See Adams, "What Alternative?" In this response, Adams holds to his position, not because he believes Welch's alternative is deficient (although he does believe that) but because he believes there is no alternative.

21. These include Psalm 1:1; Proverbs 5:23; Jeremiah 13:23; 22:21; Romans 7:22–23; 1 Corinthians 8:7; 15:33; Ephesians 2:22–32; 1 Timothy 4:7; Hebrews 5:13–14; 10:25; 1 Peter 1:18; and 2 Peter 2:14.

22. Schwab, "Critique of 'Habituation' as a Biblical Model of Change," 79.

23. Schwab, "Critique of 'Habituation' as a Biblical Model of Change," 73, 80. In 1965, Adams spent the summer working with Mowrer, which he briefly discusses in *Competent to Counsel*, xiv–xix.

24. Schwab, "Critique of 'Habituation' as a Biblical Model of Change," 80. Schwab is clear that he does not personally agree with Adams's theory of habituation, but he intends to show the error of Adams's hermeneutical approach rather than that of his theological conclusions.

25. Schwab, "Critique of 'Habituation' as a Biblical Model of Change," 82–83.

Models of Heart Motivation

Significant proposals on the centrality of heart motivation in human functioning and sanctification include those offered by Timothy S. Lane and Paul David Tripp,[26] Elyse Fitzpatrick,[27] Michael Emlet,[28] and Jeremy Pierre.[29] There is substantial overlap between each of these proposed models—for this reason, I will address them in terms of their similarities rather than the order in which they were published.

Timothy S. Lane and Paul David Tripp

The model proposed by Timothy S. Lane and Paul David Tripp is based on Jeremiah 17:5–10,[30] which reads,

> Thus says the LORD: "Cursed is the man who trusts in man and makes flesh his strength, whose heart departs from the LORD. For he shall be like a shrub in the desert, and shall not see when good comes, but shall inhabit the parched places in the wilderness, in a salt land which is not inhabited. Blessed is the man who trusts in the LORD, and whose hope is the LORD. For he shall be like a tree planted by the waters, which spreads out its roots by the river, and will not fear when heat comes; but its leaf will be green, and will not be anxious in the year of drought, nor will cease from yielding fruit. The heart is deceitful above all things, and desperately wicked; who can know it? I, the LORD, search the heart, I test the mind, even to give every man according to his ways, according to the fruit of his doings.

Explaining their model from the text, Lane and Tripp write,

---

26. Lane and Tripp, *How People Change.*

27. Fitzpatrick, *Idols of the Heart.*

28. Emlet, "Understanding the Influences on the Human Heart."

29. Pierre, *The Dynamic Heart in Daily Life.*

30. The model was first published in Timothy S. Lane and Paul David Tripp, "How Christ Changes Us by His Grace," *Journal of Biblical Counseling* 23, no. 2 (Spring 2005): 15–21. It was then republished and greatly expanded in the book *How People Change.* As Powlison noted in the foreword of the book, the model originated in a class that he taught in the 1980s titled "The Dynamics of Biblical Change," revealing that the shift in the biblical counseling movement toward heart motivation had begun even before any major works espousing it had been published. This model is also appropriated by Jeremy Lelek, although it does not play a major role in his overall proposal for counseling. See Lelek, *Biblical Counseling Basics,* 63–64.

> In verse 8, the image of Heat describes life in a fallen world. In verse
> 6, a Thorn Bush in the wasteland represents the ungodly person
> who turns away from God. Verses 5 and 7 give a clear reference to
> the Lord as the Redeemer who comforts, cleanses, and empowers
> those who trust him. We represent this part of the passage by the
> Cross to summarize all of God's redemptive activity on our behalf.
> In verses 7 and 8, we see the metaphor of a Fruit tree. It represents
> the godly person who trusts in the Lord. Verses 9 and 10 show us a
> God who does not simply focus on our behavior. Though he does
> not ignore it, his focus is on our hearts. He is the ultimate searcher
> of hearts, because they are central to the change process he under-
> takes in us as our Redeemer.[31]

Thus, Lane and Tripp deduce a view of life that involves four elements: (1) Heat: a person's daily life, with its attendant difficulties,
blessings, and temptations; (2) Thorns: a person's ungodly response to
his situation, including behavior, the heart driving the behavior, and
the consequences that result; (3) Cross: the presence of God in His
redemptive glory and love that He provides in Christ; and (4) Fruit:
a person's new, godly response to his situation, which results from
God's power at work in his heart, including the heart renewed by
grace and the behavior that follows.[32]

This model features three predominant emphases. First, it emphasizes that people are responsible for their responses to their environment. Their situation (i.e., heat) does not determine their behavior; it is
merely an occasion for their behavior. Second, this model emphasizes
the centrality of the heart. The type of fruit that arises from a person in
a given circumstance is not determined by said circumstance. Rather,
it is determined by the quality of the person's heart. If the heart is
characterized by good roots, then good fruit will arise. If it is characterized by bad roots, then bad fruit (i.e., thorns) will arise. Third, this
model emphasizes the centrality of Christ in bringing about change.
Only through the application of Christ's blessings to our lives can our
hearts be transformed from those that are characterized by bad roots
to those that are characterized by good roots. Thus, according to this

---

31. Lane and Tripp, *How People Change*, 83.
32. Lane and Tripp, *How People Change*, 83–85.

model, regeneration plants a good root in the heart, while sanctification progressively eradicates the bad roots that remain and replaces them with good roots by the power of the Spirit.

The major difference between Lane and Tripp's model and that of Adams does not lie in the overall picture it portrays. Adams would likely have agreed with their general description of human functioning. Rather, the major difference lies in the fact that this model intends to help people recognize that they have bad roots in their hearts, identify those bad roots, and work to replace them. Whereas Adams was unconcerned with identifying internal motivations, this model encourages people to probe the specifics of why they do what they do.[33] Similar to Powlison, Lane and Tripp use the language of idol worship when discussing heart motivation.[34]

Elyse Fitzpatrick

Elyse Fitzpatrick acknowledges her indebtedness to David Powlison for her understanding of heart idolatry,[35] a theme that she explores thoroughly in her book *Idols of the Heart*. She wrote this book to address the problem of habitual sins, but she roots such sins in an idolatrous heart:

> This book is written for those of you who desire to live a godly life and yet find yourself in a recurrently disappointing struggle against habitual sin. This book is written for you who find yourself constantly tripping over the same bad habit, the same embarrassing weakness, the same sinful slavery that you hoped to be free of years ago. In this book you'll learn that idolatry lies at the heart of every besetting sin that we struggle with.[36]

Like Adams, Fitzpatrick is concerned with habitual sin patterns. But, whereas Adams located the root of these sins in the body that is habituated to sin, Fitzpatrick locates it in the heart that is idolatrously worshiping something other than God.

---

33. This is clearly evidenced by the fact that the authors repeat Powlison's "X-ray questions" in their book. See Lane and Tripp, *How People Change*, 142–45.

34. Lane and Tripp, *How People Change*, 138–39.

35. Fitzpatrick, *Idols of the Heart*, 11.

36. Fitzpatrick, *Idols of the Heart*, 15.

In Fitzpatrick's model, the heart has three functions: the mind, the affections, and the will. These three functions are never isolated and always work in conjunction with one another. The mind informs the affections of the source of highest happiness; then, the affections imagine such happiness and awaken the will to choose in accordance with it.[37] Humans tend to fix functional gods in their hearts by setting their minds, affections, and wills on things other than God, thus engaging in idolatrous worship that begins in their hearts and flows out into their actions. Sanctification involves discerning the motivations of the heart by examining sinful responses to one's circumstances, both internal responses—at the level of the heart—and external ones—at the level of actions. In this model, Powlison's "X-ray Questions" help identify the idols one has set up in the heart.[38] Once such idols have been identified, they can be put to death through putting off old, sinful patterns of thinking, desiring, and choosing, and putting on new, righteous patterns of the same.[39] Thus, like Adams, Fitzpatrick portrays sanctification as a two-factor process, but the process happens at a level of depth with which Adams would have been mostly unconcerned in his counseling methodology.

The differing approaches of Adams and Fitzpatrick arise from where each locates the believer's remaining sin. Because Adams located it in the body, he focused on dehabituation and rehabituation and was largely unconcerned with motivation. Because Fitzpatrick locates indwelling sin in the heart, the motivations of the heart must be discerned in order for any put off / put on work to be effective.

Michael Emlet

Michael Emlet's model draws out the relationship between the heart and the context to which it responds. He explains, "In counseling ministry, it is critically important to understand the multiplicity of

---

37. Fitzpatrick, *Idols of the Heart*, 93–97.

38. Fitzpatrick, *Idols of the Heart*, 162–65.

39. In this sense, Fitzpatrick uses language with which Adams would agree, and she even references his work positively when discussing the put off / put on process of sanctification. See Fitzpatrick, *Idols of the Heart*, 184–86, 228n8. However, Adams would clearly part ways with Fitzpatrick when it comes to her focus on heart idolatry and motivation.

influences that test our counselees' hearts to respond in either a godly or an ungodly manner."[40] The heart is the immaterial component of human nature, the "seat of a person's spiritual-moral life."[41] Emlet identifies three interior functions of the heart: cognition, affection, and volition. "The heart thinks and remembers; the heart feels and experiences; the heart chooses and acts."[42] These three overarching functions are consistent with those identified by Fitzpatrick.

Further, Emlet identifies three categories of exterior influence upon the heart: intrapersonal, interpersonal, and extrapersonal.[43] The intrapersonal influence consists of the heart's interaction with its body. This interaction between heart and body is twofold. First, the heart always acts through the body—what the heart initiates, the body carries out in the physical world.[44] Second, the body is also a context in which the heart functions and to which it responds. Bodily weaknesses and limitations are circumstantial factors to which the morally responsible heart must respond either righteously or sinfully.[45] The interpersonal influence consists of relational factors, such as one's family and other important personal influences, both past and present.[46] The extrapersonal influence consists of broader societal factors. Comparing interpersonal and extrapersonal influence, Emlet explains, "The people around us have a more immediate, direct influence on our hearts. But the ethos of the surrounding culture exerts a mediate, perhaps more indirect influence."[47] Appropriating Calvin's description of fallen human nature as a "perpetual factory of idols,"[48] Emlet explains that humans are idol-factories surrounded by a culture comprising other idol-factories.[49] Thus, it is important to grasp

---

40. Emlet, "Understanding the Influences on the Human Heart," 47.

41. Emlet, "Understanding the Influences on the Human Heart," 48.

42. Emlet, "Understanding the Influences on the Human Heart," 48.

43. Emlet, "Understanding the Influences on the Human Heart," 47.

44. Emlet, "Understanding the Influences on the Human Heart," 48.

45. Emlet, "Understanding the Influences on the Human Heart," 49.

46. Emlet, "Understanding the Influences on the Human Heart," 51.

47. Emlet, "Understanding the Influences on the Human Heart," 51.

48. John Calvin, *Institutes of the Christian Religion*, ed. John T. McNeill, trans. Ford Lewis Battles (Philadelphia: Westminster, 1960), 1.11.8.

49. Emlet, "Understanding the Influences on the Human Heart," 51.

the tendencies of a person's surrounding culture in order to understand the responses of his heart.

Emlet's model represents a twofold shift away from that of Adams. First, like the other authors discussed in this section, Emlet focuses on discerning the motivations of the counselee's heart in order to bring about change. Second, he offers a systematic portrait of the heart's context as a means of better understanding the heart's responses. Adams, too, believed in the importance of understanding the counselee's context. For example, he had all of his counselees fill out a "Personal Data Inventory" in order to collect helpful background information about them.[50] However, such data collection was used to discern what aspects of a person's life might need to be restructured in order to address the problem being dealt with in counseling.[51] The degree to which the problem was related to other aspects of the counselee's life was determined by the degree to which the person's life might need to be restructured. In contrast, Emlet seeks to understand the complexities of counselees' lives and the responses of their hearts so that the gospel might "map onto the reality" of their circumstances.[52]

---

50. Adams, *The Christian Counselor's Manual*, 433–35.

51. Adams, *Competent to Counsel*, 155–56.

52. Emlet, "Understanding the Influences on the Human Heart," 52. In two later works, Emlet stresses the importance of understanding counselees' contexts and life experiences in order to truly address their problems. See Michael R. Emlet, *CrossTalk: Where Life & Scripture Meet* (Greensboro, N.C.: New Growth Press, 2009); Michael R. Emlet, *Saints, Sufferers, and Sinners: Loving Others as God Loves Us* (Greensboro, N.C.: New Growth Press, 2021). He argues that Christian counselees must be understood simultaneously as saints who need their identity confirmed, sufferers who need to be comforted, and sinners who need to be confronted. We must counsel them with these categories in mind because, "If we miss the fact that people have a dominant story (or stories) that shapes and directs the course of their lives, ministry will look a lot like putting out multiple brushfires.... Without considering the shaping stories of people's lives, we'll provide solution-focused counsel but perhaps miss the roots of the problem…if we don't recognize people's functional worldviews, we won't make much sense of the thoughts, attitudes, words, and actions that flow out of their overarching stories. People don't need compartmentalized solutions for compartmentalized problems," Emlet, *CrossTalk*, 79. Emlet urges counselors to connect with the experiences of their counselees in a way that is foreign to Adams's approach.

Jeremy Pierre

Jeremy Pierre directly addresses the lack of depth in Adams's approach to counseling and the heart. He argues that Adams's approach

> describes well the habitual dynamic of behavior, but this dynamic may be only the surface operation of something much deeper: a lack of faith in the gospel. Thus, a counselor's task is not summed up in the teaching of techniques to put off bad behavior patterns and put on good behavior patterns. A counselor's task addresses primarily what underlies these things.[53]

Pierre suggests two fundamental components of counseling that Adams's approach lacked. First is a continual emphasis on faith in Christ as the way to restore human functioning. He grants that "Adams has a strong view of the gospel's central role in change," but he urges that "faith must be upheld as the *continual* means by which these gospel realities are made manifest."[54] This consistent, continual emphasis on faith is missing from Adams's work. Second, such an emphasis on faith in Christ must be applied to all of the heart's functions.[55] This shifts the methodological target of counseling away from actions and toward the heart.

Like Fitzpatrick and Emlet, Pierre identifies three functions of the heart: cognition, affection, and volition. His identification of

---

53. Jeremy Pierre, "'Trust in the Lord with All Your Heart': The Centrality of Faith in Christ to the Restoration of Human Functioning" (PhD diss., The Southern Baptist Theological Seminary, 2010), 235–36. Responding to Adams's assertion that "why" questions are unnecessary in counseling, Pierre writes, "A proper understanding of the human heart sees no conflict between the *why* question and human responsibility. Why questions are heart questions. *Why* does someone choose one particular sinful behavior over another? Why does he not sin in greater ways? Why is she so faithful in one part of her life and not in another? Why does he seem so irrational in certain situations and not others? Why does he respond with such strong emotions to certain stimuli? Such questions do not threaten human responsibility, but rather shed further light into how responsible moral agents are functioning internally in response to their circumstances in the constant battle between faith and unbelief. Helping a counselee understand these dynamics can help him in turn understand how sin and its various effects are being expressed in his life. In other words, *why* questions give a more comprehensive understanding of human responsibility by seeking a more comprehensive understanding of the human heart," 17–18 (italics original).

54. Pierre, "'Trust in the Lord with All Your Heart,'" 237n77 (italics original).

55. Pierre, "'Trust in the Lord with All Your Heart,'" 220, 237n77.

these functions, however, is based upon an extensive semantic study of the words for "heart," "soul," "spirit," and "mind" in the New Testament.[56] Cognition consists of one's thoughts, beliefs, understanding, and interpretations; affection consists of one's desires, feelings, and values; and volition consists of one's commitments and choices.[57] These three functions are unified, overlapping, interrelated, and non-hierarchical.[58] When the heart fulfills these three functions properly, it achieves the singular goal for which it was designed: the worship of God.[59] In this sense, Pierre's model resembles the previous models I have discussed. All of them view humans as worshipers and the heart as determinative of what we worship.

Like Emlet, Pierre sets the heart in context. In Pierre's model, the context to which the heart responds comprises four parts: God, self, others, and circumstances.[60] Understanding the heart's dynamic response to each of these parts is vital to the process of change. Thus, helping the counselee change involves four simultaneous tasks, each of which is based upon the dynamic functions of the heart: the counselor works to read (understand the responses of the person's heart to his context), reflect (help the person understand his own responses), relate (help the person see how the gospel of Christ relates to his heart and his circumstances), and renew (call the person to new, biblical responses by faith).[61] Thus, counseling requires a deep understanding of the heart and its responses to its context, as well as a continual call to dependence upon Christ in faith, which is the only means by which the heart may be rightly and progressively restored to its purpose of worshiping God.

Pierre also lays a helpful foundation for recovering an appropriate understanding of habituation that properly considers the operations

---

56. Pierre, "'Trust in the Lord with All Your Heart,'" 20–79.

57. Pierre, *The Dynamic Heart in Daily Life*, 38–47.

58. Pierre, *The Dynamic Heart in Daily Life*, 17, 23.

59. Pierre, *The Dynamic Heart in Daily Life*, 22–23.

60. Pierre, *The Dynamic Heart in Daily Life*, 101–76. Although the general presentation of the model does not include the body, Pierre does underscore the importance of the body as part of the context in which the heart functions. See Pierre, *The Dynamic Heart in Daily Life*, 16.

61. Pierre, *The Dynamic Heart in Daily Life*, 176–239.

of the heart. Patterned heart responses create a trajectory in a person's life by which he tends to intuitively respond to particular situations in similar ways over time.[62] In other words, the heart is gradually habituated in its responses.[63] Counseling involves uncovering habituated, intuitive, sinful heart responses and changing them into righteous heart responses by faith in Christ. The difference between Pierre and Adams on this point is that Pierre seeks to uncover and replace such habituated responses at the level of the heart, whereas Adams sought to uncover and replace them at the level of bodily behavior.

Summary: Heart Motivation, Personal Responsibility, and Worship
Three observations are noteworthy regarding the above models. First, all of these models locate the source of the believer's remaining sin in the heart, whereas Adams located it in the body. Thus, these models set the heart as the methodological target of counseling, unlike that of Adams, whose methodological target was the sinfully habituated body. Furthermore, a methodological focus on the heart leads the proponents of these models to engage with the specifics of why people do what they do. The "what" that must change cannot truly be addressed until the "why" of one's sinful behavior has been determined. The interior motivations for sinful behavior must be uncovered in order to bring about change. Adams, on the other hand, engaged primarily with what his counselees did, and he only discussed motivation to ensure that they did it out of a desire to please God and not for some other, lesser goal.[64]

Second, all of the models emphasize the importance of personal responsibility. Although they each discuss circumstantial factors to varying degrees, they all stress that the heart is morally responsible

---

62. Pierre, *The Dynamic Heart in Daily Life*, 31.

63. Pierre stresses that the heart is always active and responsible, even in these habituated responses. The responses have simply become intuitive. They are "reflexive responses that arise out of the deeper structures of [people's] beliefs, values, and commitments." Pierre, *The Dynamic Heart in Daily Life*, 34.

64. In this, we could say that Adams was not concerned with uncovering sinful motivations—he was concerned that his counselees have righteous motivations for their actions.

for its responses to its context. This dispels Adams's concern that questions of "why" would undercut personal responsibility.

Third, all of the models emphasize that humans were designed for worship. This leads them to conclude that people behave in certain ways because of perceived outcomes. They worship functional gods because of what they believe those gods have to offer. Helping people change involves not only uncovering their functional gods but also discerning the thoughts and desires that led them to "worship" those particular gods through their behavior. Furthermore, the restoration of human functioning entails helping people become true worshipers of the one true God in thought, desire, word, and deed.

Efforts to Recover Habituation in Biblical Counseling

Within the past ten years, three authors have explicitly attempted to recover habituation in biblical counseling. Michael Emlet has sought to appropriate James K. A. Smith's[65] discussion of habit for the biblical counseling movement.[66] Brian Mesimer has critiqued Adams's view of habituation, but he has suggested that habit should not be abandoned. Rather, he has emphasized the necessity of incorporating habituation into a biblical counseling methodology and has relied on both historic and contemporary sources in his endeavor to revive an interest in habit.[67] Greg Gifford draws on the English Puritans in an effort to validate Adams's understanding of habit.[68] I will discuss these authors more extensively in chapter 6. In short, their attempts to reengage the topic of habituation in biblical counseling are commendable, but none of them properly and consistently distinguish between natural habits and supernatural habits—this is a vital distinction that

---

65. James K. A. Smith, *Cultural Liturgies*, vol. 1, *Desiring the Kingdom: Worship, Worldview, and Cultural Formation* (Grand Rapids: Baker Academic, 2009).

66. Emlet, "Practice Makes Perfect?."

67. Mesimer, "Habits and the Heart"; Mesimer, "Rehabilitating Habituation."

68. Gifford, "The Role of Habits in Spiritual Maturity from the Perspective of the English Puritans"; Greg E. Gifford, "John Owen's Perspective on the Effects of Habits: Habits Promote the Sanctity of the Church," *The Journal of Biblical Soul Care* 3, no. 1 (Fall 2019): 53–69; Gifford, "Jay Adams' Teaching of Habituation"; Gifford, *Heart and Habits*.

is fundamental to Owen's theology of Spirit-infused habitual grace in sanctification.

Conclusion: From "What" to "Why" to "How"

The shift in emphasis in the biblical counseling movement instigated by Powlison can be summarized simply as a shift from "what" to "why." Adams was concerned primarily with the "what" of human behavior; Powlison and those who followed him were concerned with the "why." Though this shift in focus from outward behavior to inward heart motivation was appropriate, I suggest that further development is necessary in order to appropriately understand human functioning and change. We must understand not only what behaviors people need to change and why they engage in those behaviors but also how God works by his Spirit to change people's hearts and behaviors. A historic theology of Spirit-infused habitual grace accomplishes this. Indeed, it both corrects Adams's view of habituation and unifies habituation and heart motivation. As I noted above, Pierre argues that faith in Christ must be continually emphasized in biblical counseling and that it must be applied to the breadth of the heart's functions. I suggest that a proper understanding of Spirit-infused habitual grace helps us apprehend what the Spirit is doing as He sanctifies the functions of the heart. God, by His Spirit, habitually strengthens our faith and restores our hearts to their original design, which overflows into outwardly holy lives. Understanding this process increases the confidence of both the counselor and the counselee in the task of counseling.

John Owen provided a robust explanation of Spirit-infused habitual grace, and his reliance upon this concept is evident through-out his works. His use of the concept must be understood within the framework of the Spirit's work in relation to the Father and the Son, the Spirit's work upon Christ in His humanity, and, finally, the Spirit's work upon those who have been united to Christ. I now turn to an examination of this framework.

Chapter 3

Trinitarian Agency and the Spirit's Work

According to John Owen,[1] a Spirit-infused, supernatural habit of grace is "a virtue, a power, a principle of spiritual life and grace, wrought, created, infused into our souls, and inlaid in all the faculties of them, constantly abiding and unchangeably residing in them, which is antecedent unto, and the next cause of, all acts of true holiness whatever."[2] All habits—both natural and supernatural—incline and dispose the mind, the affections, and the will toward particular acts.[3] However, natural and supernatural habits differ significantly. Everyone can acquire natural habits through repetitive acts. Such natural habits, however, cannot produce true holiness. Holiness can only come about through Spirit-infused habitual grace. Thus, natural habits acquired through natural effort may lead to an outwardly moral life, but they do not constitute true sanctification. We can only be sanctified by the Spirit's infusion and increase of habitual grace within us, which progressively inclines our souls toward obedience to God.[4]

This chapter will lay the foundation for a later discussion of Spirit-infused habitual grace in sanctification by properly grounding

---

1. Though Owen's life and historical context are important and interesting, a biographical sketch of Owen is beyond the scope of this work. For helpful modern biographies of Owen, the reader should consult Peter Toon, *God's Statesman: The Life and Work of John Owen* (Eugene, Ore.: Wipf and Stock, 2018) and Crawford Gribben, *John Owen and English Puritanism: Experiences of Defeat*, Oxford Studies in Historical Theology (New York: Oxford University Press, 2017).

2. Owen, *A Discourse Concerning the Holy Spirit*, in *Works*, 3:475.

3. Owen, *A Discourse Concerning the Holy Spirit*, in *Works*, 3:472–73.

4. Owen, *A Discourse Concerning the Holy Spirit*, in *Works*, 3:474–75. I will discuss the differences between natural and supernatural habits more fully in chapter 5.

it in the doctrine of God. Because sanctification is a work of the Spirit of God, a proper understanding of it must flow from the doctrine of God. John Owen recognized this, and, helpfully, he set his exposition of the doctrine of sanctification within a robust explanation of trinitarian agency. Furthermore, his doctrine of the simplicity of the divine nature undergirded his belief in the necessity of the prior work of God in man throughout sanctification.

The purpose of this chapter, then, is to explain how John Owen grounded the doctrine of sanctification in the doctrine of God. Believers are wholly dependent upon the Spirit of God to infuse and increase habitual grace within them for their sanctification. Understanding the nature of this dependence requires delineating between the works appropriated to each person of the Godhead, understanding the Spirit's work of sanctification in relation to His other works, and understanding how the nature of God demands our dependence upon Him. Thus, I will begin this chapter with an overview of Owen's doctrine of inseparable trinitarian operations and his explanation of the works appropriated to each person of the Trinity according to their order of subsistence. I will then provide an in-depth overview of Owen's explanation of the particular works appropriated to the Spirit. I will conclude with a discussion of Owen's argument that the perfection of God necessitates that He maintains the only purely free and independent will to which the free acts of every other will must be subordinate. For the sake of my argument, this means that no man can become holy without a prior act of God infusing habitual sanctifying grace within him.

Trinitarian Agency

Ryan McGraw notes that "Owen's trinitarian theology was the foundation of his trinitarian piety, and his trinitarian piety permeated every area of his theology."[5] He further states, "Owen's theology of the Holy Spirit illustrates some of the ways that he made the doctrine

---

5. Ryan M. McGraw, *John Owen: Trajectories in Reformed Orthodox Theology* (Cham, Switzerland: Springer International, 2017), 18.

of the Trinity the foundation of personal piety."[6] For Owen, the doctrine of the Trinity was not irrelevant to Christian life—it was vital. Thus, discussing the work of the Spirit in the sanctification of believers required that he ground this work in the doctrine of the Trinity, something he clearly set forth to do in his magisterial work on the Holy Spirit, ΠΝΕΥΜΑΤΟΛΟΓΙΑ, *or A Discourse Concerning the Holy Spirit.*[7]

Central to Owen's trinitarian theology was the doctrine of inseparable trinitarian operations. This doctrine has been described as "a regulative principle in his theological thinking."[8] He referenced the indivisible or undivided works of the Trinity in numerous works.[9] I will begin this section by outlining Owen's conception of this doctrine. This will involve explaining his conception of unity and

---

6. McGraw, *John Owen*, 135–36; cf. Matthew Barrett and Michael A. G. Haykin, *Owen on the Christian Life: Living for the Glory of God in Christ*, Theologians on the Christian Life (Wheaton, Ill.: Crossway, 2015), 58–59.

7. This work comprises volumes three and four of *The Works of John Owen*, ed. William H. Goold, 16 vols. (Edinburgh: Banner of Truth, 1967). The contents of volume three were published together by Owen in 1674 as ΠΝΕΥΜΑΤΟΛΟΓΙΑ, *or A Discourse Concerning the Holy Spirit*. Volume four comprises individual treatises that were published separately, some of which were published posthumously. However, the editor of Owen's works, William H. Goold, collated them as though they were a continuation of ΠΝΕΥΜΑΤΟΛΟΓΙΑ. Crawford Gribben, a recent biographer of Owen, apparently disagrees with Goold's decision (*John Owen and English Puritanism*, 19). However, based upon statements in prefaces to the treatises and in the treatises themselves, Goold seems to have accomplished Owen's design. See, for example, *Works*, 4:6, 355, 420.

For a summary of the material in volume three, see Suzanne McDonald, "John Owen's *Discourse on the Holy Spirit*," in *The Oxford Handbook of Reformed Theology*, ed. Michael Allen and Scott R. Swain, Oxford Handbooks (Oxford: Oxford University Press, 2020), 266–79. For a more systematic presentation of Owen's pneumatology, see Maarten Wisse and Hugo Meijer, "Pneumatology: Tradition and Renewal," in *A Companion to Reformed Orthodoxy*, ed. Herman Selderhuis, Brill's Companions to the Christian Tradition 40 (Boston: Brill, 2013), 488–514.

8. Richard W. Daniels, *The Christology of John Owen* (Grand Rapids: Reformation Heritage Books, 2004), 101.

9. See, for example, Owen, *Of Communion with God the Father, Son, and Holy Ghost*, in *Works*, 2:18, 268–69; *A Brief Declaration and Vindication of the Doctrine of the Trinity*, in *Works*, 2:407; *A Discourse Concerning the Holy Spirit*, in *Works*, 3:93, 94–95, 162, 181, 198; *A Discourse on the Holy Spirit as Comforter*, in *Works*, 4:358; *The Death of Death in the Death of Christ*, in *Works*, 10:163; *The Mystery of the Gospel Vindicated and Socinianism Examined*, in *Works*, 12:142; *Hebrews*, ed. William H. Goold (Edinburgh: Banner of Truth, 1991), 4:413–14.

distinction in the Godhead, his understanding of God's works *ad intra*, and his understanding of God's works *ad extra*. I will then provide a general overview of the works *ad extra* that Owen believed are appropriated to each person of the Godhead.

Inseparable Operations

Owen affirmed the theological assertion that *Opera Trinitatis ad extra sunt indivisa*;[10] that is, "The *ad extra* (or external) works of the Trinity are undivided."[11] This is a doctrine with a rich theological heritage stemming back to Augustine.[12] Owen summarized his conception of the doctrine thus:

____

10. Owen, *A Discourse Concerning the Holy Spirit*, in *Works*, 3:162. For a discussion of how this doctrine undergirded Owen's stress on the importance of communing with each person of the Godhead in worship, see Kelly M. Kapic, *Communion with God: The Divine and the Human in the Theology of John Owen* (Grand Rapids: Baker Academic, 2007), 162–65; McGraw, *John Owen*, 22–26. For a discussion of how this doctrine functioned among the Puritans generally, see Joel R. Beeke and Mark Jones, *A Puritan Theology: Doctrine for Life* (Grand Rapids: Reformation Heritage Books, 2012), 91–93.

11. Richard A. Muller, *Dictionary of Latin and Greek Theological Terms: Drawn Principally from Protestant Scholastic Theology*, 2nd ed. (Grand Rapids: Baker Academic, 2017), 246.

12. Though Augustine is often credited with developing this doctrine, scholars such as Lewis Ayres have shown that Augustine relied on a Latin Christian tradition that preceded him. See Lewis Ayres, *Augustine and the Trinity* (New York: Cambridge University Press, 2010). My purpose here is not to defend this doctrine, nor is it to prove Owen's reliance on the Augustinian tradition. Rather, I merely intend to expound Owen's presentation and use of the doctrine in order to show how it informed his conception of infused habitual grace. For an explanation of Augustine's presentation of the doctrine and a comparison of Owen's use of the doctrine with that of Augustine, see Kyle Claunch, "What God Hath Done Together: Defending the Historic Doctrine of the Inseparable Operations of the Trinity," *Journal of the Evangelical Theological Society* 56, no. 4 (December 2013): 781–800. For a defense of Owen's use of the doctrine and its consistency with his doctrine of the incarnation, see Kyle David Claunch, "The Son and the Spirit: The Promise of Spirit Christology in Traditional Trinitarian and Christological Perspective" (PhD diss., The Southern Baptist Theological Seminary, 2017); Tyler R. Wittman, "The End of the Incarnation: John Owen, Trinitarian Agency and Christology," *International Journal of Systematic Theology* 15, no. 3 (July 2013): 284–300; Adonis Vidu, "Trinitarian Inseparable Operations and the Incarnation," *Journal of Analytic Theology* 4 (May 2016): 106–27.

Robert Letham argues that Owen's trinitarian theology takes advantage of the trinitarian heritage of the Eastern tradition while also maintaining some of the difficulties of the Western tradition. See Robert Letham, "John Owen's Doctrine of the Trinity in Its Catholic Context," in *The Ashgate Research Companion to John Owen's Theology*, ed. Kelly M. Kapic

There is no such division in the external operations of God that any one of them should be the act of one person, without the concurrence of the others; and the reason of it is, because the nature of God, which is the principle of all divine operations, is one and the same, undivided in them all. Whereas, therefore, they are the effects of divine power, and that power is essentially the same in each person, the works themselves belong equally unto them.[13]

He urged that "every divine work, and every part of every divine work, is the work of God, that is, of the whole Trinity, inseparably and undividedly."[14] Such unity, however, does not diminish the distinction of the persons from one another and the outward divine works that terminate on each of them. He explained,

But on those divine works which outwardly are of God there is an especial impression of the order of the operation of each person, with respect unto their natural and necessary subsistence, as also

and Mark Jones, Ashgate Research Companions (New York: Routledge, 2015), 185–97. For a rebuttal to Letham and a defense of Owen's trinitarian theology, see McGraw, *John Owen*, 9–41.

Alan Spence contends that, although Owen affirmed the doctrine of inseparable operations, his theology represents a functional turn from the doctrine, which Spence believes is a positive theological development. See Alan Spence, *Incarnation and Inspiration: John Owen and the Coherence of Christology*, T & T Clark Theology (London: T & T Clark, 2007), 124–37. Brian Kay argues that strict adherence to inseparable operations in Western trinitarian theology was an unfortunate development. Rather than arguing that Owen developed Western trinitarian theology, he suggests that Owen overcame the impasse in Western theology brought about by its adherence to the doctrine of inseparable operations by drawing on an Eastern focus on the individual acts of each person. See Brian K. Kay, *Trinitarian Spirituality: John Owen and the Doctrine of God in Western Devotion*, Studies in Christian History and Thought (Eugene, Ore.: Wipf and Stock, 2008), 106–13. For a response to Spence and Kay and a defense of Owen's consistent use of the doctrine, see Wittman, "The End of the Incarnation," 285–87; Claunch, "The Son and the Spirit," 129–43.

Ryan McGraw has helpfully summarized an appropriate approach to post-Reformation Reformed trinitarian theology: "The question facing historians researching a Reformed author such as Owen should not be whether he was eastern or western, but how, as a Reformed theologian, he evaluated historical sources and how he filtered them through his Reformed understanding of Scripture." See Ryan M. McGraw, "Seeing Things Owen's Way: John Owen's Trinitarian Theology and Piety in Its Early-Modern Context," in *John Owen between Orthodoxy and Modernity*, ed. Willem van Vlastuin and Kelly M. Kapic, Studies in Reformed Theology 39 (Boston: Brill, 2019), 193.

13. Owen, *A Discourse Concerning the Holy Spirit*, in *Works*, 3:162.

14. Owen, *A Discourse Concerning the Holy Spirit*, in *Works*, 3:94.

with regard unto their internal characteristical properties, whereby we are distinctly taught to know them and adore them.[15]

Understanding Owen's use of this doctrine requires discussing his presentation of the essential unity of the Godhead and the distinction of the persons, the works of God *ad intra,* and the works of God *ad extra.*

Unity and distinction. A clear statement of Owen's doctrine of the Trinity can be found at the beginning of *The Doctrine of the Holy Trinity Explained and Vindicated.*[16] The "substance of the doctrine of the Trinity" is that "God is one; — that this one God is Father, Son and Holy Ghost;—that the Father is the Father of the Son; and the Son, the Son of the Father; and the Holy Ghost, the Spirit of the Father and the Son; and that, in respect of this their mutual relation, they are distinct from the other."[17] God is one with regard to His essence—or nature—and He is three with regard to His persons. Thus, there is unity in God with regard to the divine nature and distinction with regard to divine personhood.

In proving the oneness of God, Owen appealed primarily to Deuteronomy 6:4 and Isaiah 44:6–8, both of which, he asserted, prove that God is one in nature while also implying a plurality of persons.[18] Further, Owen maintained the simplicity of God's nature.[19] God is

---

15. Owen, *A Discourse Concerning the Holy Spirit,* in *Works,* 3:94–95.

16. In Owen, *Works,* 2:365–453.

17. Owen, *The Doctrine of the Holy Trinity Explained and Vindicated,* in *Works,* 2:377.

18. Owen, *The Doctrine of the Holy Trinity Explained and Vindicated,* in *Works,* 2:381. He wrote, "And although there be no more absolute and sacred truth than this, that God is one, yet it may be evinced that it is nowhere mentioned in the Scripture, but that, either in the words themselves or the context of the place, a plurality of persons in that one sense is intimated."

19. Owen, *A Display of Arminianism,* in *Works,* 10:19–20, 44; *The Mystery of the Gospel Vindicated and Socinianism Examined,* in *Works,* 12:71–72. Beeke and Jones have noted that a proper understanding of divine simplicity is essential to explaining the unity and power of God. See Beeke and Jones, *A Puritan Theology,* 62. They quote Charnock, who said, "Where there is the greatest simplicity, there is the greatest unity; and where there is the greatest unity, there is the greatest power." Quoted from *The Existence and Attributes of God,* in *The Works of Stephen Charnock* (Edinburgh: Banner of Truth, 1997), 2:124. For further discussion of Owen's doctrine of divine simplicity, see Carl R. Trueman, *John Owen: Reformed Catholic, Renaissance Man,* Great Theologians (Aldershot, England: Ashgate,

singular and simple in nature, but He subsists in three distinct persons. Owen defined a divine person as "the divine essence, upon the account of an especial Property, subsisting in an especial manner."[20] He proved God's subsistence in three persons by showing that Scripture portrays the Father, the Son, and the Holy Spirit each as God, as the author of divine operations, and as the object of divine worship.[21] Each person to whom is ascribed the name of God, any of the divine properties of God, or the works of God must have the nature of God.[22] The persons are simultaneously distinct and inseparable.[23] Thus, each person is God, yet each person is also distinct from the other two persons.[24] Such distinction means not only that the persons can be differentiated from one another but also that they each have particular works ascribed to them. These works can be divided into God's works *ad intra* and *ad extra*.[25]

God's works *ad intra*. Owen defined God's works *ad intra* as "those internal acts in one person whereof another person is the object." Such acts "are natural and necessary, inseparable from the being and existence of God."[26] The works of God *ad intra* are the primary means by which the persons are distinguished from one another. Commenting on the reference to Jesus as the Son of God in

---

2007), 38–39; Christopher Cleveland, *Thomism in John Owen* (Burlington, Vt.: Ashgate, 2013), 52–60. See also the discussion below.

20. Owen, *The Doctrine of the Holy Trinity Explained and Vindicated*, in *Works*, 2:407.

21. For his biblical and theological defense of the deity of the Father, the Son, and the Holy Spirit, see Owen, *The Doctrine of the Holy Trinity Explained and Vindicated*, in *Works*, 2:381–404. For his extended defense of the deity and personhood of the Spirit, see Owen, *A Discourse Concerning the Holy Spirit*, in *Works*, 3:64–92.

22. Owen, *A Discourse Concerning the Holy Spirit*, in *Works*, 3:89–90.

23. Owen affirmed the doctrine of divine *circumincession*, or *perichoresis*, which states that the persons of the Godhead interpenetrate one another by virtue of their shared nature in a way that does not diminish their distinction (*The Mystery of the Gospel Vindicated and Socinianism Examined*, in *Works*, 12:73). For a further discussion on the significance of this doctrine in Owen's theology, see McGraw, *John Owen*, 23.

24. Owen, *The Mystery of the Gospel Vindicated and Socinianism Examined*, in *Works*, 12:72.

25. For definitions of these terms drawn from their common use among Protestant scholastic theologians, see Muller, *Dictionary of Latin and Greek Theological Terms*, 244.

26. Owen, *A Discourse Concerning the Holy Spirit*, in *Works*, 3:66–67.

Hebrews 4:14, Owen provided a glorious meditation on the *ad intra* relations of the persons of the Godhead:

> Here the sacred truth of the *trinity of persons* in the divine nature or essence openeth itself unto the creatures. The nature, the essence, or being of God, is absolutely and numerically one. All the natural and essential properties of that being are absolutely and essentially the same; and all the operations of this divine essence or being, according to its properties, are undivided, as being the effects of one principle, one power, one wisdom. Hence it could not by any such acts be manifested that there was more than one person in that one nature or being. But now, in these actings of the persons of the Trinity in such ways as firstly respect themselves, or their operations "ad intra," where one person is as it were the object of the other persons' acting, the sacred truth of the plurality of persons in the same single, undivided essence is gloriously manifested. The Son undertaking to the Father to become a high priest for sinners, openly declares the distinction of the Son, or eternal Word, from the person of the Father. And in these distinct and mutual actings of the persons of it is the doctrine and truth of the holy Trinity most safely contemplated.[27]

For Owen, the simple reference to Jesus as both the great High Priest and the Son of God was enough to prove a plurality of coequal divine persons in whom the divine nature subsists.

The *ad intra* acts of the persons upon one another are their eternal relations of origin. The Father eternally begets the Son, the Son is eternally begotten of the Father, and the Spirit eternally proceeds from them both.[28] The Father is so only with reference to the Son, the Son is so only with reference to the Father, and the Holy Spirit is so only with reference to the Father and the Son.[29] The Father knows and loves the Son, the Son knows and loves the Father, and the Spirit

---

27. Owen, *Hebrews*, 4:413–14 (italics original).

28. Owen, *The Doctrine of the Holy Trinity Explained and Vindicated*, in *Works*, 2:405. Owen provided an extended defense of the eternal generation of the Son from the Father in *The Mystery of the Gospel Vindicated and Socinianism Examined*, in *Works*, 12:184–200, and of the eternal procession of the Spirit from the Father and the Son in *A Discourse Concerning the Holy Spirit*, in *Works*, 3:59–63.

29. Owen, *The Doctrine of the Holy Trinity Explained and Vindicated*, in *Works*, 2:381; *A Discourse Concerning the Holy Spirit*, in *Works*, 3:60–61.

is the medium of such acts, the "mutual love of the Father and the Son, knowing them as he is known."[30] The persons' eternal relations of origin determine their eternal order of subsistence. The Father is the first person because He begets the Son, the Son is the second person because He is begotten of the Father, and the Spirit is the third person because He proceeds from them both.[31]

God's works *ad extra*. God's works *ad extra* are external works of God, "which are voluntary, or effects of will and choice, and not natural or necessary."[32] The persons of the Godhead, in their order of operation *ad extra*, follow their eternal and natural order of subsistence *ad intra*.[33] In the *ad extra* operations of the Trinity, the persons operate in inseparable unity, although particular works in the economy of salvation are attributed to particular persons relative to their order of subsistence *ad intra*.

The *ad extra* operations are of two types. The first type are those external acts in which the object of the act is another person of the Godhead. In such acts, "the person that is the object of these actings is not considered absolutely as a divine person, but with respect unto some peculiar dispensation and condescension."[34] Such acts are synonymous with the missions of the divine persons, each of which corresponds to the *ad intra* order of subsistence. As the Father eternally begets the Son, so also does He send the Son into the world to take on human nature for the redemption of man. As the Spirit eternally proceeds from the Father and the Son, so also do the Father and the Son send Him into the world to impart to the church the blessings of Christ's accomplished redemption.[35]

---

30. Owen, *A Discourse Concerning the Holy Spirit*, in *Works*, 3:67; cf. *Posthumous Sermons, 1760*, in *Works*, 9:614 (also referred to as Owen's *Sacramental Discourses*).

31. Owen, *A Discourse Concerning the Holy Spirit*, in *Works*, 3:91–92.

32. Owen, *A Discourse Concerning the Holy Spirit*, in *Works*, 3:67.

33. Owen, *A Discourse Concerning the Holy Spirit*, in *Works*, 3:91, 198–99; Owen, *Hebrews*, 2:34; 3:34–35.

34. Owen, *A Discourse Concerning the Holy Spirit*, in *Works*, 3:67.

35. Also of note is Owen's discussion of the Son as the principal object of the Father's love by the Spirit. Owen argued that, because the Son is the principal object of the Father's love *ad intra*, so also is the Son, incarnate in His humanity, the "first and full object of the

The second type of works *ad extra* are those works that are special acts toward the creatures, all of which are simultaneously attributed to God *qua* His divine nature as well as appropriated to individual persons of the Godhead according to their order of subsistence. Owen explained the importance of understanding this concept: "None who have learned the first principles of the doctrine of Christ, but can tell you what works are ascribed peculiarly to the Father, what to the Son, and what to the Holy Ghost."[36] I now turn to a discussion of the particular external works attributed to each person of the Trinity.

Appropriation of Divine Works

In discussing the appropriation of divine works, it is important to distinguish between the principle out of which an act arises and the end on which it terminates.[37] The principle out of which every trinitarian work *ad extra* arises is the divine nature, and the end on which it terminates is one of the particular persons. Therefore, Owen explained, "There is no such division in the external operations of God that any one of them should be the act of one person, without the concurrence of the others; and the reason of it is, because the nature of God, which is the principle of all divine operations, is one and the same, undivided in them all."[38] In the work of redemption, we have all that we have from the Father, through the Son, by the Spirit.[39] That which the Father purposed to do, the Son purchased and procured, and the Spirit applies.[40]

---

love of the Father in those acts of it which are 'ad extra.'" See *A Declaration of the Glorious Mystery of the Person of Christ*, in *Works*, 1:144–50.

36. Owen, *A Discourse Concerning the Holy Spirit*, in *Works*, 3:67.

37. Wittman explains the importance of the historic use of the terms *principium* and *terminus*, which refer to these two concepts, and he notes that, although Owen does not use these terms explicitly, the concepts are present in his discussion of *ad extra* trinitarian works. He concludes, "Far from innovating or weakening the received grammar of trinitarian theology, Owen is in basic continuity with the Augustinian tradition as it came through Aquinas and was articulated by Reformed Orthodoxy." See "The End of the Incarnation," 294–300.

38. Owen, *A Discourse Concerning the Holy Spirit*, in *Works*, 3:162.

39. Owen, *A Discourse Concerning the Holy Spirit*, in *Works*, 3:198–99.

40. Owen, *A Discourse Concerning the Holy Spirit*, in *Works*, 3:158–59.

For the sake of my argument, I am particularly concerned with the works appropriated to the Spirit. However, a brief overview of the works appropriated to the Father and the Son will be helpful in preparation for a larger discussion of the work of the Spirit. Regarding the works appropriated to the Father, Owen wrote, "The foundation of the whole glorious work of the salvation of the church was laid in the sovereign will, pleasure, and grace of God, even the Father."[41] In the Father, there originally resides authority, love, and power, all of which are required for the work of redemption and are directed by infinite wisdom. He reveals His authority, love, and power thus:

> He sent the Son, as he gives the Spirit, by an act of sovereign authority. And he sent the Son from his eternal love;—he loved the world, and sent his Son to die. This is constantly assigned to be the effect of the love and grace of the Father. And he wrought in Christ, and he works in us, with respect unto the end of this mystery, with the "exceeding greatness of his power," Eph. 1:19.[42]

The Son "puts the whole authority, love, and power of the Father in execution."[43] In carrying out the will of the Father in time, the Son assumed to Himself a human nature.[44] This was a work that was distinctly suitable to Him and not to the Father or the Spirit.[45] The Spirit

---

41. Owen, *Hebrews*, 2:507.

42. Owen, *A Declaration of the Glorious Mystery of the Person of Christ*, in *Works*, 1:219.

43. Owen, *A Declaration of the Glorious Mystery of the Person of Christ*, in *Works*, 1:219.

44. Owen made the seemingly controversial claim that "the only singular immediate act of the person of the Son on the human nature was the assumption of it into subsistence with himself." *A Discourse Concerning the Holy Spirit*, in *Works*, 3:160. I will explain and defend this statement in light of Owen's orthodox Christology in the next chapter.

45. Owen explained, "Wherefore, this work of our redemption and recovery being the especial effect of the authority, love, and power of the Father—it was to be *executed* in and by the person of the Son; as the application of it unto us is made by the Holy Ghost. Hence it became not the person of the Father to assume our nature;—it belonged not thereunto in the order of subsistence and operation in the blessed Trinity. The authority, love, and power whence the whole work proceeded, were his in a peculiar manner. But the execution of what infinite wisdom designed in them and by them belonged unto another. Nor did this belong unto the person of the Holy Spirit, who, in order of divine operation following that of his subsistence, was to perfect the whole work, in making application of it unto the church when it was wrought. Wherefore it was every way suited unto divine wisdom—unto the order of the Holy Persons in their subsistence and operation—that this work should be undertaken and accomplished in the person of the Son." *A Declaration of*

brings about the "perfecting application of the whole [work of redemption] unto all its proper ends."[46] He is the "immediate, peculiar, efficient cause of all external divine operations."[47] I now turn to a fuller discussion of His work.

The Work of the Spirit

This book focuses on the Spirit's sanctifying work of infusing habitual grace within believers. Yet, this is not the only work that the Spirit does. In this section, I will set the Spirit's work of sanctification within the overall work of the Spirit. Doing so will help to distinguish the work of the Spirit in sanctification from His other works, thus enabling me to discuss His work of infusing habitual grace with greater clarity.

Owen's presentation of the work of the Spirit is divided into two overarching heads: the work of the Spirit in the old creation and the work of the Spirit in the new creation. By old creation, Owen meant those works that are of nature, and by new creation, he meant those works that are of grace.[48] The former refers to the works of God whereby He created the world and continues to sustain it;[49] the latter

---

the Glorious Mystery of the Person of Christ, in *Works* 1:220 (italics original). Kapic notes that Owen's line of reasoning led him to a different conclusion than that of Aquinas regarding the fittingness of the Son becoming incarnate. See Kapic, *Communion with God*, 75. For a further discussion of Owen on the fittingness of the Son's incarnation, see Sinclair B. Ferguson, "John Owen and the Doctrine of the Person of Christ," in *John Owen: The Man and His Theology: Papers Read at the Conference of the John Owen Centre for Theological Study, September 2000*, ed. Robert W. Oliver (Phillipsburg, N.J.: P&R, 2002), 87–88.

46. Owen, *A Declaration of the Glorious Mystery of the Person of Christ*, in *Works*, 1:219; cf. 1:94, 96, 101, 159, 206; cf. Barrett and Haykin, *Owen on the Christian Life*, 76–79, 161–63.

47. Owen, *A Discourse Concerning the Holy Spirit*, in *Works*, 3:161.

48. Owen, *A Discourse Concerning the Holy Spirit*, in *Works*, 3:95. It is important to note that Owen distinguished grace in multiple ways. Here, it is distinguished from nature, but in the discussion below, it will be distinguished from gifts. The former use is broader and indicates God's work toward the church in general whereby He works out His plan of redemption; the latter is narrower and indicates God's sanctifying work of infusing habitual grace within particular members of the church.

49. Owen, *A Discourse Concerning the Holy Spirit*, in *Works*, 3:94–99, 103. As scriptural support for the Spirit's work in creation and providence, he cites Genesis 1:2, Job 26:13; Psalms 8:3 (cf., Matt. 12:28 and Luke 11:20); 19:1; and 104:29–30.

refers to the works of God whereby He redeems fallen humanity by grace and restores the image of God in them.[50] With regard to both heads, the Spirit is the immediate, efficient, and perfecting cause of all. Owen's chief concern is the work of the Spirit toward the new creation, which is nothing more than the founding, building up, and finishing of the church of God.[51] That is, he was primarily concerned with the work of the Spirit toward Christ and His church.

There are two types of this work: the Spirit's work of infusing and increasing habitual grace and the Spirit's work of bestowing gifts.[52] Both of these must be considered first with regard to Christ in His

---

50. Owen, *A Discourse Concerning the Holy Spirit*, in *Works*, 3:102. For discussions of the Spirit's restoration of the image of God in Owen's works, see Sinclair B. Ferguson, *John Owen on the Christian Life* (Edinburgh: Banner of Truth, 1987), 65–67; Steve Griffiths, *Redeem the Time: Sin in the Writings of John Owen* (Fearn, Scotland: Mentor, 2001), 29–44; Kapic, *Communion with God*, 35–66; Suzanne McDonald, "The Pneumatology of the 'Lost' Image in John Owen," *Westminster Theological Journal* 71, no. 2 (Fall 2009): 323–35; Andrew M. Leslie, *The Light of Grace: John Owen on the Authority of Scripture and Christian Faith*, Reformed Historical Theology 34 (Göttingen, Germany: Vandenhoeck & Ruprecht, 2015), 160–74. See also chapter 5 below.

51. Owen, *A Discourse Concerning the Holy Spirit*, in *Works*, 3:104–5.

52. Owen summarized the entirety of the work of the Spirit in and toward men under three headings: "sanctifying grace," "especial gifts," and "evangelical privileges" (*A Discourse Concerning the Holy Spirit*, in *Works*, 3:206). William H. Goold, the editor of Owen's collected works, noted that the first heading serves as a summary of books III through VIII of *ΠΝΕΥΜΑΤΟΛΟΓΙΑ* (*Works*, 3:207–651 and 4:1–419) and that the second heading is a summary of book IX (*Works*, 4:420–520; see *Works*, 4:352 for Goold's note). Because book IX (*A Discourse of Spiritual Gifts*) is the last book of *ΠΝΕΥΜΑΤΟΛΟΓΙΑ*, and because it was published posthumously, it may be that Owen intended to produce further works that would elucidate the third heading, "evangelical privileges." However, Nathaniel Mather, in his preface to the 1692 joint publication of *A Discourse on the Holy Spirit as Comforter* and *A Discourse of Spiritual Gifts*, wrote, "These two discourses, with those formerly published, make up all that Dr Owen perfected or designed on this subject of the Spirit" (*Works*, 4:354). Therefore, it may also be that Owen's work on spiritual gifts truly did complete his intended treatment of the subject of the Holy Spirit. Furthermore, Owen seems to have determined to limit his particular treatment of the Holy Spirit to graces and gifts, noting that he dealt extensively with the privileges given to believers by the Holy Spirit in *Of Communion with God the Father, Son and Holy Ghost* (*Works*, 2:1–275) and *The Doctrine of the Saints' Perseverance Explained and Confirmed* (*Works*, 11:1–666; for Owen's reference to these works, see *Works*, 4:383). Evangelical privileges, then, seem to be benefits that arise out of the grace and gifts we receive by the Spirit. In light of this, I will treat grace and gifts as the primary headings of Owen's treatment of the work of the Holy Spirit, and any particular privileges that I may need to mention will fall under one of these two headings.

human nature and then with regard to His church. The Spirit is the immediate, peculiar, and efficient cause of all God's works of grace and gifts toward Christ in His human nature and toward the church.[53] Owen stressed the importance of understanding this: "And this belongs unto the establishment of our faith, that he who prepared, sanctified, and glorified the human nature, the natural body of Jesus Christ, the head of the church, hath undertaken to prepare, sanctify, and glorify his mystical body, or all the elect given unto him of the Father."[54]

It is here that I come to my primary concern regarding Owen's doctrine of the Holy Spirit. In Christ's human nature and in the church, the Spirit carries out His sanctifying work of infusing and increasing habitual grace. In chapter 4 I will discuss the Spirit's gracious work in the human nature of Christ, and in chapter 5 I will discuss His gracious work in believers. In preparation for those discussions, however, it is necessary to bring greater clarity to the Spirit's work of infusing habitual grace by defining it and distinguishing it from His gifts. It will then be necessary to explain the continuity and discontinuity of the Spirit's work of infusing grace and bestowing gifts between the Old and New Testaments.

Defining the Spirit's Work of Grace

The Spirit's work of grace in the believer is synonymous with His infusion and increase of habitual grace in the soul. This work is begun at regeneration, continued through sanctification, and perfected in glorification. Owen defined regeneration as

---

53. Owen, *A Discourse Concerning the Holy Spirit*, in *Works*, 3:161.

54. Owen, *A Discourse Concerning the Holy Spirit*, in *Works*, 3:189. Ferguson further elucidates Owen's point: "Owen understands that Jesus was the recipient and bearer of the Spirit both *prior to* our becoming the recipients of the Spirit and also *with a specific view to* our reception of the Spirit. Furthermore, the relationship formed between the divine Spirit and the incarnate Mediator is determinative of the character of the ministry of the Holy Spirit to all believers." See Sinclair B. Ferguson, "John Owen and the Doctrine of the Holy Spirit," in *John Owen: The Man and His Theology: Papers Read at the Conference of the John Owen Centre for Theological Study, September 2000*, ed. Robert W. Oliver (Phillipsburg, N.J.: P&R, 2002), 108.

the infusion of a new, real, spiritual principle into the soul and its faculties, of spiritual life, light, holiness, and righteousness, disposed unto and suited for the destruction or expulsion of a contrary inbred, habitual principle of sin and enmity against God, enabling unto all acts of holy obedience, and so in order of nature antecedent to them.[55]

Such a work is necessary because, "without an infused habit of internal inherent grace, received from Christ by an efficacious work of the Spirit, no man can believe or obey God, or perform any duty in a saving manner, so as it should be accepted with him."[56] This work of regeneration is continuous with sanctification.[57] Owen defined sanctification thus: "in the sanctification of believers, the Holy Ghost doth work in them, in their whole souls, their minds, wills, and affections, a gracious, supernatural habit, principle, and disposition of living unto God; wherein the substance or essence, the life and being, of holiness doth consist."[58] In regeneration, the Spirit plants a seed, or habit, of grace within the soul of the believer that the same Spirit continues to grow through sanctification. Regeneration and sanctification are also continuous with glorification, such that the habit of grace that is infused at regeneration is increased in sanctification and perfected in glorification.[59]

Distinguishing Grace from Gifts
Owen published one of the only discourses on spiritual gifts ever produced by the Puritans, a work titled *Holy Spirit and His Work, as a*

---

55. Owen, *A Discourse Concerning the Holy Spirit*, in *Works*, 3:219; cf. 3:220, 222, 224.

56. Owen, *A Discourse Concerning the Holy Spirit*, in *Works*, 3:292.

57. Owen, *A Discourse Concerning the Holy Spirit*, in *Works*, 3:325; cf. Henk van den Belt, "*Vocatio* as Regeneration: John Owen's Concept of Effectual Calling," in *John Owen between Orthodoxy and Modernity*, ed. Willem van Vlastuin and Kelly M. Kapic, Studies in Reformed Theology 39 (Boston: Brill, 2019), 150.

58. Owen, *A Discourse Concerning the Holy Spirit*, in *Works*, 3:468–69.

59. Owen, *A Discourse Concerning the Holy Spirit*, in *Works*, 3:183, 189, 207, 336–37. For further discussion of Owen on regeneration and sanctification, see Ferguson, *John Owen on the Christian Life*, 41–66; Barrett and Haykin, *Owen on the Christian Life*, 163–74; Randall C. Gleason, *John Calvin and John Owen on Mortification: A Comparative Study in Reformed Spirituality*, Studies in Church History 3 (New York: Peter Lang, 1995), 95–108.

Comforter and as the Author of Spiritual Gifts.[60] Early in this discourse, he outlined the distinction between the infused grace of the Spirit and the bestowed gifts of the Spirit, which is not only central to my argument but also a significant aspect of his pneumatology and his theology of the Christian life.[61] Before describing the differences between these two works of the Spirit, it is important to note their similarities.

Similarities between sanctifying grace and spiritual gifts. Owen offered four similarities between grace and gifts.[62] First, both sanctifying graces and spiritual gifts have been purchased by Christ for His church.[63] On this point, Owen made clear that he referred to those gifts that are peculiar to Christ's church under the new covenant. They are those gifts whereby Christ lays the foundation of and edifies the church and demonstrates His power and exercises His rule in the church.[64] Such gifts were secured by Christ for the church and are superior to all gifts of common grace that men might receive by the Spirit for the purpose of increasing moral, civil, or political abilities. Furthermore, the gifts to which Owen referred here are distinct even from those that were given to men under the old covenant as

---

60. J. I. Packer remarks that this is the only full-scale treatment by a major Puritan writer of which he is aware. See *A Quest for Godliness: The Puritan Vision of the Christian Life* (Wheaton, Ill.: Crossway, 1990), 219. For a further analysis of Owen's discussion of grace and gifts, see Ferguson, *John Owen on the Christian Life*, 202–4.

61. Ferguson, *John Owen on the Christian Life*, 202.

62. This discussion is located in John Owen, *A Discourse of Spiritual Gifts*, in *Works*, 4:425–28. Owen used "grace" (singular) and "graces" (plural) interchangeably. Both refer to the Spirit's infusion of a regenerating and sanctifying habit of grace in the soul of the believer. His interchangeable use of the terms reveals the holistic nature of the Spirit's work in the soul. The Spirit infuses a habit of grace (singular) in the soul at regeneration that is like a seed. That seed is the root of all sanctification, and, as one grows, the operations of that seed begin to affect the whole soul, producing the fruits of righteousness. The work of the Spirit, then, can be viewed with regard to the root (singular) or the fruits (plural). Thus, "grace" (singular) often refers to the seed or root implanted by the Spirit out of which all holiness arises, and "graces" (plural) often refers to those varied operations or fruits in the soul that have arisen out of it. Further, since all holiness is worked by the Spirit, outward righteous actions can sometimes be referred to as "graces" (plural) because they are visible results of the Spirit's underlying infusion and increase of grace within the believer's soul.

63. Owen, *A Discourse of Spiritual Gifts*, in *Works*, 4:425.

64. Here, Owen cited Acts 1:4, 8; 2:33; and 2 Corinthians 10:3–6 (*A Discourse of Spiritual Gifts*, in *Works*, 4:426).

preparation for the new. The gifts of all the Old Testament prophets fall short of those received by John the Baptist, and yet even his gifts were inferior to the gifts received by the one who is "least in the kingdom of heaven" (Matt. 11:11).[65] With his assertion that these gifts are peculiar to the church under the new covenant, Owen indicated the distinct spheres in which the Spirit distributes gifts. Before the revelation of the gospel, the Spirit distributed extraordinary gifts among His people to prepare them for the gospel.[66] During that time, He also distributed ordinary gifts for the upholding and ruling of the natural order, which He continues to do today, even after the revelation of the gospel.[67] But, under the new covenant, the gifts that He gives to the church have been peculiarly secured by Christ, and such gifts share this in common with the Holy Spirit's work of grace.

Second, both sanctifying graces and spiritual gifts have the Holy Spirit as their immediate efficient cause.[68] Consistent with the order of subsistence of the persons of the Trinity, the Son procures both graces and gifts for the church, and the Spirit applies them to the church.

Third, both sanctifying graces and spiritual gifts "are designed unto the good, benefit, ornament, and glory of the church."[69] Owen made a further distinction here between the church believing and the church professing.[70] Grace is infused into the church believing in order to give it invisible life, and gifts are bestowed upon the church professing in order to give it visible life. The church believing

---

65. Owen, *A Discourse of Spiritual Gifts*, in *Works*, 4:426.

66. Owen cited Balaam as an example of somebody in the Old Testament who received the extraordinary gift of prophecy, showing that the Spirit has the freedom to distribute any gifts to whomever He chooses, even those outside of the covenant people of God. Balaam could receive such a gift and still be an enemy of God because gifts do not by their nature necessitate saving grace, as will be discussed below (*A Discourse Concerning the Holy Spirit*, in *Works*, 3:141–42).

67. Owen, *A Discourse Concerning the Holy Spirit*, in *Works*, 3:6; *A Discourse of Spiritual Gifts*, in *Works*, 4:425. He cited Cyrus as an example of a ruler "out of the pale of the church" who received such gifts (*A Discourse Concerning the Holy Spirit*, in *Works*, 3:103, 149).

68. Owen, *A Discourse of Spiritual Gifts*, in *Works*, 4:427.

69. Owen, *A Discourse of Spiritual Gifts*, in *Works*, 4:427.

70. Owen, *A Discourse of Spiritual Gifts*, in *Works*, 4:427.

is referred to in Ephesians 5:25–27 as the subject of Christ's work of sanctification and cleansing with the word, "that He might present her to Himself a glorious church, not having spot or wrinkle or any such thing, but that she should be holy and without blemish." The church professing is referred to in Ephesians 4:16 as a body of members who mutually build one another up "for the edifying of itself in love." In both senses, that which Christ gives by His Spirit benefits the church.[71]

Fourth, both saving graces and spiritual gifts are communicated to the church out of the bounty of Christ.[72] All saving grace that is infused is a freely bestowed gift from Christ.[73] Every gift that is bestowed is not a grace in the believer but a grace toward the believer, "proceeding from gracious favor and bounty."[74]

Differences between sanctifying grace and spiritual gifts. Owen outlined seven differences between sanctifying graces and spiritual gifts.[75] First, sanctifying graces are fruits of the Spirit's work *in* men, whereas spiritual gifts are effects of the Spirit's work *upon* them.[76] Owen argued that, wherever the Spirit works, there also is His presence:

> [God] doth not only give and send his Spirit unto them to whom he designs so great a benefit and privilege, but he actually collates and bestows him upon them. He doth not send him unto them, and leave it in their wills and power whether they will receive him or no, but he so effectually collates and puts him in them or upon them as that they shall be actually made partakers of them.... So, then, where God intendeth unto any the benefit of his Spirit, he will actually and effectually collate him upon them.[77]

---

71. Owen, *A Discourse of Spiritual Gifts*, in *Works*, 4:427–28.

72. Owen, *A Discourse of Spiritual Gifts*, in *Works*, 4:428.

73. Here, he cites Matthew 13:11 and Philippians 1:29 (Owen, *A Discourse of Spiritual Gifts*, in *Works* 4:428).

74. Owen, *A Discourse of Spiritual Gifts*, in *Works*, 4:428. He cites Romans 12:6 and Ephesians 4:7, which describe the gifts given by Christ as that which flows out of His grace.

75. This discussion is located in Owen, *A Discourse of Spiritual Gifts*, in *Works*, 4:428–38.

76. Owen, *A Discourse of Spiritual Gifts*, in *Works*, 4:428–29.

77. Owen, *A Discourse Concerning the Holy Spirit*, in *Works*, 3:112–13.

However, when God gives or sends His Spirit, He does so in different manners and for different ends. Commenting on John 14:17, where Jesus promises that the Spirit who was already with the disciples would one day be in them, Owen wrote, "our Lord Jesus Christ promiseth to send the Holy Ghost unto his disciples as a comforter, whom they had received before as a sanctifier."[78] Their new reception of Him would be for a different purpose than their previous reception of Him. Owen further explained, "But in every coming of his, he is sent for one especial work or another; and this sufficiently manifests that in his gifts and graces he is not common unto all."[79] The graces and gifts imparted by the Spirit have distinct ends. With regard to graces, the Spirit conforms the believer to the image of Christ, which is "the principal end for which he is promised."[80] One may receive gifts, however, without receiving infused, sanctifying grace. Such a person partakes of the Spirit, but not in such a way that results in his being sanctified and conformed to the image of Christ.

Second, saving grace proceeds from the eternal, electing love of God, whereas gifts proceed from His temporary election of individuals to particular offices in the church or works in the world.[81] One can receive gifts related to temporary election without being eternally elected. Judas, who for a season was endowed with the same gifts as the other apostles, was not ordained by God unto eternal life.[82] All who receive grace according to eternal election will receive gifts according to their calling in the church, but not all who receive gifts necessarily receive grace by God's decree.

Third, saving grace belongs to the internal form and essence of the new covenant, whereas gifts belong to the external administration of it.[83] The distinction between the internal grace of the covenant and the external administration of it is vital in preventing theological confusion:

---

78. Owen, *A Discourse Concerning the Holy Spirit*, in *Works*, 3:111.
79. Owen, *A Discourse Concerning the Holy Spirit*, in *Works*, 3:111.
80. Owen, *A Discourse of Spiritual Gifts*, in *Works*, 4:429.
81. Owen, *A Discourse of Spiritual Gifts*, in *Works*, 4:429–31.
82. Owen, *A Discourse of Spiritual Gifts*, in *Works*, 4:430.
83. Owen, *A Discourse of Spiritual Gifts*, in *Works*, 4:431–32.

> For all the promises of the plentiful effusion of the Spirit under the new testament, which are frequently applied unto him as he works and effects evangelical gifts, extraordinary and ordinary, in men, do belong unto the new covenant,—not as unto its internal essence and form, but as unto its outward administration. And if you overthrow this distinction, that the covenant is considered either with respect unto its internal grace or its external administration, every thing in religion will be cast into confusion. Take away internal grace, as some do, and the whole is rendered a mere outside appearance; take away the outward administration, and all spiritual gifts and order thereon depending must cease.[84]

Some who partake of the internal grace of the covenant do not partake of its external administration. Owen explained that this is particularly true of elect infants who die before their baptism.[85] Moreover, some who belong to the outward administration of the covenant by virtue of the spiritual gifts they have received never partake of its internal grace.

Fourth, grace is immediately related to Christ's mediatorial office as priest, whereas gifts are immediately related to His mediatorial office as king.[86] The Spirit's work of sanctification specifically applies what Christ has accomplished according to His priestly office. His kingship should not be separated from this, "for by his kingly power he makes effectual the fruits of his oblation and intercession."[87] Gifts, however,

---

84. Owen, *A Discourse of Spiritual Gifts*, in *Works*, 4:432.

85. Owen, *A Discourse of Spiritual Gifts*, in *Works*, 4:432. Owen's view of baptism is somewhat complicated. Gribben notes that his early writings seem to indicate that he held to a form of baptismal regeneration but that he later changed his view (*John Owen and English Puritanism*, 51, 63; cf. Owen, *Two Short Catechisms*, in *Works*, 1:469; *A Display of Arminianism*, in *Works* 10:80–81). This apparent change is supported by Owen's description of baptism as a sign of regeneration rather than a cause of it in a posthumously published tract titled *Of Infant Baptism and Dipping*, in *Works*, 16:260. In this tract, he argued that all children of believers are capable of the grace signified in baptism and, therefore, should be baptized. Furthermore, he suggests that all children of believers who die in infancy are certainly regenerated. Thus, he argues that all children of believers should be baptized, not because they are regenerated through baptism, but because they are capable of being regenerated and may already have been regenerated.

86. Owen, *A Discourse of Spiritual Gifts*, in *Works*, 4:432–33.

87. Owen, *A Discourse of Spiritual Gifts*, in *Works*, 4:432.

proceed exclusively from His kingly office, whereby He continues the visible administration of His kingdom and builds up the church.

Fifth, infused habitual grace is permanent, whereas gifts are temporary.[88] Gifts may be completely lost, but grace can only be diminished. Owen identified gifts as one of those things that are lost by the apostasy described in Hebrews 6:4–6, which concerns those who have shared in the Holy Spirit.[89] In his commentary on these verses, he explained, "The Holy Ghost is present with many as unto powerful operations, with whom he is not present as to gracious inhabitation; or, many are made partakers of him in his spiritual gifts who are never made partakers of him in his saving graces."[90] Those who receive gifts but not grace can fall away, but those who partake of the gracious indwelling of the Spirit will never fall away.

Sixth, saving grace is primarily for the good of the one who receives it, whereas gifts are primarily for the good of others.[91] Owen cautioned, however, that one should not oversimplify this distinction. Although graces are primarily for personal benefit, they also benefit others through the example of our godly living, through the fruitful outworking of our gracious dispositions, and through the adorning of the gospel. Although gifts are primarily given for the edification of others, they also benefit the one upon whom they are bestowed.

Seventh, gifts affect only the mind, whereas saving graces affect the whole soul.[92] Like many Reformed Orthodox theologians, Owen distinguished between the theoretical intellect and the practical intellect. Gifts only affect the theoretical intellect.[93] "They are intellectual abilities, and no more."[94] In contrast, the gracious operations of the

---

88. Owen, *A Discourse of Spiritual Gifts*, in *Works*, 4:434–35.

89. Owen, *A Discourse of Spiritual Gifts*, in *Works*, 4:435.

90. Owen, *Hebrews*, 5:81.

91. Owen, *A Discourse of Spiritual Gifts*, in *Works*, 4:435–36.

92. Owen, *A Discourse of Spiritual Gifts*, in *Works*, 4:436–37.

93. Owen, *A Discourse of Spiritual Gifts*, in *Works*, 4:437; cf. *A Discourse Concerning the Holy Spirit*, in *Works* 3:280–82. For a discussion of the theoretical and the practical intellect in Puritan thought, see Paul Helm, *Human Nature from Calvin to Edwards* (Grand Rapids: Reformation Heritage Books, 2018), 79–84, 111–19.

94. Owen, *A Discourse of Spiritual Gifts*, in *Works*, 4:437. Importantly, Owen made room for those gifts that are not intellectual, such as miracles and tongues. He argued that

Spirit bring about an actual transformation of the soul that inclines a person toward holiness.[95] Gifts merely grant an intellectual capacity to an individual, one that may be temporary, whereas grace produces an inward change that results in practical obedience.

The mutual benefits of sanctifying grace and spiritual gifts. Owen called sanctifying grace "the only proper soil for gifts to flourish in."[96] Grace prevents the abuse of gifts and adorns their expression with the beautiful fruit of the gospel. Furthermore, gifts promote the increase and operation of grace through the edification of the mind.[97] Christians, therefore, should not be discouraged from pursuing gifts because of their temporal and limited nature. Rather, they should pursue gifts to their proper end and seek the Spirit's work of grace to undergird them.

The Work of the Spirit in the Old and New Testaments:
Discontinuity and Continuity

The preceding discussion regarding the distinction between grace and gifts has demonstrated the priority of infused habits of grace over spiritual gifts, in that habits of grace are permanent fixtures of the soul and result in actual, personal holiness, whereas spiritual gifts are temporary and primarily promote the holiness of others.[98] Owen demonstrated this contrast further by asserting the continuity of the Spirit's gracious operations in believers from the Old Testament to the New Testament. In this section, I will discuss, first, Owen's understanding

---

such gifts only have a transient operation on those who are given them, whereas all others have an actual residence in the individual and affect the intellect.

95. Owen, *A Discourse of Spiritual Gifts,* in *Works,* 4:437.

96. Owen, *A Discourse of Spiritual Gifts,* in *Works,* 4:438.

97. Owen, *A Discourse of Spiritual Gifts,* in *Works,* 4:438.

98. This is not to say that gifts are unimportant by any means. Gifts serve to build up the body of Christ. However, it is to say, as Owen did, that an abundance of gifts where grace is absent will still result in condemnation. Such is the argument of Paul in 1 Corinthians 13:1–2: "Though I speak with the tongues of men and of angels, but have not love, I have become sounding brass or a clanging cymbal. And though I have the gift of prophecy, and understand all mysteries and all knowledge, and though I have all faith, so that I could remove mountains, but have not love, I am nothing." To have the greatest spiritual gifts without the love that springs from an internal habit of grace will result in no personal gain.

of the works of the Spirit that are discontinuous between the Old and New Testaments and, second, his understanding of the continuity of Spirit-infused habitual grace between the Old and New Testaments.

Discontinuity. Two axioms guide Owen's consideration of the works of the Spirit that are peculiar to the Old Testament. First, every excellent work of men—whether by an extraordinary enablement exceeding the abilities of their nature or by an improvement of the abilities of their nature—is brought about by the Holy Spirit, who is its immediate operator and efficient cause. Second, the works of the Spirit that are peculiar to the Old Testament were preparation for the work accomplished in and by Christ in His incarnation.[99]

The works of the Spirit that are peculiar to the Old Testament are of two kinds. The first kind are extraordinary giftings that exceed men's natural abilities. Such works include prophecy,[100] the writing

---

99. Owen, *A Discourse Concerning the Holy Spirit*, in *Works*, 3:126. Owen's overall understanding of the relationship between the covenants has been the subject of much debate. For his own summary of the major differences between the old and new covenants, see *Hebrews*, 6:87–98. For discussions of Owen's understanding of the relationship between the covenants, see Ferguson, *John Owen on the Christian Life*, 20–32; Sebastian Rehnman, "Is the Narrative of Redemptive History Trichotomous or Dichotomous? A Problem for Federal Theology," *Dutch Review of Church History* 80, no. 3 (January 2000): 296–308; Richard C. Barcellos, "John Owen and New Covenant Theology: Owen on the Old and New Covenants and the Functions of the Decalogue in Redemptive History in Historical and Contemporary Perspective," *Reformed Baptist Theological Review* 1, no. 2 (July 2004): 12–46; Sebastian Rehnman, *Divine Discourse: The Theological Methodology of John Owen*, Texts and Studies in Reformation and Post-Reformation Thought (Grand Rapids: Baker Academic, 2002), 162–76; Trueman, *John Owen*, 67–99; Beeke and Jones, *A Puritan Theology*, 293–303; Christopher Earl Caughey, "Puritan Responses to Antinomianism in the Context of Reformed Covenant Theology: 1630–1696" (PhD diss., Trinity College Dublin, 2013), 101–28; Willem J. van Asselt, "Covenant Theology as Relational Theology: The Contributions of Johannes Cocceius (1603–1669) and John Owen (1618–1683) to a Living Reformed Theology," in *The Ashgate Research Companion to John Owen's Theology*, ed. Kelly M. Kapic and Mark Jones, Ashgate Research Companions (New York: Routledge, 2015), 65–84; Ryan M. McGraw, *A Heavenly Directory: Trinitarian Piety, Public Worship and a Reassessment of John Owen's Theology*, Reformed Historical Theology 29 (Göttingen, Germany: Vandenhoeck & Ruprecht, 2014), 140–86.

100. Prophecy refers to the divinely inspired prediction of future events or the declaration of the mind of God. Such prediction or declaration is brought about by God, who prepares and elevates the minds of men and enables them to speak or write His word. Prophecies were revealed by God to men through an articulate voice (Ex. 33:11; Num.

of Scripture,[101] and miracles.[102] The second kind of works are gifts whereby the Spirit brings about an extraordinary improvement of ordinary abilities.[103] These include political gifts directed toward ruling and civil government, gifts of moral virtue such as courage and fortitude, gifts of bodily strength, intellectual gifts for the purpose of artistry and craftsmanship, and intellectual gifts for the purpose of preaching the Word of God.[104] Such works are preparation for the work of the Spirit in and upon Christ and the church under the new covenant.

The peculiar work of the Spirit in the New Testament centers on the gospel, "or the new creation of all things in and by Jesus Christ."[105] Owen believed that the distinct advantage of living under the new covenant consists in a fuller revelation of God and His plan of redemption and a wider outpouring of the Spirit on the people of God. In the work done in and by Christ in His incarnation, more light is cast upon the Trinity, and God's plan of redemption is fully revealed.[106] Furthermore, "the plentiful effusion of the Spirit is that which was principally prophesied of and foretold as the great privilege and pre-eminence of the gospel church-state."[107] As discussed

---

12:8; 1 Kings 19:12–18); dreams and visions in their sleep (Gen. 15:12–16; Dan. 10:9); waking visions, that is, outward representations unto their eyes (Gen. 18:1–2; Ex. 3:2; Josh. 5:13–14); or inward representations unto their minds (1 Kings 22:19–22; Isaiah 6; Ezekiel 1). Sometimes, prophecy was accompanied by symbolic actions (Isa. 20:1–3; Jer. 13:1–5; Ezek. 4:1–3; 12:3–4) or physical transportation to another location (Ezek. 8:3; 11:24). See *A Discourse Concerning the Holy Spirit*, in *Works*, 3:126–39.

101. Owen described the writing of Scripture as a distinct species of prophecy in which the minds of the writers were fully assured of the divine inspiration of their writing. See *A Discourse Concerning the Holy Spirit*, in *Works* 3:143–45.

102. Miracles are immediate effects of the Holy Spirit that are beyond the power of natural causes. The individuals who performed them did not inherently possess the power whereby the miracles were wrought, nor did this power reside in them. They were merely "organs of the Holy Ghost." Such miracles were meant to improve the reputation of and confirm the ministry of the person by whom they were wrought. See *A Discourse Concerning the Holy Spirit*, in *Works*, 3:145–46.

103. Owen, *A Discourse Concerning the Holy Spirit*, in *Works*, 3:148–49.

104. Owen, *A Discourse Concerning the Holy Spirit*, in *Works*, 3:147–50.

105. Owen, *A Discourse Concerning the Holy Spirit*, in *Works*, 3:152.

106. Owen, *A Discourse Concerning the Holy Spirit*, in *Works*, 3:152, 157–58.

107. Owen, *A Discourse Concerning the Holy Spirit*, in *Works*, 3:153; cf. *A Discourse of Spiritual Gifts*, in *Works*, 4:421.

above, under the old covenant, the Spirit granted gifts only to specific individuals in order to prepare the way for the revelation of the gospel under the new covenant. However, under the new covenant, the Spirit bestows gifts on all believers.[108] Moreover, the new covenant church not only receives clearer revelation and a wider outpouring of gifts but also the ministry of the Holy Spirit as Comforter.[109] Finally, the blessings of the Spirit have a wider outpouring under the new covenant, in that they are given to the Gentiles in greater number.[110]

Continuity. Owen believed that the primary distinction between the Old and New Testaments is not the Spirit's working of grace but rather His wider outpouring and His revelation of the nature and plan of God. He argued for the continuity of the gracious work of regeneration and sanctification under the new covenant, under the old covenant, and prior to the establishment of the old covenant, "even from the foundation of the world."[111] In other words, the Spirit

---

108. Owen, *A Discourse Concerning the Holy Spirit*, in *Works*, 3:153–54.

109. Owen, *Hebrews*, 6:95–96; *A Discourse Concerning the Holy Spirit*, in *Works*, 3:111; *A Discourse on the Holy Spirit as Comforter*, in *Works*, 4:357–58.

110. Owen, *A Discourse Concerning the Holy Spirit*, in *Works*, 3:114–15; *A Discourse of the Work of the Holy Spirit in Prayer*, in *Works*, 4:261–63.

111. Owen, *A Discourse Concerning the Holy Spirit*, in *Works*, 3:210. Owen further argued that Old Testament saints were not only regenerated by the Spirit but also indwelt by Him (*The Doctrine of the Saints' Perseverance Explained and Confirmed*, in *Works*, 11:331). See James M. Hamilton Jr.'s discussion of this in *God's Indwelling Presence: The Holy Spirit in the Old and New Testaments*, New American Commentary Studies in Bible and Theology (Nashville: B&H, 2006), 10–13. Note, however, that Owen's understanding of indwelling may be more complex than Hamilton suggests. Owen distinguished the Spirit's personal presence from His omnipresence (*A Discourse on the Holy Spirit as Comforter*, in *Works*, 4:384). Scripture teaches that the Spirit is personally present in the location of His particular works. That which must be determined with regard to the question of indwelling is not only *where* the Spirit is personally present but also *how* He is personally present, i.e., to what end He is personally present (*A Discourse Concerning the Holy Spirit*, in *Works* 3:111). He was personally present with all Old Testament saints to the end of their regeneration and sanctification. Regarding New Testament saints, He is present to this end as well as to other ends that fulfill particular promises of His work under the new covenant.

Such a view on indwelling as Owen's is not merely compatible with the convictions of pedobaptists, who view the old and new covenants as two administrations of the same covenant of grace. Reformed Baptists have also made the case for Old Testament indwelling. For example, Nehemiah Coxe (d. 1689) wrote, "And none can have Union to [Christ] but by the *indwelling of his holy Spirit*; and wherever the Spirit of God applies the Blood of

infused regenerating and sanctifying habitual grace in Old Testament saints just as He does in New Testament saints.

In proving this point, Owen refers to Jesus's interaction with Nicodemus in John 3:1–21.[112] After he hears Jesus teach that one must be born again, Nicodemus asks, "How can these things be?" (v. 9). Jesus reproves him for being a "teacher of Israel" who does not understand the necessity of the new birth (v. 10). Expounding upon Jesus's intention in these words, Owen wrote, "Dost though take upon thee to teach others what is their state and condition, and what is their duty towards God, and art ignorant thyself of so great and fundamental a doctrine, which thou mightest have learned from the Scripture?"[113] Thus, Jesus reproves Nicodemus because he had enough light in the Old Testament Scriptures to know of the necessity of regeneration. Owen concluded, "This doctrine, therefore,—namely that every one who would enter into the kingdom of God must be born again of the Holy Spirit,—was contained in the writings of the Old Testament."[114]

Owen argued that the promises of God under the old covenant— that He would circumcise the hearts of His people, remove their hearts of stone and give them hearts of flesh, and write His law upon their hearts—all refer to regeneration.[115] Such promises describe the

---

Christ for the *Remission* of Sins he doth it also for the *purging of the Conscience from dead Works to serve the living God*," in *A Discourse of the Covenants That God Made with Men before the Law* (London: John Darby, 1681), 87 (italics and capitalization original). Richard Barcellos explains that, in this quote, Coxe refers to believers prior to the incarnation of Christ. See "Guest Post: No Communion and No Christ? Part 3," *Petty France* (blog), April 8, 2020, https://pettyfrance.wordpress.com/2020/04/08/guest-post-no-communion-and-no -christ-part-3/.

Modern Reformed Baptist pastor Geoffrey Thomas has similarly written, "The Holy Spirit indwelt all true Old Testament believers. No one can be born again, believe, repent, or make one step of spiritual progress without the inward work of the Holy Spirit. In fact, no one can persevere in faith for one second without the ongoing internal work of the Holy Spirit—neither in the Old Testament nor in the New Testament." *The Holy Spirit* (Grand Rapids: Reformation Heritage Books, 2011), 23.

112. Owen, *A Discourse Concerning the Holy Spirit*, in *Works*, 3:210. Beeke and Jones note that other Puritans frequently appealed to this text to argue for the necessity of regeneration (*A Puritan Theology*, 465).

113. Owen, *A Discourse Concerning the Holy Spirit*, in *Works*, 3:210.

114. Owen, *A Discourse Concerning the Holy Spirit*, in *Works*, 3:210.

115. Owen, *A Discourse Concerning the Holy Spirit*, in *Works*, 3:210.

nature of God's work in all stages of redemption history. All who are regenerate for all time have been brought out of the same state and into the same state by the same cause.[116] He explained, "The elect of God were not regenerate one way, by one kind of operation of the Holy Spirit, under the Old Testament, and those under the New Testament [by] another."[117]

We may better understand Owen's argument for the regeneration of Old Testament saints if we consider it alongside his doctrine of justification. He viewed regeneration as prior to justification in the *ordo salutis*.[118] Justification occurs on the basis of faith, and faith can only be produced by the Spirit's work of regeneration.[119] Furthermore, the object of justifying faith has always been "the Lord Jesus Christ himself, as the ordinance of God, in his work of mediation for the recovery and salvation of lost sinners, and as unto that end proposed in the promise of the gospel."[120] Old Testament saints believed in the person and work of Christ as progressively revealed by the promises of God, beginning in the garden of Eden in Genesis 3:15.[121] Like New Testament saints, they could only be justified by faith in the person and work of Christ, and such faith could only be produced in them by the Spirit's work of regeneration.

Though saints before and after the revelation of the gospel understood the nature of the work of regeneration to varying extents, they both had revealed to them the necessity of regeneration and had experienced regeneration itself. Thus, the Spirit infused regenerating

---

116. Owen, *A Discourse Concerning the Holy Spirit*, in *Works*, 3:215–16.

117. Owen, *A Discourse Concerning the Holy Spirit*, in *Works*, 3:214.

118. Owen, *A Practical Exposition upon Psalm 130*, in *Works*, 6:597; cf. Ferguson, *John Owen on the Christian Life*, 35–36; Barrett and Haykin, *Owen on the Christian Life*, 215; J. V. Fesko, "John Owen on Union with Christ and Justification," *Themelios* 37, no. 1 (April 2012): 12.

119. Owen was quite concerned with proving that regeneration is wholly a work of the Spirit and that conversion is a fruit of true regeneration. See Owen, *A Discourse Concerning the Holy Spirit*, in *Works*, 3:320–37; *A Display of Arminianism*, in *Works*, 10:100–8.

120. Owen, *The Doctrine of Justification by Faith*, in *Works*, 5:85–86.

121. Owen, *The Doctrine of Justification by Faith*, in *Works*, 5:27. See also McGraw's analysis of the function of Genesis 3:15 in Owen's Old Testament interpretation in *John Owen*, 43–70.

and sanctifying grace in the Old Testament as He did in the New, and He bestowed gifts sparingly among God's people in the Old Testament but upon all of God's people in the New.

The Work of the Spirit: Summary and Conclusion

In this section, I have provided an overview of Owen's understanding of the work of the Spirit in order to highlight the nature of the Spirit's infusion of habitual grace in the soul of the believer. The Spirit's work of grace is not unique to the new covenant. Rather, the Spirit worked regeneration and sanctification in Old Testament saints through infusing and increasing a habit of grace within them, just as He does within New Testament saints. With the coming of Christ and the writing of the New Testament, believers receive a fuller revelation of this work, which was discernible, though somewhat veiled, in the Old Testament. Unique to the New Testament is the wider outpouring of the Spirit upon the Gentiles, the wider outpouring of gifts upon all the members of the church, and the peculiar work of the Holy Spirit as the Comforter of the church.

Owen's distinction between saving grace and spiritual gifts is a key component of his theology. Overall, gifts are temporary, operate only upon the theoretical intellect, and are primarily for the benefit of others. Infused habitual grace, however, is permanent (it may be diminished, but it is never fully removed), operates upon the whole soul, and is primarily for the benefit of those who receive it.

The purpose of this section for the present work has been to isolate the work of the Spirit in sanctification from all of His other works, thus providing a clearer understanding of how Spirit-infused habitual grace relates to sanctification. I have summarized Owen's argument that the Spirit is the immediate, efficient cause of all God's external works, and I have further summarized what these particular works are. Sanctification differs from all of the works attributed to the Spirit in that it brings about a stable renovation of human nature by removing indwelling sin and increasing one's inclination toward righteousness. The Spirit accomplishes this through infused habitual grace.

Habitual Grace and Divine Simplicity

To conclude this overview of Owen's presentation of the work of the Spirit, I now turn to his discussion of infused habits in relation to the nature of God. He argued that the infusion of habitual grace in sanctification is a necessary outworking of God's simplicity. Because God in His nature is pure and simple act, He must be a prior agent to all creaturely acts. Thus, in order for a person to be moved toward holiness, God must, through His Spirit, infuse a habit of grace within that person, and He must similarly bring that habit of grace to fruition.[122] In this section, I will first discuss Owen's understanding of divine being and action, after which I will discuss human action relative to divine action.

Divine Being and Action

Divine simplicity is the doctrine that, although the essence, attributes, and eternal acts of God can be distinguished, they do not differ in any real sense. All are synonymous with the being of God.[123] Owen summarized his doctrine of divine simplicity with four assertions.[124] First, God is simple in His essence because of "his absolute independence and firstness in being and operation."[125] Were God to have a complex

---

122. Carl Trueman has described well the significance of Owen's understanding of the nature of God for salvation. He writes, "For Owen, God can be described using the scholastic notion of pure or simple act. This means that God is fully actualized being, with no potential to change, and no cause either logically or ontologically anterior to himself. This concept lies at the heart of scholastic formulations of the doctrine of divine immutability, and has obvious implications for, among other things, the relationship of God to time, God's simplicity, and thus also for the nature of language about God. While such a definition of God might appear very abstract and impersonal…the attributes which are implied by God's being as pure act are employed by Owen primarily to provide the necessary metaphysical basis for the reliability of God's saving purposes." See *The Claims of Truth: John Owen's Trinitarian Theology* (Carlisle, England: Paternoster Press, 1998), 111–12.

123. James E. Dolezal, *All That Is in God: Evangelical Theology and the Challenge of Classical Christian Theism* (Grand Rapids: Reformation Heritage Books, 2017), 40–44.

124. These assertions are found in Owen's response to Socinian theologian John Biddle in Owen, *The Mystery of the Gospel Vindicated and Socinianism Examined*, in *Works*, 12:71–72. For a lengthy discussion of Owen's doctrine of divine simplicity and its Thomistic roots, see Cleveland, *Thomism in John Owen*, 27–68.

125. Owen, *The Mystery of the Gospel Vindicated and Socinianism Examined*, in *Works*, 12:71.

nature composed of parts or accidents, He could not be the first and highest Being, as such parts or accidents would be prior to Him in existence—thus, He would not be God. Second, God is simple in His essence because His essence and His being are "absolutely and perfectly one and the same."[126] His essence is His existence. Third, the attributes of God "are all of them essentially the same with one another, and every one the same with the essence of God itself."[127] If they are distinct from one another or from God Himself, then there is eternal power that exists outside of God. Fourth, God must be simple and pure act in His essence.[128] If He is not, then there is potentiality in God and, therefore, a lack of perfection and self-sufficiency in Him.

Put simply, "God is pure act of being, without any potentiality."[129] The simplicity of God's nature is directly related to His immutability. God is the God "with whom there is no variation or shadow of turning" (James 1:17). He is the Lord who does not change (Mal. 4:16), the One who eternally is who He is (Ex. 3:14).[130] As He Himself is unchangeable, so also is His will, because it is essential to who He is. Owen explained, "The eternal acts of his will not really differing from his unchangeable essence, must needs be immutable."[131] Furthermore, "The essence of God, then, being a most absolute, pure, simple act or substance, his will consequently can be but simply one."[132] Thus, His decrees are unchanging because His being is unchanging.

Also related to simplicity is Owen's affirmation of divine aseity. God is uncaused and independent as well as self-sufficient. Regarding God's independence, Owen wrote, "Everything that is independent of any else in operation is purely active, and so consequently a god; for

---

126. Owen, *The Mystery of the Gospel Vindicated and Socinianism Examined*, in *Works*, 12:72.

127. Owen, *The Mystery of the Gospel Vindicated and Socinianism Examined*, in *Works*, 12:72.

128. Owen, *The Mystery of the Gospel Vindicated and Socinianism Examined*, in *Works*, 12:72.

129. Cleveland, *Thomism in John Owen*, 27.

130. Owen, *A Display of Arminianism*, in *Works*, 10:20; *The Mystery of the Gospel Vindicated and Socinianism Examined*, in *Works*, 12:72.

131. Owen, *A Display of Arminianism*, in *Works*, 10:20.

132. Owen, *A Display of Arminianism*, in *Works*, 10:44.

nothing but a divine will can be a pure act, possessing such a liberty by virtue of its own essence."[133] God is also self-sufficient with regard to His own eternal blessedness, meaning that nothing can be taken away from Him or added to Him.[134] All of His external works are independent and free, and they arise from His own eternal blessedness.

Four conclusions follow from God's independence and self-sufficiency. First, because such qualities are essential to divinity, no human can share them. Second, any potential for change is foreign to the nature of God because it requires that God may be acted upon by another being. To act upon God is to be greater than God. Third, if no other being can act upon God, then God's agency must be prior to all creaturely acts. Fourth, as creatures, human beings require the prior action of God upon them in order for their wills to be moved because they are imperfectly potential by nature.

Human Action Relative to the Divine

According to Owen, human wills have a twofold dependence upon God. First, as discussed above, by virtue of their creation they are imperfectly potential and dependent upon the providence of God in order to act. Second, by virtue of their corruption by sin they are dependent upon God's grace in order for their acts to be good.[135] Although the human will is subservient to the providence of God, it is still free, for it is a "spontaneous appetite of what seemeth good unto it."[136] It is "free from all outward compulsion and inward necessity," yet in freely choosing what it judges to be good, it always infallibly complies with the providence of God.[137] The will as the internal principle of operation is both active and free, but this freedom is bound by

---

133. Owen, *A Display of Arminianism*, in *Works*, 10:119–20.

134. Owen, *A Declaration of the Glorious Mystery of the Person of Christ*, in *Works*, 1:324–25.

135. Owen, *A Display of Arminianism*, in *Works*, 10:118–19; cf. Trueman, *The Claims of Truth*, 112. Note also, however, Owen's belief that, even before the fall, Adam and Eve were supernaturally inclined toward good by grace (*A Display of Arminianism*, in *Works*, 10:85). I will discuss this further in chapter 5.

136. Owen, *A Display of Arminianism*, in *Works*, 10:119. Owen cites Prosper of Aquitaine for this definition.

137. Owen, *A Display of Arminianism*, in *Works*, 10:119.

the premotion of God. For without the premotion of God, a created will could not act.[138]

Consequent to the fall, every human will in its natural state is unable to do good. Therefore, the will depends upon the supernatural grace of God in order for its acts to be good. Every act proceeds from an underlying habit, or principle, which inclines the will toward that act.[139] The fallen man is habitually inclined toward sin.[140] His mind is darkened (Eph. 4:18), his affections are corrupted (Gen. 6:5), and his will is enslaved (John 8:34).[141] Owen explained,

> The will, though in itself radically free, yet in respect of the term or object to which in this regard it should tend, is corrupted, inthralled, and under a miserable bondage; tied to such a necessity of sinning in general, that though unregenerate men are not

---

138. Trueman summarizes well Owen's argument regarding the freedom of the human will within the bounds of God's providential control: "This argument has a twofold significance for Owen. First, it allows him to safeguard human freedom within a deterministic framework. Depending once again on faculty psychology, Owen argues that the human will is radically free and self-determined with respect to its internal principle of operation, i.e., its own desires and ambitions. Thus, if a human being chooses to act in a particular manner it is because that individual's own intellect and will lead in that direction. Second, this does not negate God's purpose or his control over human action: God uses humans to fulfill his purposes by moving them in a manner consistent with their own internal principle of operation. Thus there is, from a human perspective, a happy coincidence of God's plan and human willing which preserves the former's sovereignty and the latter's freedom." See *The Claims of Truth*, 117.

139. Owen argued that one of the fundamental flaws of Arminianism is its denial of the necessity of a supernaturally infused habit of grace prior to conversion. Thus, Arminians believed that one could perform the act of faith and repentance by virtue of one's natural faculties. In contrast, Owen argued that man's fallenness requires a supernaturally infused habit of grace to be implanted within him, which then enables him to perform the act of faith and repentance (*A Display of Arminianism*, in *Works*, 10:125).

140. In *The Nature, Power, Deceit, and Prevalency of the Remainders of Indwelling Sin in Believers*, Owen delineated between a habitual inclination toward sin and a habitual propensity toward sin. This distinction is determined by the ruling principle of the heart. Unbelievers have a habitual inclination toward sin because sin is the ruling principle of their hearts. Believers, however, only have a habitual propensity toward sin because the Sprit has infused a habit of grace within them that serves as the ruling principle of the heart and inclines them toward righteousness (*Works*, 6:190). I will discuss this further in chapter 5.

141. Owen, *A Display of Arminianism*, in *Works*, 10:126–27.

restrained to this or that sin in particular, yet for the main they can do nothing but sin.[142]

All the acts of sinful men are themselves tainted by sin because they proceed from an indwelling, ruling habit of sin. Because of this, a simple change in one's actions cannot produce righteousness. A change in the underlying habit, or principle, out of which the actions arise is required.[143]

Herein lies the necessity of regeneration. Man cannot overcome his habitual inclination toward sin apart from a supernatural work of regeneration wherein God, by His Spirit, infuses a habit of grace within the soul. Such a habit of grace is "that spiritual vital principle that is infused into us by the Holy Spirit, that new creation and bestowing of new strength, whereby we are made fit and able for the producing of spiritual acts, to believe and yield evangelical obedience."[144] Thus, the human will depends upon divine providence generally for all of its acts and upon divine grace specifically for all of its righteous acts. In order to act at all, the human will requires the prior agency of God, and, in order to act for good, it requires a Spirit-infused habit of grace to change its inclinations.

Although there is an immediate change of the inclinations upon the Spirit's infusion of habitual grace, this change is not complete. In the ongoing work of sanctification, the Spirit progressively works from this principle to cleanse the soul from sin and increasingly incline it toward righteousness. This progressively growing inclination is, itself, the restoration of the image of God.[145] But it is not as though the Spirit begins the work and allows the human to complete it. The Spirit is operative in the beginning, He carries it forward, and He completes it. Regeneration is merely an initial reception of habitual grace. The work must be increased and carried forward from there by the Holy Spirit: "The actual supplies of the Spirit are the waterings that are the

---

142. Owen, *A Display of Arminianism*, in *Works*, 10:128.

143. Cleveland, *Thomism in John Owen*, 85–86.

144. Owen, *A Display of Arminianism*, in *Works*, 10:135.

145. Owen, *A Discourse Concerning the Holy Spirit*, in *Works*, 3:386; cf. Kapic, *Communion with God*, 58–64.

immediate cause of its increase. It wholly depends on continual influences from God. He cherisheth and improves the work he hath begun with new and fresh supplies of grace every moment."[146] The human always depends upon the divine for continual supplies of grace.

Conclusion

In this chapter, I have sought to appropriately ground the doctrine of sanctification in the doctrine of God. Specifically, I have explained how John Owen's understanding of sanctifying, Spirit-infused habitual grace arises out of his trinitarian theological framework and his argument for divine simplicity. Owen held to a classical understanding of trinitarian inseparable operations and divine appropriations, which led him to conclude that the Spirit is the immediate, efficient cause of all the external works of God. The Spirit works from the Father, through the Son, and in and upon the human nature of Christ and His church. Furthermore, Owen's affirmation of divine simplicity led him to the conclusion that humans are completely dependent upon God in their actions, both in their natural state and in the state of grace.

The purpose, then, of this chapter has been to show that God graciously effects sanctification by His Spirit. He carries out this work by infusing and increasing habitual grace within the soul of the believer. It is a work in which man is completely dependent upon God's prior gracious operations through His Spirit. This is fundamental to a proper approach to biblical counseling because it emphasizes that habituation is a work of the Spirit and that this work occurs at a deeper level than that of behavior. Sanctification does not occur merely at the level of the acts, and it does not lie within our own power. Rather, it begins at the level of the habits of the soul as the Spirit infuses and increases habitual grace within the believer, progressively inclining him more and more toward holiness. In order for an act to be truly holy, it must proceed from a gracious habit infused by the Spirit. This provides counselors with a proper understanding of what is actually happening in the work of sanctification they seek

---

146. Owen, *A Discourse Concerning the Holy Spirit*, in *Works*, 3:393.

to promote. Furthermore, it grounds their work in a knowledgeable dependence upon the Spirit. Growing in our understanding of His work helps to increase our faith in His work. In the next chapter, I will seek to further explain the work of the Spirit in sanctification by discussing Owen's presentation of the Spirit's gracious work in the human nature of Christ as the paradigm for the sanctification of the members of His church.

The Spirit's Work in Christ's Human Nature

The Trinity and the incarnation are two of the most difficult doctrines for Christians to understand, and yet they provide the theoretical grounding for some of the most practical aspects of the Christian life. John Owen devoted numerous pages of his works to their precise exposition, not only doctrinally but also experientially.[1] Owen's doctrinal exposition was never far removed from experimental application. This was particularly the case in his exposition of the work of the Spirit. He grounded his teaching in the work of the Spirit in the Trinity and in the incarnation in order to show that these doctrines are foundational to understanding how the Spirit works in the lives of individual believers.[2] Such doctrinal precision was meant to help believers better examine their experience of the Spirit's work in their own souls.

---

1. The use of the words "experiential" and "experimental" among the Puritans did not convey an elevation of experience over truth. Rather, it was a common theme of their preaching and theological writing that emphasized their belief that true doctrine must be experienced in practical piety. Joel Beeke explains, "The Puritans' experiential faith is not the same as experientialism, which makes experience the end-all, thereby losing its biblical moorings. This is common in contemporary Pentecostalism. Rather, experiential Reformed Christianity addresses how the Holy Spirit brings the truth of God's Word into the experience of the Christian, both in terms of what he ought to be *idealistically* as a believer in Christ (e.g., Rom. 6:10–23 and chap. 8) and what he finds himself to be *realistically* in his holy war against sin (e.g., Rom. 7:14–25). All this is meant to be God-centered and not experience-centered—that is to say, the goal of the believer's examination of his own experience is to trace the Spirit's work in his own soul so as to give glory to God." See Joel R. Beeke, *Puritan Reformed Theology: Historical, Experiential, and Practical Studies for the Whole of Life* (Grand Rapids: Reformation Heritage Books, 2020), 127–28 (italics original).

2. McGraw, *John Owen*, 136.

In the previous chapter, I showed how Owen grounded the sanctifying work of the Spirit in the doctrine of God, specifically regarding the Spirit's work in relation to the Father and the Son and regarding the simplicity of divine being and action. In the present chapter, I will outline Owen's understanding of the work of the Spirit in the incarnation, with a particular focus on His work of infusing habitual grace in the human nature of Christ. As Carl Trueman has noted, if the sinless Son of God in His human nature depended upon the Spirit's work of grace, how much more should the church, with her remaining corruption, consciously depend upon this same work of the Spirit.[3] The Spirit's work in Christ, the head of the Church, is foundational for and paradigmatic of the Spirit's work in the members of His church.[4]

The purpose of this chapter, then, is to ground the doctrine of sanctification in the person and work of Christ. I will begin this chapter by explaining the classical christological framework that undergirded Owen's explanation of the Spirit's work of grace in Christ's human nature. Owen remained consistent with the Christology of the early church in guarding the full deity and the full humanity of Christ. Like the early church, he recognized the significance of the full humanity of Christ for the work of redemption and the Christian life. Next, I will outline his exposition of the Spirit's work of infusing habitual grace in the human nature of Christ. Christ's full humanity meant that He underwent true human development, both in a natural and in a supernatural sense. Thus, He grew naturally as He developed physical and psychological capacities, and He grew supernaturally as the Spirit perfectly sanctified every newly emerging natural capacity

---

3. Carl Trueman, "The Spirit and the Word Incarnate: John Owen's Trinitarian Christology," in *The Holy Spirit and Reformed Spirituality: A Tribute to Geoffrey Thomas*, ed. Joel R. Beeke and Derek W. H. Thomas (Grand Rapids: Reformation Heritage Books, 2013), 35.

4. Richard Daniels has also noted the practical nature of Owen's Christology, writing, "What is true of the practical emphasis in Puritan theology in general is especially true of Owenian Christology. The strong practical emphasis of Owen's Christology is not an interesting sidelight, but one of its distinguishing characteristics. In a deliberate attempt to build his theological edifice upon Christ, Owen firmly secures his practical divinity upon the foundation of Christology, and shows that Christ's person is the center for Christian ethics. In so doing, Owen secures his Puritan practice from dislodging the theological foundation upon which it was built," in *The Christology of John Owen*, 17.

through increasing habitual grace within His soul. Finally, as noted above, Owen's doctrinal exposition was never far removed from practical, experiential application. Thus, I will conclude this chapter by outlining the practical value of Owen's conception of the Spirit's work in the incarnation.

Owen's Classical Christology

Owen was suspicious of ecumenical councils because of their tendency to utilize their supposed authority to distort the truth. He believed so strongly in God's preservation of the truth for His church by His Spirit that he doubted the necessity of such councils, which presumed to authoritatively set down the boundaries of orthodoxy on behalf of the church.[5] Nevertheless, Owen's publication of his own catechisms,[6] his work as one of the primary architects of the Savoy Declaration,[7] and his public endorsement of the doctrines enumerated in the Church of England's Thirty-Nine Articles[8] evidence his

---

5. In his preface to ΧΡΙΣΤΟΛΟΓΙΑ: *or, A Declaration of the Glorious Mystery of the Person of Christ—God and Man,* he wrote, "Such was the watchful care of Christ over the church, as unto the preservation of this sacred, fundamental truth, concerning his divine person, and the union of his natures therein, retaining their distinct properties and operations, that—notwithstanding all the faction and disorder that were in those primitive councils, and the scandalous contests of many of the members of them; notwithstanding the determination contrary unto it in great and numerous councils—the faith of it was preserved entire in the hearts of all that truly believed, and triumphed over the gates of hell…the church, without any disadvantage to the truth, may be preserved without such general assemblies, which in the following ages, proved the most pernicious engines for the corruption of the faith, worship, and manners of it. Yea, from the beginning they were so far from being the only way of preserving truth, that it was almost constantly prejudiced by the addition of their authority unto the confirmation of it. Nor was there any one of them wherein 'the mystery of iniquity' did not work, unto the laying of some rubbish in the foundation of that fatal apostasy which afterwards openly ensued." See Owen, *Works,* 1:12.

6. Owen, *Two Short Catechisms,* in *Works,* 1:462–94.

7. See Andrew Thomson's biographical sketch of Owen in *Works,* 1:lxvii–lxx.

8. Owen, *Truth and Innocence Vindicated,* in *Works,* 13:551–52. It is important to note that Crawford Gribben believes that Owen may have wavered in his support for the use of confessions of faith in the 1660s due to statements made in his *A Vindication of the Animadversions on "Fiat Lux"* (1664) (Gribben, *John Owen and English Puritanism,* 10, 221–22). Regardless, it is clear that Owen continued to believe in the importance of systematizing and expounding the faith once for all delivered to the saints for the benefit of the church. Such is evidenced by his thorough treatments of the person and work of the Holy Spirit

support for formally systematizing the doctrines of the church for her benefit. Furthermore, with regard to his Christology, though Owen did not refer to the ecumenical councils as an authoritative ground for his argumentation, he refuted all of the early christological heresies in a way that was consistent with the both the Nicene Creed (325/381)

---

and the person of Christ in the 1670s. Furthermore, in ΣΥΝΕΣΙΣ ΠΝΕΥΜΑΤΙΚΕ, *or, The Causes, Ways, and Means of Understanding the Mind of God as Revealed in His Word, with Assurance Therein* (1678), Owen affirmed that the sole use of ecclesiastical means (i.e., the tradition of the church, the church fathers, or other theological writers) in the interpretation of Scripture "is in due consideration and improvement of that light, knowledge, and understanding in, and those gifts for the declaration of, the mind of God in the Scripture, which he hath granted unto and furnished them withal who have gone before us in the ministry and work of the gospel" (*Works*, 4:228). Owen consistently maintained a commitment to the Protestant affirmation of the magisterial authority of Scripture and the ministerial authority of the church. Thus, his seemingly anticreedal statements should be read in light of his disapproval of the use of creeds to authoritatively bind the consciences of men but not necessarily of their use as ministerial aids to understanding and declaring the mind of God as revealed in Scripture.

Furthermore, Owen does seem to have embraced something akin to what Gregg Allison has recently termed the "presumptive authority" of the early ecumenical creeds. That is, the historical theological consensus of the church on core doctrines should not be rejected without significant biblical warrant to do so. Scripture has supreme authority, but the theological tradition should be given presumptive ministerial authority. See Gregg R. Allison, "The *Corpus Theologicum* of the Church and Presumptive Authority," in *Revisioning, Renewing, Rediscovering the Triune Center: Essays in Honor of Stanley J. Grenz*, ed. Derek J. Tidball, Brian S. Harris, and Jason S. Sexton (Eugene, Ore.: Cascade Books, 2014), 319–39. Evidence of such an approach in Owen's writings can be seen in his discussion of the theological terms used by the early church to explain the incarnation. Owen wrote, "Wherefore, as our faith is not confined unto any one of these words or terms, so as that we should be obliged to believe not only the things intended, but also the manner of its expression in them; so, in as far as they explain the thing intended according unto the mind of the Holy Ghost in the Scripture, and obviate the senses of men of corrupt minds, they are to be embraced and defended as useful helps in teaching the truth" (*A Declaration of the Glorious Mystery of the Person of Christ*, in *Works*, 1:227). Thus, Owen asserted that Scripture maintains supreme authority for the faith and practice of the church but that the church's traditional explanation of scriptural doctrines should be received to the extent that it is useful in communicating the truth and refuting error. Carl Trueman summarizes Owen's approach well: "Claiming that scripture is authoritative is not the same as agreeing on what scripture says.... There is therefore a need for interpretation...and Owen used the church tradition as an aid in trying to discern what scripture itself authoritatively says, an approach which in no way places tradition on an equal or superior level to scripture," in Trueman, *John Owen*, 10–11n26; cf. Trueman, "The Spirit and the Word Incarnate," 31–32.

and the Chalcedonian Definition (451).[9] In this section, I will detail the consistency of Owen's Christology with the theological categories of classical Chalcedonian Christology.[10] These categories include word-man Christology, the person-nature distinction, *enhypostasia*, the *communicatio idiomatum*, the *extra Calvinisticum*, and Dyothelitism. I will thereby demonstrate that Owen carefully guarded the full deity and humanity of Christ in a way that maintained christological orthodoxy and provided the appropriate framework for him to thoroughly expound upon the Spirit's work in Christ's human nature.

Word-Man Christology

Two significant christological frameworks were evident in the church leading up to the Council of Chalcedon in 451: the "word-flesh" (*logos-sarx*) christological framework and the "word-man" (*logos-anthrōpos*) christological framework. Gerald Bray describes well the word-flesh Christology as expressed by one its primary proponents, Apollinarius:

> Apollinarius taught that the incarnation was the union of the divine spirit of the Son with human flesh, taken from the womb of the Virgin Mary. The Son did not enter an already existing man, as the adoptianists claimed, nor did he unite with flesh on the basis that he too was a creature, as the Arians believed. Instead, the divine *logos* became a man by taking on human flesh. Jesus did not have a human mind, soul, or will, because the *logos* did not need them— he had their divine equivalents already.[11]

Therefore, according to the word-flesh Christology, the incarnation is a simple union of the divine *logos* with a human body analogous to the union between soul and body in a normal human being. Christ becomes man not by incarnating a full human nature with an immaterial soul and a material body but by uniting Himself in all His divine

---

9. Owen, *A Declaration of the Glorious Mystery of the Person of Christ*, in *Works*, 1:37–40, 226–35.

10. For a further discussion of the consistency of Owen's Christology with Chalcedon, see Claunch, "The Son and the Spirit," 143–45.

11. Gerald Bray, *God Has Spoken: A History of Christian Theology* (Wheaton, Ill.: Crossway, 2014), 327.

spiritual capacities with the physical body of a human being.[12] The proponents of the theology that would later come to characterize the Chalcedonian Definition argued that this word-flesh Christology led to a Christ who was not fully man. Therefore, He could not serve as the perfect Redeemer of humanity, nor could He have lived a truly human life.[13]

In opposition to the word-flesh Christology, the word-man Christology held that, in order for Christ to be the perfect Redeemer of humanity, He had to take upon Himself the full essence of what it is to be human. This meant that the divine *logos* took upon Himself not just a material human body but also an immaterial human soul with all of the faculties contained therein. The Chalcedonian Definition upheld the word-man Christology and condemned the word-flesh Christology of Apollinarianism by maintaining that Christ is "a true and complete human being, with body, soul, mind, and will."[14]

Owen makes the same assertion in his larger catechism. Answering the question "How prove you that [Christ] was a perfect man?" he wrote, "By the Scriptures assigning to him those things which are required to a perfect man; as, first, a body, Luke 24:39; Heb. 2:17, 10:5; 1 John 1:1; secondly, a soul, Matt. 26:38; Mark 14:34;—and therein, first, a will, Matt. 26:39; secondly, affections, Mark 3:5; Luke 10:21; thirdly, endowments, Luke 2:52."[15] "Perfect" here means that Christ was a complete—or true—man. He had to be such in order that "the nature which had offended might suffer, and make satisfaction,

---

12. Describing Apollinarian Christology, Aloys Grillmeier writes, "Incarnation, as it must be envisaged in Christ, only comes about if divine pneuma and earthly sarx together form a substantial unity in such a way that the man in Christ first becomes man through the union of these two components." See *Christ in Christian Tradition*, vol. 1, *From the Apostolic Age to Chalcedon (451)*, trans. John Bowden (Atlanta: Westminster John Knox Press, 1975), 331.

13. Stephen J. Wellum, *God the Son Incarnate: The Doctrine of Christ*, Foundations of Evangelical Theology (Wheaton, Ill.: Crossway, 2016), 296.

14. Gregg R. Allison, *Historical Theology: An Introduction to Christian Doctrine* (Grand Rapids: Zondervan, 2011), 373.

15. Owen, *Two Short Catechisms*, in *Works*, 1:479. By "endowments" Owen meant a mind capable of increasing in understanding. Hence his reference to Luke 2:52, "And Jesus increased in wisdom and stature, and in favor with God and men."

and so that he might be every way a fit and sufficient Savior for men."[16] Owen further stated, "His divine nature was not unto him in the place of a soul, nor did immediately operate the things which he performed, as some of old vainly imagined; but being a perfect man, his rational soul was in him the immediate principle of all his moral operations, even as ours are in us."[17] Such a statement directly contradicts the Apollinarian word-flesh Christology and affirms the word-man Christology.

Thus, Owen agreed with the view of Gregory of Nazianzus, who famously asserted, "For that which He has not assumed He has not healed; but that which is united to His Godhead is also saved. If only half Adam fell, then that which Christ assumes may be half also; but if the whole of his nature fell, it must be united to the whole nature of Him that was begotten, and so be saved as a whole."[18] In order to be the Savior of humanity, Christ had to have a complete human nature, including both a body and a soul, with its mind, affections, and will.

Person-Nature Distinction

In addition to helping develop a proper word-man Christology, engaging with the word-flesh Christology of Apollinarius gave the church terms and concepts to use and define, such as the terms *hypostasis* (person) and *physis* (nature).[19] Refuting Apollinarius led the church to develop the person-nature distinction: Christ, in His incarnation, is one person (*hypostasis*) subsisting in two natures (*physis*). Chalcedon affirmed that Christ took upon Himself a full human nature without taking a human person (*anhypostasia*).[20] Asserting that Christ did not take upon Himself a human person was not

---

16. Owen, *Two Short Catechisms*, in *Works*, 1:479; cf. Owen, *Hebrews*, 3:461.

17. Owen, *A Discourse Concerning the Holy Spirit*, in *Works*, 3:169.

18. Gregory of Nazianzus, "To Cledonius the Priest Against Apollinarius (Epistle 101)," in *A Select Library of Nicene and Post-Nicene Fathers of the Christian Church*, series 2, vol. 7, *Cyril of Jerusalem, Gregory Nazianzen*, ed. Philip Schaff and Henry Wace (New York: Christian Literature, 1894), 440.

19. Grillmeier, *Christ in Christian Tradition*, 1:346–47.

20. Philip Schaff, *The Creeds of Christendom, with a History and Critical Notes*, vol. 1, *The History of Creeds* (New York: Harper & Brothers, 1919), 30–32.

intended to communicate that Christ was not fully human; rather, it was intended to show that Christ did not take upon Himself a human nature that could have existed independently of His divine person. "When the Son became incarnate, he did not assume a fully existing man, i.e., a human person and nature, but instead added to himself a human nature and gave to that human nature its 'person' in and through the person of the Son."[21]

Owen's comments on Hebrews 2:16 show that his Christology accords with the Chalcedonian conception of the person-nature distinction and the anhypostatic human nature of Christ prior to His incarnation. He wrote,

> The Lord Jesus Christ is truly God and man in one person; and this is fully manifested in these words. For, 1. There is supposed in them his *pre-existence* in another nature than that which he is said here to assume. He *was* before, he *subsisted* before, or he could not have taken on him what he had not. This was his divine nature.... 2. He assumed, he took to himself, another nature, "of the seed of Abraham," according unto the promise. So, continuing what he was, he became what he was not. For, 3. He took this to be his *own nature*.... And therefore, 6. This is done without a *multiplication of persons* in him; for the human nature can have no personality of its own, because it was taken to be the nature of another person who was pre-existent unto it, and by assuming of it prevented its proper personality.[22]

Thus, he affirmed that the Son eternally subsisted as a person in the divine nature and that His human nature had no personal subsistence in itself before the assumption of it by His own person. Furthermore, he avoided Nestorianism by asserting that the union itself does not create a union of multiple persons but, rather, a union of two natures in one person.[23]

---

21. Wellum, *God the Son Incarnate*, 316.

22. Owen, *Hebrews*, 3:461–62 (italics original); cf. Owen, *A Declaration of the Glorious Mystery of the Person of Christ*, in *Works*, 1:228; *A Discourse Concerning the Holy Spirit*, in *Works*, 3:161.

23. For a further discussion of these aspects of Owen's Christology, see Trueman, *The Claims of Truth*, 154–57; Daniels, *The Christology of John Owen*, 273–76.

Enhypostasia

Adding even greater clarity to the doctrine that Christ's human nature was without personhood (*anhypostasia*) prior to its being assumed by the person of the Son, later theologians began to utilize the term *enhypostasia* in order to emphasize the singular acting subject in Christ as the divine Son who acts through and *in*-personates two natures, one divine and the other human.[24] This makes clear that Christ's humanity is not "a mere attribute, an accident of his existence."[25] Rather, He is truly man because His person subsists in a human nature just as much as it subsists in the divine nature. Macleod explains, "He thinks and loves and wills as a man, as surely as he thinks, loves and wills as God."[26]

Owen spoke similarly of the relationship between the person and the human nature of Christ:

> But he took it to be *his own nature*; which it could no ways be but by personal union, causing it to subsist in his own person. And he is therefore a true and perfect man: for no more is required to make a complete and perfect man but the entire nature of man subsisting; and this is in Christ as a man, the human nature having a subsistence communicated unto it by the Son of God."[27]

Thus, we can say not only that the Son took upon Himself a human nature that was not previously united to any person (*anhypostasia*) but also that He assumed a human nature such that it truly became His own (*enhypostasia*).[28]

---

24. Wellum, *God the Son Incarnate*, 318.

25. Donald Macleod, *The Person of Christ*, Contours of Christian Theology (Downers Grove, Ill.: InterVarsity Press, 1998), 202.

26. Macleod, *The Person of Christ*, 202. Wellum expresses this similarly: "Since it is the divine Son who gave a personal identity to Christ's human nature and is now able to live, think, will, and act in and through his human nature (and his divine nature), we can say that the Son is now able to live a fully human life (and a divine life)." See Wellum, *God the Son Incarnate*, 323.

27. Owen, *Hebrews*, 3:461 (italics original).

28. For a further discussion of the doctrine of *enhypostasia* in Owen's theology, see Daniels, *The Christology of John Owen*, 275–76, 521.

The Communicatio Idiomatum

From Chalcedon was also derived what became known as the *communicatio idiomatum*. This doctrine describes the communication of the attributes of Christ's natures to His person. Wellum notes two traditional points of agreement among the orthodox regarding this doctrine. First, each of Christ's natures retains its own attributes, and, second, the attributes of each nature are predicated to the Son by virtue of Him being their acting subject.[29] Thus, what is true of the Son *qua* His human nature can be said to be true of Him as a person, and vice versa *qua* His divine nature. The natures are united in His person, and their attributes are communicated to His person without being communicated to one another.[30]

Although the Latin term never appears in Owen's works, the *communicatio idiomatum* as a theological concept is fundamental to his Christology.[31] He was clear that, upon the union of the divine and human natures in Christ's person, no "mixture or confusion of natures ensue, or of the essential properties of them; for he took the seed of Abraham to be his human nature, which if mixed with the divine it could not be."[32] Thus, he clearly held to a Reformed, rather than a Lutheran, view of the relationship between the two natures of Christ.[33]

---

29. Wellum, *God the Son Incarnate*, 437.

30. Note that Calvin and Luther, along with their respective traditions, disagreed regarding this doctrine as it pertains to the Lord's Supper. Luther argued that certain of Christ's divine attributes (i.e., omnipotence, omniscience, and omnipresence) are communicated to His human nature such that Christ's physical body can be present in the Lord's Supper in, with, and under the elements. Calvin, on the other hand, rejected this view and maintained the Chalcedonian conception of the *communicatio*, arguing that there is no communication of attributes between the natures. Thus, Calvin argued that Christ is not physically present in the Lord's Supper but, rather, that He is present by means of His Spirit. See Macleod, *The Person of Christ*, 196–99; Wellum, *God the Son Incarnate*, 328–32.

31. Daniels, *The Christology of John Owen*, 284–85. For an analysis of Owen's use of the *communicatio* relative to Christ's prophetic office in particular, see Trueman, *The Claims of Truth*, 169–79.

32. Owen, *Hebrews*, 3:462; cf. Owen, *A Declaration of the Glorious Mystery of the Person of Christ*, in *Works*, 1:228, 229–30, 234; *A Discourse Concerning the Holy Spirit*, in *Works*, 3:161.

33. Ferguson, "John Owen and the Doctrine of the Person of Christ," 90; Daniels, *The Christology of John Owen*, 312–13; Barrett and Haykin, *Owen on the Christian Life*, 99n40.

Owen also asserted that the attributes and acts of the natures are predicated to the person, such that all that the Son is and does in each nature truly is an attribute and act of His person. Regarding the attributes, he wrote, "Each nature operates in him according unto its essential properties."[34] As God, Christ is infinite, omniscient, omnipotent, and omnipresent, and His divine acts accord with these attributes. As man, He is finite, locally present, and capable of death, and His human acts accord with such. The acts themselves are also predicated to His person. Owen explained,

> *The perfect, complete work of Christ, in every act of his mediatory office,*—in all that he did as the King, Priest, and Prophet of the church,—in all that he did and suffered,—in all that he continueth to do for us, in or by virtue of whether nature soever it be done or wrought,—is not to be considered as the act of this or that nature in him alone, but it is the act and work of the whole person,—of him that is both God and man in one person.[35]

Although Scripture sometimes attributes certain works to Christ's divine or human nature in particular, every work is ultimately a work of His person.[36] Furthermore, every human work that Christ performs in carrying out His mediatorial office has worth and dignity communicated unto it because He is also divine.[37]

The Extra Calvinisticum

The *extra Calvinisticum* (the *extra*) is the doctrine that "the Word is fully united to but never totally contained within the human nature

---

34. Owen, *A Declaration of the Glorious Mystery of the Person of Christ*, in *Works*, 1:234 (italics original).

35. Owen, *A Declaration of the Glorious Mystery of the Person of Christ*, in *Works*, 1:234.

36. For example, Colossians 1:16 states that all things were created by Christ. This clearly cannot be true of Christ in His human nature, because Christ did not have a human nature when the universe was created. Though such a statement is not true of Him in His human nature, it is true of Him in His divine nature and is, therefore, also true of His person. Conversely, in Matthew 24:36, Christ says that the Son does not know the day nor the hour of His second coming. This statement is true of His human nature, which is limited and finite. However, in His divine nature He is omniscient, knowing all things exhaustively. Therefore, though the statement is not true of Him in His divine nature, it is true of Him in His human nature and is, therefore, also true of His person.

37. Owen, *A Declaration of the Glorious Mystery of the Person of Christ*, in *Works*, 1:233.

and therefore, even in incarnation, is to be conceived of as beyond or outside of (*extra*) the human nature."[38] As Wellum explains, this doctrine is built upon the previous christological categories inherent in Chalcedon. The Son *in*-personates two natures such that He is the acting subject of both. The natures remain distinct from the person, and their attributes are not shared with each other. Yet, the attributes and acts of each nature are predicated to the person. Thus, although Christ assumes and is personally united to a human nature, He remains fully God and united with the Father and the Spirit as He always has been eternally, and He continues to uphold the universe by the word of His power (Col. 1:15–17; Heb. 1:1–3).[39]

Owen clearly held to the *extra*, and he included it in his explanation of the hypostatic union.[40] He wrote, "The divine nature knows all things, upholds all things, rules all things, acts by its presence everywhere; the human nature was born, yielded obedience, died, and rose again. But it is the same person, the same Christ, that acts all these things,—the one nature being his no less than the other."[41] As Trueman has shown, Owen further employed the *extra* in his refutation of the Socinians, who sought to limit Christ's kingship to His mediatorial office.[42] In contrast, Owen argued that Christ's mediatorial kingship must be set within the context of His divine kingship. Even as His mediatorial kingship was connected to His humiliation and exaltation, His divine kingship never ceased.[43] Thus, as a divine person, He is not fully contained or restrained by His human nature.

---

38. Muller, *Dictionary of Latin and Greek Theological Terms*, 116 (italics original).

39. Wellum, *God the Son Incarnate*, 332–33. For a summary of the widespread use of the doctrine of the *extra*—prior to its being associated with Calvin—see E. David Willis, *Calvin's Catholic Christology: The Function of the So-Called Extra Calvinisticum in Calvin's Theology*, Studies in Medieval and Reformation Thought 2, ed. Heiko A. Oberman (Leiden: Brill, 1967), 1–60; Wellum, *God the Son Incarnate*, 333–38.

40. Ferguson, "John Owen and the Doctrine of the Person of Christ," 90; Barrett and Haykin, *Owen on the Christian Life*, 90n41.

41. Owen, *A Declaration of the Glorious Mystery of the Person of Christ*, in *Works*, 1:234.

42. Trueman, *The Claims of Truth*, 180–85.

43. Owen, *The Mystery of the Gospel Vindicated and Socinianism Examined*, in *Works*, 12:373.

Dyothelitism

Dyothelitism is the doctrine that Christ has two wills, one divine and one human. It was affirmed by the church at the Third Council of Constantinople (681), and the contrasting view of Monothelitism (i.e., Christ has one will) was condemned.[44] Dyothelitism is consistent with the word-man Christology that prevailed at Chalcedon, and it is important for Christ's work of redeeming humanity because He must assume an entire human nature in order to redeem human natures that are fallen in their entirety.

Owen agreed with the church's condemnation of Monothelitism as heretical.[45] Also, as I have demonstrated above, he affirmed that Christ had a human will, and he maintained the distinction between Christ's two natures. Moreover, he so strongly asserted the singularity and the unity of the divine will that passages like Jesus's prayer in Matthew 26:39 would destroy his understanding of the divine nature if Christ only had one will.[46] Thus, he clearly and consistently interpreted such a passage as evidence that Jesus has a human will distinct from the divine will.[47]

The Spirit and the Incarnation

By detailing the consistency of Owen's Christology with classical Chalcedonian Christology, I have laid the groundwork for a discussion of the pneumatological emphasis of his Christology. Owen did not seek to innovate in his Christology. As I have shown, he consistently employed Chalcedonian christological categories in his discussion of the person and work of Christ. He did, however, seek to develop the church's understanding of the work of the Spirit in and upon the human nature of Christ, in order to more clearly explain the

---

44. For a summary of the Monothelite–Dyothelite controversy, see Wellum, *God the Son Incarnate*, 338–48.

45. Owen, *A Declaration of the Glorious Mystery of the Person of Christ*, in *Works*, 1:15; *A Vindication of the Animadversions on "Fiat Lux,"* in *Works*, 14:234.

46. Owen, *Hebrews*, 2:88.

47. Owen, *Two Short Catechisms*, in *Works*, 1:479.

teaching of the Scriptures and to more clearly display the practical implications of Christ's assumption of a human nature for believers.[48]

In this section, I will first discuss Owen's guiding principles for understanding the Spirit's work in and upon Christ's human nature. Second, I will discuss the Spirit's sanctifying work in preparing Christ's human nature for its assumption. Third, I will discuss the Spirit's work in Christ's life, ministry, sacrifice, and exaltation. Such work includes His ongoing sanctification of Christ through infused habitual grace as well as His gifting of Christ for the work of ministry. As in the previous chapter, my discussion of the Spirit's work of imparting gifts is intended to clarify and distinguish His work of infusing habitual grace.

Guiding Principles

A key christological challenge for the church throughout the ages has been understanding the means by which Christ was endowed with grace to perform the tasks of His mediatorial office. Was grace communicated directly from His divine nature to His human nature by virtue of the hypostatic union? Owen answered this question in the negative, and he has been identified as one who uniquely, yet faithfully, pointed to the work of the Spirit, rather than the grace of union, as the means by which Christ was endowed with such grace.[49]

In light of this challenge, Owen offered six guiding principles for understanding the Spirit's work in and upon the human nature of Christ.[50] First, "the only singular immediate act of the person of the Son on the human nature was the assumption of it into subsistence

---

48. On the orthodoxy of Owen's view, Beeke and Jones have argued that "Owen's understanding of the Spirit's work in Christ is the consistent outworking of the Reformed insistence on both the integrity and perfection of the two natures and the unity of the person." See Beeke and Jones, *A Puritan Theology*, 341.

On the practical significance of Owen's Spirit-centered Christology, see Kapic, *Communion with God*, 88–93; Ferguson, "John Owen and the Doctrine of the Holy Spirit," 108; Trueman, *The Claims of Truth*, 179; Trueman, "The Spirit and the Word Incarnate," 35. See also the discussion below.

49. Macleod, *The Person of Christ*, 195–96; Wellum, *God the Son Incarnate*, 327–28.

50. These guiding principles are found in Owen, *A Discourse Concerning the Holy Spirit*, in *Works*, 3:160–62.

with himself."[51] This is perhaps the most misunderstood aspect of Owen's Christology among modern readers. Oliver Crisp in particular has misread this statement, leading him to false conclusions regarding Owen's Christology.

Crisp believes that by limiting the immediate acts of the Son on the human nature to the assumption, Owen has, in effect, made the Spirit the acting subject of the incarnation rather than the Son.[52] Crisp's erroneous conclusion likely lies primarily in his failure to properly consider the context of Owen's statement. As I mentioned above, Owen sought to answer the question of how grace is communicated from the divine nature to the human nature of Christ so that He may fulfill the tasks of His mediatorial office. Owen's answer was that grace was not communicated from the divine nature to the human nature by virtue of the hypostatic union, for this would undermine the *communicatio idiomatum*. Rather, the internal habitual grace and the gracious bestowal of gifts from the divine nature to Christ's human nature are communicated immediately by the Holy Spirit. The person of the Son *qua* His divine nature only acts upon the human nature immediately when He assumes this nature to Himself. In actively assuming the human nature, the person of the Son gives subsistence to it, and He continually remains the acting subject of it in all of its ordinary operations.[53] All supernatural operations of grace from the divine nature, however, are directly mediated by the person of the Spirit to the human nature. Thus, Owen avoided Crisp's claims that his emphasis on the work of the Spirit undermines the agency of the Son in the incarnation.[54]

---

51. Owen, *A Discourse Concerning the Holy Spirit*, in *Works*, 3:160.

52. Oliver D. Crisp, "John Owen on Spirit Christology," *Journal of Reformed Theology* 5, no. 1 (January 2011): 16–19. This article has been republished in Oliver D. Crisp, *Revisioning Christology: Theology in the Reformed Tradition* (New York: Routledge, 2011), 91–109.

53. See Owen's discussion of assumption and union in *A Declaration of the Glorious Mystery of the Person of Christ*, in *Works*, 1:224–26.

54. For a more thorough engagement with Crisp on this issue, see Claunch, "The Son and the Spirit," 145–52.

The second guiding principle is that the only necessary conse-quent of the Son's assumption of a human nature is "the personal union of Christ, or the inseparable subsistence of the assumed nature of the person of the Son."[55] This principle is further proof that Owen affirmed the doctrine of *enhypostasia*—the person of the Son in-personates the human nature such that it is inseparably and undeni-ably His nature.

Third, "all other actings of God in the person of the Son toward the human nature were voluntary, and did not necessarily ensue on the union mentioned; for there was no transfusion of the properties of one nature into the other, nor real physical communication of divine essential excellencies unto the humanity."[56] Owen's affirmation of the *communicatio idiomatum* here further supports the notion that his focus is the communication of grace from the divine nature to the human nature. He made clear that such communication does not occur through a transfusion of properties that results from the Son's assumption of a human nature into hypostatic union with the divine nature. Owen used as an example the revelation given by Christ to the apostle John in the book of Revelation.[57] It is not that Christ in His human nature had such knowledge inherently, as though it were com-municated to Him through the hypostatic union. Rather, it had to be communicated to Him by other means—namely, by the Holy Spirit. Such communications were voluntary and not necessary. They were voluntarily communicated to the human nature mediately from the Father through the Son and immediately by the Spirit. They were not necessary, in that they did not result from an immediate transference of properties from the divine nature to the human nature by virtue of the hypostatic union.

Fourth, Owen reasserted that the work of the Spirit is framed by the doctrines of inseparable operations and appropriation of divine works: "The Holy Ghost…is the immediate, peculiar, efficient cause of all external divine operations: for God worketh by his Spirit, or in

---

55. Owen, *A Discourse Concerning the Holy Spirit*, in *Works*, 3:160.
56. Owen, *A Discourse Concerning the Holy Spirit*, in *Works*, 3:161.
57. Owen, *A Discourse Concerning the Holy Spirit*, in *Works*, 3:161.

him immediately applies the power and efficacy of the divine excellencies unto their operation; whence the same work is equally the work of each person."[58]

Fifth, "The Holy Spirit is the Spirit of the Son, no less than the Spirit of the Father…. And hence is he the immediate operator of all the divine acts of the Son himself, even on his own human nature."[59] This point further refutes Crisp's assertion that Owen made the Spirit the acting subject of the incarnation. Owen stated that the Spirit is the immediate operator of all the *divine* acts of the Son *on* Christ's human nature, but this does not include the *personal* acts of the Son *through* His human nature. The Son remains the acting subject of His human nature, but all divine operations of grace and bestowal of gifts in and upon the human nature are carried out immediately by the Spirit.

Finally, Owen reaffirmed that even though such divine works upon the Son's human nature are appropriated to the Spirit, the persons of the Godhead remain inseparably united in their external works. He explained, "The immediate actings of the Holy Ghost are not spoken of him absolutely, nor ascribed unto him exclusively, as unto the other persons and their concurrence in them."[60] Though the Spirit is the immediate operator of all divine works upon the human nature of the Son—with the exception of the assumption—the Father and the Son remain perfectly united with the Spirit in such works.

To summarize Owen's guiding principles for understanding the Spirit's work in and upon the human nature of Christ, the Son *qua* His divine nature assumes a human nature to Himself. At the moment of the assumption, the Son becomes the acting subject of the human nature. In assuming and uniting to Himself the human nature, the Son does not immediately communicate grace from the divine nature to the human nature by virtue of the union. That is, the natures remain distinct and do not communicate any of their properties to each other. Rather, all gracious operations of the divine nature in and upon the human nature of Christ are the immediate work of

---

58. Owen, *A Discourse Concerning the Holy Spirit*, in *Works*, 3:161–62.
59. Owen, *A Discourse Concerning the Holy Spirit*, in *Works*, 3:161.
60. Owen, *A Discourse Concerning the Holy Spirit*, in *Works*, 3:162.

the person of the Holy Spirit.[61] Thus, like all humans, Christ in His human nature depended upon the Holy Spirit's infusion and increase of habitual grace and bestowal of spiritual gifts.

The Spirit's Preparatory Work before the Assumption

The Spirit's work in and upon the human nature of Christ did not begin after the assumption. Rather, He worked before the assumption to prepare the human nature. Owen described two works of the Spirit that prepared the human nature for its assumption by God the Son. First was "the framing, forming, and miraculous conception of the body of Christ in the womb of the blessed Virgin."[62] Second was the instantaneous sanctification of the human nature of Christ.[63]

Miraculous conception. The miraculous conception was a creative work of God and was immediately and efficiently carried out by the Holy Spirit. Though the Father designated that the Son would assume a human nature (Heb. 10:5), and though the Son voluntarily did so (Heb. 2:14), the Spirit was the immediate operator who created this nature (Matt. 1:18, 20; Luke 1:35).[64] As the Spirit hovered over the face of the waters at the first creation, so the Spirit overshadowed Mary in the creation of the human nature of Christ, the firstborn of the new creation.[65] This creative act was not like the very first creative act, when God produced matter out of nothing. Rather, it was like the creation of man and woman, both of whom were formed from pre-existing substances, the man from the dust and the woman from the

---

61. Trueman notes the fittingness of this concept: "Christ in His human nature cannot draw immediately on the divine attributes of the second person but must learn to depend on the work of the Trinitarian God as mediated to the created realm by the Spirit. So He must be filled with the Spirit, guided by the Spirit, and taught to depend upon the Spirit.... This is entirely consistent with the general Trinitarian principle that governs God's relationship to the created realm—the Spirit is seen as the direct agent of, and in, creation. Christ's human nature is a creature; thus, the Spirit is the medium by which God acts upon it." See Trueman, "The Spirit and the Word Incarnate," 34–35.

62. Owen, *A Discourse Concerning the Holy Spirit*, in *Works*, 3:162.

63. Owen, *A Discourse Concerning the Holy Spirit*, in *Works*, 3:168.

64. Owen, *A Discourse Concerning the Holy Spirit*, in *Works*, 3:163.

65. Owen, *A Discourse Concerning the Holy Spirit*, in *Works*, 3:166.

rib of the man. Likewise, the Spirit miraculously created the human nature of Christ out of the substance of Mary's body.[66] The Son assumed the body and the soul prepared by the Spirit at the instant of their creation. Thus, although the Son's assumption of the human nature logically follows the Spirit's creation of it, no actual time elapsed between the two acts.[67] This further supports the doctrine of *enhypostasia*: from the moment of its creation, Christ's human nature was truly His.

Owen explained that the miraculous conception also guarded the sinlessness of Christ. Humans born of natural generation have original sin or corruption transmitted to them from Adam through their parents. Furthermore, having been in the loins of Adam morally (i.e., federally) at the time of his fall into sin, they have his guilt imputed to them. Because Christ in His human nature was miraculously conceived and not born by ordinary generation, He does not have Adam's guilt imputed to Him nor does He have Adam's corruption transmitted to Him.[68]

Instantaneous sanctification. Concurrent with the miraculous conception was the Spirit's instantaneous sanctification of Christ's human nature.[69] This sanctifying work meant that the human nature was "filled with grace according to the measure of its receptivity."[70] In a natural sense, Christ's human nature was spotless and upright, just as Adam's was on the day of his creation. However, a supernatural infusion of habitual grace was also required, such that the faculties of Christ's human soul could function continually for the glory of God. Thus, the Spirit instantaneously infused a habit of grace in the human nature of Christ, a habit that the Spirit would continually increase throughout Christ's life and ministry. Owen explained,

---

66. Owen, *A Discourse Concerning the Holy Spirit*, in *Works*, 3:163–64.

67. Owen, *A Discourse Concerning the Holy Spirit*, in *Works*, 3:165.

68. Owen, *A Discourse Concerning the Holy Spirit*, in *Works*, 3:168.

69. Thus, the logical order of the works is: (1) the miraculous conception by the Spirit, (2) the instantaneous sanctification by the Spirit, and (3) the assumption by the Son. However, all of the works occur at the same instant.

70. Owen, *A Discourse Concerning the Holy Spirit*, in *Works*, 3:168.

This work of sanctification, or the original infusion of all grace into the human nature of Christ, was the immediate work of the Holy Spirit; which was necessary unto him: for let the natural faculties of the soul, the mind, the will, the affections, be created pure, innocent, undefiled—as they cannot be otherwise immediately created of God,—yet there is not enough to enable any rational creature to live to God; much less was it all that was in Jesus Christ. There is, moreover, required hereunto supernatural endowments of grace, superadded unto the natural faculties of our souls. If we live unto God, there must be a principle of spiritual life in us, as well as of life natural. This was the image of God in Adam, and was wrought in Christ by the Holy Spirit.[71]

Thus, Owen believed that any human—including Christ—requires both natural and supernatural endowments in order to live perfectly unto God. These endowments include a soul that is naturally spotless and a supernaturally infused principle of grace that habitually conforms the soul unto God.[72] This is the image of God that was lost in Adam and that was worked in Christ by the Holy Spirit instantaneously at the moment of the miraculous conception.[73]

The Spirit's Work in Christ's Life, Ministry, Death, Resurrection, and Exaltation

Because the miraculous conception, the instantaneous sanctification,

---

71. Owen, *A Discourse Concerning the Holy Spirit*, in *Works*, 3:168–69. This is a further indication that Owen believed that Adam required, even in his prefallen state, supernatural grace in order to live unto God. Furthermore, this quote strongly suggests that Owen largely identified the image of God with this supernaturally infused habit, which was lost at the fall and is restored to the elect in Christ.

72. Regarding the supernatural infusion of grace in the unfallen human natures of Adam and Christ, McDonald remarks, "What at first might appear to be Owen's somewhat speculative account of the role of the Spirit toward unfallen Adam is therefore intimately bound to an understanding of the person and work of the Spirit towards Christ and towards us, as this may be inferred from the NT witness." See McDonald, "The Pneumatology of the 'Lost' Image in John Owen," 327.

73. See Owen's discussion of the image of God in Christ in *A Declaration of the Glorious Mystery of the Person of Christ* (*Works*, 1:169–78). See also Griffiths, *Redeem the Time*, 41–43; McDonald, "The Pneumatology of the 'Lost' Image in John Owen." I will further discuss Owen's understanding of the image of God in Christ below, and I will examine his understanding of the image of God in man in the next chapter.

and the assumption and hypostatic union all occurred simultaneously, the Son was perfectly habitually inclined toward God in every capacity of His humanity from the moment He took on a human nature. However, this was not the end of the Spirit's work in and upon the human nature of Christ. Christ in His human nature continually depended upon the Spirit for the grace and the gifts that were necessary to fulfill His mediatorial office. These included inward operations of grace for a holy life and the bestowal of gifts for an anointed ministry.[74]

Grace for a holy life. The immediate sanctification of Christ's human nature before its assumption provided the foundation upon which the Spirit continued to work throughout Christ's life.[75] As a true human, Christ had a human soul with real human faculties, which

---

74. Owen also discussed the Spirit's work in the resurrection and in the glorification of the body of Christ, but this is beyond the scope of my discussion here. See Owen, *A Discourse Concerning the Holy Spirit*, in *Works*, 3:181–83.

The general heads of sanctifying grace and anointing with gifts are consistent with the Westminster Confession of Faith 8.3. J. V. Fesko explains that the use of such language in reference to Christ was debated at the Westminster Assembly, although the nature of this debate is unknown. See J. V. Fesko, *The Spirit of the Age: The 19th-Century Debate over the Holy Spirit and the Westminster Confession* (Grand Rapids: Reformation Heritage Books, 2017), 65–68. However, Fesko cites Thomas Goodwin, a member of the Assembly with the Independent party, whose language in his own published work is consistent with both the Westminster Confession of Faith and Owen. Goodwin wrote, "In respect of sanctifying that human nature of Christ, it was the Holy Ghost who made him Christ, that anointed him with himself, and all his graces: Isa. xi. 2, 'The Spirit of the Lord shall rest upon him, the Spirit of knowledge and the fear of the Lord.' The graces of Christ, as man, are attributed to this Spirit, as the immediate author of them; for although the Son of God dwelt personally in the human nature, and so advanced that nature above the ordinary rank of creatures, and raised it up to that dignity and worth, yet all his habitual graces, which even his soul was full of, were from the Holy Ghost. The Holy Spirit is therefore said to be 'given him without measure.' And this inhabitation of the Holy Ghost did in some sense and degree concur to constitute him Christ, which, as you know, is the anointed one of God: Acts iv. 27, 'Thy holy child Jesus, whom thou hast anointed.' Anointed with what? Acts x. 38, 'God anointed Jesus with the Holy Ghost.' Now, then, if the Spirit made him Christ, and concurred in this respect to make him the anointed of God, much more is it he that makes us Christians." See Thomas Goodwin, *The Work of the Holy Ghost in Our Salvation*, in *The Works of Thomas Goodwin* (Grand Rapids: Reformation Heritage Books, 2006), 6:50.

75. Owen, *A Discourse Concerning the Holy Spirit*, in *Works*, 3:169.

consisted of a mind, affections, and a will.[76] Throughout His life, He experienced real natural development in these faculties—this natural development was accompanied by the gracious internal workings of the Holy Spirit, which habitually inclined them perfectly unto righteousness. It is helpful to quote Owen at length here:

> That the Lord Christ, as man, did and was to exercise all grace by the rational faculties and powers of his soul, his understanding, will, and affections; for he acted grace as a man, "made of a woman, made under the law." His divine nature was not unto him in the place of a soul, nor did immediately operate the things which he performed, as some of old vainly imagined; but being a perfect man, his rational soul was in him the immediate principle of all his moral operations, even as ours are in us. Now, in the improvement and exercise of these faculties and powers of his soul, he had and made a progress after the manner of other men; for he was made like unto us "in all things," yet without sin. In their increase, enlargement, and exercise, there was required a progression in grace also; and this he had continually by the Holy Ghost: Luke 2:40, "The child grew, and waxed strong in spirit." The first clause refers to his body, which grew and increased after the manner of other men; as verse 52, he "increased in stature." The other respects the confirmation of the faculties of his mind,—he "waxed strong in spirit," So, verse 52, he is said to "increase in wisdom and stature." He was πληρούμενος σοφίας, continually "filling and filled" with new degrees "of wisdom," as to its exercise, according as the rational faculties of his mind were capable thereof; an increase in these things accompanied his years, verse 52. And what is here recorded by the evangelist contains a description of the accomplishment of the prophecy before mentioned, Isa. 11:1–3. And this growth in grace and wisdom was the peculiar work of the Holy Spirit; for as the faculties of his mind were enlarged by degrees and strengthened, so the Holy Spirit filled them up with grace for actual obedience.[77]

Christ experienced normal human growth in the whole of His human nature.[78] This growth was not synthetic, nor was it a mere appear-

---

76. Kapic, *Communion with God*, 93–94.

77. Owen, *A Discourse Concerning the Holy Spirit*, in *Works*, 3:169–70.

78. For a further discussion of the human development of Jesus, see Benjamin B. Warfield, "The Emotional Life of Our Lord," in *The Person and Work of Christ*, ed. Samuel G. Craig (Philadelphia: P&R, 1950), 91–145; Benjamin B. Warfield, "The Human Develop-

ance of growth. It was true human growth and was accompanied by true, gracious, internal habitual workings of the Spirit. The infusion of habitual grace that occurred simultaneous to the creation and assumption of His human nature was continually increased according to the capacity of His human soul and was always perfectly operating upon the faculties of His soul by the Spirit, resulting in continual outward works of righteousness.[79]

Furthermore, as a real human, Christ could have real human experiences—such as pain, tiredness, and hunger—and new objects could be presented to the faculty of His understanding.[80] Thus, as I have asserted above, Christ was not omniscient in His human nature. His mental capacities were limited just as His physical capacities were. However, the limitation of His human capacities was perfectly compatible with "the highest holiness and purity of human nature."[81] Owen further explained the relationship between Christ's true experience of new things in His human nature and His perfect holiness by the Spirit:

> In the representation, then, of things anew to the human nature of Christ, the wisdom and knowledge of it was *objectively* increased, and in new trials and temptations he *experimentally* learned the new exercise of grace. And this was the constant work of the Holy Spirit in the human nature of Christ. He dwelt in him in fulness; for he received him not by measure. And continually, upon all occasions, he gave out of his unsearchable treasures grace for exercise in all duties and instances of it. From hence was he habitually holy,

---

ment of Jesus," in *Selected Shorter Writings of Benjamin B. Warfield*, ed. John E. Meeter (Phillipsburg, N.J.: P&R, 1980), 1:158–66; Philip Eveson, "The Inner or Psychological Life of Christ," in *The Forgotten Christ: Exploring the Majesty and Mystery of God Incarnate*, ed. Stephen Clark (Nottingham, England: InterVarsity Press, 2007), 191–231.

79. Ferguson describes this well: "There is, by definition, a progress in our Lord's humanity and correspondingly progress in his holiness—not from sin to holiness as such, but from *holiness* to *holiness*, in a manner commensurate with the natural progress within his humanity." See Ferguson, "John Owen and the Doctrine of the Holy Spirit," 110 (italics original).

80. Owen, *A Discourse Concerning the Holy Spirit*, in *Works*, 3:170.

81. Owen, *A Discourse Concerning the Holy Spirit*, in *Works*, 3:170.

and from hence did he exercise holiness entirely and universally in all things.[82]

To summarize, the Son of God in His divine nature is—as He always has been and always will be—omniscient (along with all of His other divine properties). However, in His human nature He is limited in His knowledge such that He truly does develop as He comes to a knowledge of new objects and experiences. Yet, the whole of His human experience is characterized by inward habitual holiness and outward acts of righteousness, which are completely enabled by the presence and work of the Spirit within Him.[83] It is the fullness of grace in Christ's human nature—this progressively increasing, habitual holiness—that represents to us the perfection of the image of God in man.[84]

This discussion of the experience of Christ as it pertains to His natural human experience and His supernatural reception of the gracious work of the Spirit is particularly relevant to His temptation and His sacrifice. He is a sympathetic High Priest who "was in all points tempted as we are, yet without sin" (Heb. 4:15; cf. 2:17–18). By the power of the Spirit He withstood every temptation, which enabled Him to identify with us in our weakness and temptation and to serve

---

82. Owen, *A Discourse Concerning the Holy Spirit*, in *Works*, 3:170–71.

83. Again, Ferguson is helpful: "The Messiah who died on the cross did not come immediately from heaven to the cross. Rather, he developed from his (literally) embryonic condition in the womb, through the natural processes of growth, accompanied by the development of holiness in the power of the Spirit, to become a mature man in his thirties. In him uniquely, ongoing growth in obedience and in the fruit of the Spirit were perfectly commensurate with the natural development of all human characteristics." See Ferguson, "John Owen and the Doctrine of the Holy Spirit," 111.

Trueman similarly explains, "The humanity [of Christ] receives its personhood or its subsistence from its union with the Logos, but the divine attributes are not communicated directly to the human nature. Instead, the human nature can receive knowledge through empirical means—education, observation, experience—and through the work of the Holy Spirit mediating such knowledge to the nature. Christ really learns obedience as an incarnate person because the human nature grows, develops, and learns throughout His earthly life. Christ really feels the devil's temptation because His humanity does not enjoy full access to divine power simply by virtue of the union." See Trueman, "The Spirit and the Word Incarnate," 37.

84. Owen, *Posthumous Sermons, 1756*, in *Works*, 9:483; cf. Daniels, *The Christology of John Owen*, 288–90.

as our merciful and faithful High Priest.[85] His perfect holiness also enabled Him to offer Himself to God as a perfect sacrifice for sinners (Heb. 9:14).[86] This pertains to both His active obedience and His passive obedience. Regarding His active obedience, the habitual grace infused and continually increased within Him by the Spirit enabled Him to obey His Father perfectly and, thus, to prepare Himself to be a perfect sacrifice.[87] Furthermore, the gracious empowerment of the Spirit enabled Him to voluntarily take upon Himself the wrath of God in His suffering.[88] Thus, in His entire life and death, Christ was empowered in His human nature as the gracious internal operations of the Holy Spirit habitually inclined Him toward righteousness such that He could carry out His perfect work.

Gifts for an anointed ministry. As discussed in the previous chapter, the Spirit's infusion of habitual grace must be distinguished from His bestowal of gifts. This distinction must also be maintained when discussing the work of the Spirit in the human nature of Christ. The Spirit anointed Christ "with those extraordinary powers and gifts which were necessary for the exercise and discharging of his office on earth."[89] Such gifts have particular reference to the discharge of His prophetic office and the confirmation of His ministry through miraculous works. The Spirit's anointing of Christ for the discharge of His prophetic office is prophesied in Isaiah 61:1 and confirmed in Luke 4:18–19.[90] This anointing occurred at Christ's baptism (Matt. 3:13–17)

---

85. Owen, *A Discourse Concerning the Holy Spirit*, in *Works*, 3:174–75. Owen explained that one of the primary differences between Christ's temptations and ours is that all of Christ's temptations were external rather than internal. Sinful humans have temptations that arise both from their remaining indwelling sin (i.e., their flesh) and from external sources such as the world and the devil. Christ, as a perfectly holy man, has no indwelling sin out of which internal temptations can arise. He did, however, truly experience external temptations, just as we do. See Owen, *Hebrews*, 3:477–81; cf. Kapic, *Communion with God*, 94–97.

86. Owen, *A Discourse Concerning the Holy Spirit*, in *Works*, 3:176.

87. Owen, *A Discourse Concerning the Holy Spirit*, in *Works*, 3:176–77.

88. Owen, *A Discourse Concerning the Holy Spirit*, in *Works*, 3:177.

89. Owen, *A Discourse Concerning the Holy Spirit*, in *Works*, 3:171.

90. Owen, *A Discourse Concerning the Holy Spirit*, in *Works*, 3:171.

and empowered Him for His public ministry.[91] Both Christ's ministry of proclamation and His miraculous works were empowered by the gifting of the Holy Spirit. Thus, Owen believed that Christ performed the miracles of His earthly ministry by the power of the Holy Spirit rather than doing so immediately through His divine nature.[92] Such miracles served to confirm His identity as the Son of God who was sent into the world to save sinners. In concluding this section, then, it is clear that Christ in His human nature depended upon the Spirit both for the Spirit's internal workings of habitual grace—such that He continually increased in holiness according to the capacities of His human nature—and for the Spirit's bestowal of gifts for the discharge and confirmation of His anointed ministry.

The Practical Value of Owen's Pneumatological Christology

Having shown that Owen held to a classical, orthodox Christology, and having explained his understanding of the work of the Spirit in the incarnation within the context of this Christology, I now turn to a discussion of the practical value of Owen's pneumatological Christology. Owen's emphasis on the work of the Spirit in the incarnation can be traced back to his overall emphasis on the centrality of the person of Christ. He was concerned that so few professing Christians had "an acquaintance with, and a love unto, the person of Christ."[93] Too many seek to follow Christ merely for the benefits they think they

---

91. Owen, *A Discourse Concerning the Holy Spirit*, in *Works*, 3:171–72; Ferguson, "John Owen and the Doctrine of the Holy Spirit," 111–12.

92. The way in which Christ performed His earthly miracles is a topic of significant theological debate. Oliver Crisp, for example, has argued that the conventional view of Christ's miracles is that "Christ was able to perform miracles in virtue of the action of his divine nature in and through his human nature in the hypostatic union." See Oliver D. Crisp, *Divinity and Humanity: The Incarnation Reconsidered*, Current Issues in Theology 5 (New York: Cambridge University Press, 2007), 25. Crisp cites Alan Spence ("Christ's Humanity and Ours: John Owen," in *Persons, Divine and Human: King's College Essays in Theological Anthropology*, ed. Christoph Schwöbel and Colin E. Gunton [Edinburgh: T & T Clark, 1991]) in an attempt to prove that Owen held to an unconventional view of Christ's miracles. However, others have shown that Owen's view is actually quite conventional and orthodox (e.g., Beeke and Jones, *A Puritan Theology*, 341–43; Claunch, "The Son and the Spirit," 195–98).

93. Owen, *Posthumous Sermons, 1756*, in *Works*, 9:478.

may receive from Him without duly considering the excellency of His person.[94] Furthermore, Owen believed that contemplating the person of Christ is central to the practical outworking of the Christian faith.[95] The whole of the duties of the Christian religion may be reduced to the practical uses of the person of Christ.[96] Such contemplation of the person of Christ should not be limited to the excellency of His divinity; it should also include a due consideration of the excellency of His humanity.[97] In a sermon on Psalm 45:2 that he preached at

94. Owen, *Posthumous Sermons, 1756*, in *Works*, 9:478.

95. Barrett and Haykin have noted, "It would be difficult to overemphasize the importance of the person of Christ in John Owen's theology. Owen's understanding of Christ penetrates his theology as a whole, giving each of his writings a Christ-centered, gospel-saturated flavor. But what is often forgotten is that many of his works on the person of Christ are intended to be applied to the Christian life. For Owen, this is the purpose of Christology. Not only is Christ to be studied, but our study of Christ should lead us to worship him and consequently to live out our lives for his glory." See Barrett and Haykin, *Owen on the Christian Life*, 89.

96. Owen, *A Declaration of the Glorious Mystery of the Person of Christ*, in *Works*, 1:104; cf. Barrett and Haykin, *Owen on the Christian Life*, 103. "Practical uses" refers to the Puritan method of moving from theoretical, doctrinal exposition to practical application, or "uses." The typical pattern of Puritan preaching was an explanation of the text, a statement and exposition of a doctrine from the text, and uses—or an application—of the doctrine. This method was explained by William Perkins (1558–1602) in England in his work *The Art of Prophesying* (*The Works of William Perkins*, ed. Joel R. Beeke and Derek W. H. Thomas, vol. 10, ed. Joseph A. Pipa Jr. and J. Stephen Yuille [Grand Rapids: Reformation Heritage Books, 2020], 281–356). The method of moving from doctrine to uses often characterized Puritan writings as well, and this is largely due to the fact that ninety percent of Puritan books were adaptations of sermons (Beeke and Jones, *A Puritan Theology*, 704). Packer notes that this method of preaching and writing contributed to the great length of Puritan expositions (Packer, *A Quest for Godliness*, 73). Owen himself summarized the importance of joining doctrine and uses in his commentary on Hebrews 12: "*Doctrine* and *use* were the apostle's method; and must, at least virtually, be theirs also who regard either sense, or reason, or experience, in their preaching. It would be an uncouth sermon that should be without doctrine and use" (*Hebrews*, 7:218). Thus, the doctrinal expositions of the person of Christ in Owen's writings are often accompanied by practical uses. See, for example, *A Declaration of the Glorious Mystery of the Person of Christ*, in *Works*, 1:104–78; *Posthumous Sermons, 1756*, in *Works*, 9:476–84.

97. This is not to say that Owen undervalued the practical usefulness of the divinity of Christ in the Christian life. Christ's divinity is the ground of our worship of Him. *A Declaration of the Glorious Mystery of the Person of Christ*, in *Works*, 1:104–18. However, the focus of this chapter is the work of the Spirit in the human nature of Christ, which is why I will focus on the practical usefulness of this particular aspect of the doctrine of the person of Christ.

Stadham on June 14, 1674, Owen made this statement regarding the fullness of grace in the human nature of Christ: "It is what I have as much thought of as any one thing."[98] Owen considered the Spirit's communication of habitual grace to the human nature of Christ to be of central importance to the Christian life.

In this section, I will outline key insights from Owen on the practical usefulness of the Spirit's infusion of habitual grace in the human nature of Christ for Christian living. The usefulness of this doctrine centers on the Spirit's immediate work of displaying the image of God in Christ. With regard to the practical outworking of our faith, Christians must constantly seek to behold the glory of the image of God in Christ and to pursue conformity unto the image of God in Christ.

Beholding the Glory of the Image of God in Christ
The image of God is central to Owen's understanding of God's work of redemption.[99] It is because the image of God was lost in Adam that Christ—the true image of God—assumed a human nature. He could thereby reveal the image of God to man and restore the image of God in man.[100] According to Owen, the image of God in Christ is revealed through the Spirit's unmeasured infusion of habitual grace in His human nature. There are three primary ways in which we benefit from beholding the glory of the image of God as revealed to us in Christ.

First, as we behold the glory of the image of God in Christ, we see revealed in Him that into which we are being continually conformed. Owen explained that Christ received habitual grace in His human nature by the Spirit so that "he might be the pattern and example of the renovation of the image of God in us, and of the glory that doth ensue thereon. He is in the eye of God as the idea of what he intends in us, in the communication of grace and glory; and he ought to be

---

98. Owen, *Posthumous Sermons, 1756*, in *Works*, 9:480.

99. See the next chapter for a further discussion of the image of God in man.

100. He explained, "It carrieth in it a great condecency unto divine wisdom, that man should be restored unto the image of God by him who was the essential image of the Father; (as is declared in our discourse;) and that he was made like unto us, that we might be made like unto him, and unto God through him." See Owen, *A Declaration of the Glorious Mystery of the Person of Christ*, in *Works*, 1:25–26; cf. Kapic, *Communion with God*, 42–45.

so in ours, as unto all that we aim at in a way of duty."[101] In the mind of God, Christ is the pattern according to which He is transforming us—therefore, the image of God in Christ should be in our minds as well. At regeneration, the Spirit infuses a principle of faith-enabling habitual grace in us, which enables us to discern the glory of the image of God in Christ.[102] As we behold the excellency of Christ in the fullness of grace communicated to Him by the Spirit, we see that into which God by His Spirit is conforming us. As Owen explains, "Faith will cast the soul into the form or frame of the thing believed."[103] As we behold by faith the glory of the image of God in Christ, which was revealed through the Spirit's infusion of habitual grace in Him, we are transformed into that same image by the Spirit's same gracious work.[104]

Second, as we behold the glory of the image of God in Christ, we see revealed in Him the process by which we are continually being transformed. As has been shown above, Christ in His human nature experienced natural human development in which all of His natural faculties, according to the measure of their receptivity, were supernaturally habitually inclined toward righteousness by the gracious internal work of the Spirit. As we participate in the ordinary means of grace by faith in Christ, the Spirit carries out that same work in us. Owen explained,

> That which God intends for us in the internal communication of grace, and in the use of all the ordinances of the church, is, that we may come unto the "measure of the stature of the fulness of Christ," Eph. iv. 13. There is a fulness of all grace in Christ. Hereunto are we

---

101. Owen, *A Declaration of the Glorious Mystery of the Person of Christ*, in *Works*, 1:170; cf. *Posthumous Sermons, 1756*, in *Works*, 9:480–83. Owen similarly wrote elsewhere, "We are to know Christ so as to labour after conformity unto him. And this conformity consists only in a participation of those graces whose fulness dwells in him. We can, therefore, no other way regularly press after it, but by an acquaintance with and due consideration of the work of the Spirit of God upon his human nature." See Owen, *A Discourse Concerning the Holy Spirit*, in *Works*, 3:188.

102. Owen, *A Declaration of the Glorious Mystery of the Person of Christ*, in *Works*, 1:173.

103. Owen, *A Declaration of the Glorious Mystery of the Person of Christ*, in *Works*, 1:169.

104. Griffiths similarly explains, "Owen suggested that Christ is the prototype of the glory that is to be bestowed on all believers in the renovation of their nature. Since the image of God in the covenant of works has been lost, humanity has no comprehension of it outside of its representation in Christ revealed through the Scriptures." See Griffiths, *Redeem the Time*, 42.

to be brought, according to the measure that is designed unto every one of us.[105]

The work that the Spirit does in us is distinct from the work that He does in Christ in two ways. First, as Owen states, Christ received the Spirit without measure, while we receive Him to a measured extent. Second, Christ proceeded, as Ferguson notes, "from holiness to holiness,"[106] whereas we proceed from sin to holiness. Nevertheless, the difference between the Spirit's work in Christ and His work in us is quantitative, not qualitative. We are habitually inclined toward righteousness by the same Spirit, through the same efficient cause, as was Christ—namely, the Holy Spirit as He works through the means of grace.[107]

Third, as we behold the glory of the image of God in Christ, we look forward to the eschatological fulfillment of the Christian life: the beatific vision. As we contemplate the glory of the image of God in Christ by faith in the here and now, we are prepared for our glorified state, in which we will behold the glory of the image of God in Christ by sight for eternity. Owen provides three key reflections regarding the eternal, eschatological significance of the image of God in Christ as displayed in His humanity. First, "the person of Christ, in and by his human nature, shall be for ever the immediate head of the whole glorified creation."[108] Second, Christ in His human nature "shall be the means and way of communication between God and his glorified saints for ever."[109] Third, "the person of Christ, and therein his human nature, shall be the eternal object of divine glory, praise, and worship."[110] Thus, the significance of the fullness of grace in the human nature of Christ joins regeneration, sanctification, and glorification. At regeneration, we behold Christ by faith for the first time; in sanctification, we continually grow in our capacity to behold Him by

---

105. Owen, *A Declaration of the Glorious Mystery of the Person of Christ*, in *Works*, 1:171.

106. Ferguson, "John Owen and the Doctrine of the Holy Spirit," 110.

107. I will discuss the Spirit's work through the means of grace in the Christian life more thoroughly in the next chapter.

108. Owen, *A Declaration of the Glorious Mystery of the Person of Christ*, in *Works*, 1:271.

109. Owen, *A Declaration of the Glorious Mystery of the Person of Christ*, in *Works*, 1:271.

110. Owen, *A Declaration of the Glorious Mystery of the Person of Christ*, in *Works*, 1:272.

faith; and, in glorification, we will behold Him by sight. As the Spirit habitually conforms us to the image of Christ in His work of grace, He moves us progressively nearer to our glorified state, in which we will be perfectly conformed to the image of Christ as we behold His glory by sight for eternity.[111]

Conformity unto the Image of God in Christ

Owen argued that beholding the image of the glory of God in Christ by faith leads to conformity unto Christ. Such conformity is twofold. First, it consists of "internal conformity unto his habitual grace and holiness," which is "the fundamental design of the Christian life."[112] Second, this conformity consists in "following the example of Christ in all duties toward God and men."[113] Therefore, conformity unto Christ comprises grace and duty. The relationship between grace and duty is a great mystery of the Christian life, and a failure to adequately explain this relationship has led to many a theological distortion. As I argued in the first chapter of this work, such an imbalanced explanation of the relationship between grace and duty underlies the error of Jay Adams's theology of sanctification. Moreover, the heart-motivational models, developed within the biblical counseling movement after Adams, need to further develop said relationship. Therefore, the next chapter will comprise an in-depth explanation of Owen's conception of the relationship between the Spirit's internal work of infusing habitual grace and the duties of the Christian life.

---

111. McDonald summarizes this dynamic well: "In Owen's view, the Christological and pneumatological dynamic of the Christian life here and now, and our eternal salvation, is contained in a nutshell [in 1 Cor. 3:18; 4:6]. We are to be conformed more and more to Christ, the image of God, through the work of the Spirit, and one of the chief ways in which we are formed, and transformed, is by beholding the glory of the Lord, now, partially and by faith, and then at the eschatological consummation by sight as we see face to face and know as we are known." See Suzanne McDonald, "Beholding the Glory of God in the Face of Jesus Christ: John Owen and the 'Reforming' of the Beatific Vision," in *The Ashgate Research Companion to John Owen's Theology*, ed. Kelly M. Kapic and Mark Jones, Ashgate Research Companions (New York: Routledge, 2015), 142–43.

112. Owen, *A Declaration of the Glorious Mystery of the Person of Christ*, in *Works*, 1:169–70.

113. Owen, *A Declaration of the Glorious Mystery of the Person of Christ*, in *Works*, 1:175.

Chapter 5

Habitual Grace in the
Souls of Believers

Up to this point, I have located Owen's doctrine of infused habitual grace in sanctification within the context of his doctrine of God and his Christology. In this chapter, I will locate the doctrine within his anthropology. In order to do this, I will first discuss Owen's basic anthropology by expounding his conception of nature and grace with regard to the image of God in man. Second, I will discuss more fully how infused habitual grace functions in sanctification. This will involve distinguishing Owen's understanding of infused habitual grace from that of Roman Catholicism as well as discussing how infused habitual grace relates theologically to Owen's anthropology. Finally, I will discuss the relationship between the Spirit's work of infusing and increasing habitual grace in the believer and the duty of Christian obedience.

This chapter concludes my direct treatment of Owen. It is the final step in laying out a robust doctrine of sanctification that properly references God in His nature and personality, Christ in His true humanity, and man in his dependence upon God in creation and redemption. In the final two chapters of this work, I will discuss the practical use of this doctrine for the ministry of the Word among the people of God today, specifically as it pertains to the biblical counseling movement.

Nature and Grace

What man is by nature must be distinguished from what he is by grace. Such a discussion lies at the intersection of anthropology and sanctification and brings me again to Owen's understanding of the image of God. In the previous chapter, I discussed the image of God in Christ. In this section, I will discuss Owen's understanding of the image of God in man. Is the image of God something that man has by nature or by grace? Answering this question in light of Owen's theology is not easy. However, I suggest that Owen's understanding of the image of God was consistent with the understanding of nature and grace held by many of his Reformed contemporaries.[1] Owen believed that man requires a supernatural habit of grace to be infused into his soul by the Spirit in order for his natural faculties to operate righteously.[2] Thus, for him, the image of God necessarily has a gracious—or supernatural—component to it. This gracious component was his primary emphasis when discussing the image of God, yet he still believed that a "relic" of the image remained in the fallen man.[3] This discussion is important because it sets the context for Owen's understanding of the necessity of Spirit-infused habitual grace, and it demonstrates the connection between habitual grace and the restoration of the image of God in man. In short, Owen believed that grace restores and perfects nature such that the fallen man becomes what God intended him to be through the gracious renovation of his natural constitution.[4] In discussing Owen's view, I will first outline his understanding of the natural constitution of man, after which I will move to his gracious emphasis on the image of God in man.

---

1. Thus, I agree with Andrew M. Leslie in *The Light of Grace*, 164–67. Leslie explains that the Reformed followed Aristotle in distinguishing the soul substantially and accidentally. He writes regarding Francis Turretin, "Turretin is typical amongst Reformed scholastics in defining the *imago* both in terms of the soul's natural essence and formal powers—whether its intellectual and volitional faculties, or its spiritual and intrinsically corruptible, immortal essence—*and* its concreated, accidental gifts, chiefly, its original righteousness. The Reformed scholastics saw no difficulty in following the Aristotelian paradigm of distinguishing the soul's essence, powers, and the various qualities and habits which were accidental to the soul's natural state. Echoing traditional scholasticism, then, they could in a restricted sense call these accidental qualities 'gifts' or 'graces' added to nature rather than flowing from it, provided they were held to have been naturally concreated with that essence." Leslie, *The Light of Grace*, 165.

2. Owen, *A Discourse Concerning the Holy Spirit*, in *Works*, 3:168–69.

3. Owen, *A Discourse Concerning the Holy Spirit*, in *Works*, 3:580.

4. Ferguson, *John Owen on the Christian Life*, 218–19.

The Natural Constitution of Man

Like his Reformed and Puritan contemporaries, Owen consistently employed faculty psychology in his discussion of the human soul. Faculty psychology is a way to conceptually describe the power of the soul by which a person acts in the world. Kapic has provided the most thorough description of Owen's employment of faculty psychology and has shown that he consistently identified three faculties within the soul: the intellect, the will, and the affections.[5] Such faculties are conceptual distinctions that describe the unified power of the soul. The soul with its faculties, combined with a body, is simply a description of what constitutes a human nature.[6] Owen viewed the soul as a unified entity. He understood it to be synonymous with the scriptural term "heart."[7] Thus, the faculties are not different components that

---

5. Kapic, *Communion with God*, 45–57; Kelly M. Kapic, "John Owen's Theological Spirituality: Navigating Perceived Threats in a Changing World," in *John Owen between Orthodoxy and Modernity*, ed. Willem van Vlastuin and Kelly M. Kapic, Studies in Reformed Theology 39 (Boston: Brill, 2019), 69–74.

The faculty psychology of the Reformation and post-Reformation tradition has been a subject of much debate in recent years. For an overview of the tradition and a summary of the recent debate, see Helm, *Human Nature from Calvin to Edwards*; Paul Helm, *Reforming Free Will: A Conversation on the History of Reformed Views on Compatibilism (1500–1800)*, Reformed Exegetical and Doctrinal Studies (Fearn, Scotland: Mentor, 2020).

Note also that several authors in the biblical counseling movement have used this same threefold faculty psychology. See Fitzpatrick, *Idols of the Heart*; Emlet, "Understanding the Influences on the Human Heart"; Pierre, "'Trust in the Lord with All Your Heart'"; Pierre, *The Dynamic Heart in Daily Life*.

6. This description of human nature is easily discerned in Owen's discussion in his catechism of what it means for Christ to have a human nature. The Scriptures assign to Christ "those things which are required to a perfect man; as, first, a body, Luke 24:39; Heb. 2:17, 10:5; 1 John 1:1; secondly, a soul, Matt. 26:38; Mark 14:34;—and therein, first, a will, Matt. 26:39; secondly, affections, Mark 3:5; Luke 10:21; thirdly, endowments, Luke 2:52." See Owen, *A Declaration of the Glorious Mystery of the Person of Christ*, in *Works*, 1:479.

7. Owen, *The Nature, Power, Deceit, and Prevalency of the Remainders of Indwelling Sin in Believers*, in *Works*, 6:170. Owen wrote, "The *heart* in the Scripture is variously used; sometimes for the *mind and understanding*, sometimes for the *will*, sometimes for the *affections*, sometimes for the *conscience*, sometimes for the *whole soul*. Generally, it denotes *the whole soul of man* and all the faculties of it, not absolutely, but as they are all one principle of moral operations, as they all concur in our doing good or evil. The mind, as it inquireth, discerneth, and judgeth what is to be done, what refused; the will, as it chooseth or refuseth and avoids; the affections, as they like or dislike, cleave to or have an aversation from, that which is proposed to them; the conscience, as it warns and determines,—are all together

make up the soul—rather, they are distinct descriptions of the soul's power. Among the soul's distinct faculties, Owen believed that the intellect maintains a particular primacy over the will and the affections.[8] He also believed that the soul and the body have a vital union, which is only temporarily dissoluble by death.[9] In what follows, I will discuss each of the faculties of the soul individually, after which I will examine the relationship of the soul to the body.

Intellect. For Owen, the intellect—or the mind—is the directive faculty of the soul.[10] It leads the will and the affections in the way that they should go according to its reason.[11] He explained the relationship between the mind, the will, and the affections before and after the fall as follows:

> God created [the faculties] all in a perfect harmony and union. The mind and reason were in perfect subjection and subordination to God and his will; the will answered, in its choice of good, the discovery made of it by the mind; the affections constantly and evenly followed the understanding and will. The mind's subjection to God was the spring of the orderly and harmonious motion of the soul and all the wheels in it. That being disturbed by sin, the rest

called the *heart*. And in this sense it is that we say the seat and subject of this law of sin is the heart of man" (italics original). It is important to note that, although Owen seemed to indicate here that he viewed the conscience as a fourth faculty of the soul, the conscience does not function this way in his writings on the whole. He likely viewed the conscience as a function of the intellect. See his discussion of the work of the Spirit—on the mind, the conscience, and the affections—that is preparatory unto regeneration in Owen, *A Discourse Concerning the Holy Spirit*, in *Works*, 3:238–40; cf. 280. See also below.

8. Owen, *The Nature, Power, Deceit, and Prevalency of the Remainders of Indwelling Sin in Believers*, in *Works*, 6:254.

9. Owen, *A Declaration of the Glorious Mystery of the Person of Christ*, in *Works*, 1:282.

10. Owen, *A Discourse Concerning the Holy Spirit*, in *Works*, 3:330. Derek Thomas explains, "Owen and his contemporaries believed that the way to the human heart is via the mind." He notes that this is why they placed such a heavy emphasis on meditation and spiritual-mindedness. See Derek W. H. Thomas, "John Owen and Spiritual-Mindedness: A Reflection on Reformed Spirituality," in *The Holy Spirit and Reformed Spirituality: A Tribute to Geoffrey Thomas*, ed. Joel R. Beeke and Derek W. H. Thomas (Grand Rapids: Reformation Heritage Books, 2013), 130.

11. Owen expounded a great deal upon his understanding of this rational faculty and its relationship to the affections in his *The Nature, Power, Deceit, and Prevalency of the Remainders of Indwelling Sin in Believers*. See Owen, *Works*, 6:153–322.

of the faculties move cross and contrary one to another. The will chooseth not the good which the mind discovers; the affections delight not in that which the will chooseth; but all jar and interfere, cross and rebel against each other. This we have got by our falling from God. Hence sometimes the will leads, the judgment follows. Yea, commonly the affections, that should attend upon all, get the sovereignty, and draw the whole soul captive after them. And hence it is, as I said, that the heart is made up of so many contradictions in its actings. Sometimes the mind retains its sovereignty, and the affections are in subjection, and the will ready for its duty. This puts a good face upon things. Immediately the rebellion of the affections or the obstinacy of the will takes place and prevails, and the whole scene is changed. This, I say, makes the heart deceitful above all things: it agrees not at all in itself, is not constant to itself, hath no order that it is constant unto, is under no certain conduct that is stable; but, if I may so say, hath a rotation in itself, where ofttimes the feet lead and guide the whole.[12]

Although the mind can no longer perfectly guide the will and the affections because they are corrupted by sin, the mind still maintains sovereignty over the soul because the operations of the affections and the will are limited by the amount of light that the mind has received. Thus, sin is most prevalent in minds that are most deceived. A mind that has received a great deal of light can still be resisted by the corrupted will and affections.[13] However, a mind that is deceived and heavily clouded by darkness will necessarily lead the will and the affections into sin. Owen wrote,

The ground of this efficacy of sin by deceit is taken from the faculty of the soul affected with it. Deceit properly affects the *mind*; it is the mind that is deceived. When sin attempts any other way of entrance into the soul, as by the affections, the mind, retaining its right and

---

12. Owen, *The Nature, Power, Deceit, and Prevalency of the Remainders of Indwelling Sin in Believers*, in *Works*, 6:173.

13. Owen included a whole chapter in book 3 of ΠΝΕΥΜΑΤΟΛΟΓΙΑ on the works of the Holy Spirit that are preparatory unto regeneration. He explained that, before conversion, the mind can be enlightened, the conscience convicted, and the affections somewhat disentangled from sin, yet, while sin remains the ruling principle of the will, a person will not choose God. This is why the supernatural infusion of grace into the soul by the Holy Spirit in regeneration is necessary for conversion. See Owen, *A Discourse Concerning the Holy Spirit*, in *Works*, 3:228–42. See also the discussion below on the will.

sovereignty, is able to give check and control unto it. But where the mind is tainted, the prevalency must be great; for the mind or understanding is the leading faculty of the soul, and what that fixes on, the will and affections rush after, being capable of no consideration but what that presents unto them. Hence it is, that though the entanglement of the affections unto sin be ofttimes most troublesome, yet the deceit of the mind is always most dangerous, and that because of the place that it possesseth in the soul as unto all its operations. Its office is to guide, direct, choose, and lead; and "if the light that is in us be darkness, how great is that darkness!"[14]

Owen explained elsewhere that "nothing in the soul, nor the will and affections can will, desire, or cleave unto any good, but what is presented unto them by the mind, and as it is presented. That good, whatever it be, which the mind cannot discover, the will cannot choose nor the affections cleave unto."[15] A mind that does not understand good will necessarily lead to a will and affections that are inclined to choose and love evil.

Like many of his Reformed contemporaries, Owen divided the mind into the theoretical intellect and the practical intellect.[16] As it is theoretical, the mind is contemplative, perceiving and discerning those things which are proposed unto it.[17] As it is practical, the mind has power "to direct the whole soul, and determine the will unto actual operation, according to its light."[18] The Puritans generally viewed the conscience not as a separate faculty but as an exercise of the mind's practical reasoning.[19] The conscience convicts and excuses the actions of the soul, and it is both limited and aided in doing so by the amount of light that the theoretical intellect has received.[20] Thus, the intellect

---

14. Owen, *The Nature, Power, Deceit, and Prevalency of the Remainders of Indwelling Sin in Believers*, in *Works*, 6:213 (italics original).

15. Owen, *A Discourse Concerning the Holy Spirit*, in *Works*, 3:281.

16. Helm, *Human Nature from Calvin to Edwards*, 79.

17. Owen, *A Discourse Concerning the Holy Spirit*, in *Works*, 3:280.

18. Owen, *A Discourse Concerning the Holy Spirit*, in *Works*, 3:281.

19. Packer, *A Quest for Godliness*, 109; Beeke and Jones, *A Puritan Theology*, 911–12; Beeke, *Puritan Reformed Theology*, 320; Helm, *Human Nature from Calvin to Edwards*, 111–23.

20. Owen, *A Discourse Concerning the Holy Spirit*, in *Works*, 3:239.

perceives and judges that which is presented unto it, and as it does this, it guides the soul in all of its moral and spiritual operations.

Will. Explaining the difference between the mind and the will, Owen wrote, "Now, the will is the ruling, governing faculty of the soul, as the mind is the guiding and leading."[21] Just as the will and the affections are limited by the amount of light that the mind has received, so the whole soul is limited by the direction in which the will is inclined. Thus, the will, in Owen's thinking, is like the rudder of a ship, while the mind is like the ship's captain. The whole ship is limited in its voyage by the captain's knowledge of the seas and his skill in navigation. However, the captain is also limited by the degree to which his rudder can turn. If his ship is pointed in the wrong direction, and if his rudder is locked and unable to turn, then his ship will be unchangeably inclined to travel in the wrong direction. Such a situation describes an unregenerate man. His soul is inclined toward sin, and he has no power to change his own will.[22] He might acquire a great degree of knowledge, and he might even begin to value what is good in his affections, but he cannot change his will and turn himself toward righteousness.[23] In regeneration, the Spirit enlightens the mind, frees

---

21. Owen, *A Discourse Concerning the Holy Spirit*, in *Works*, 3:238.

22. So far as I can tell, Owen himself did not depict the will as the rudder of a ship in any of his writings. He did, however, use a nautical illustration for sanctification, describing it as the right ordering of the mind, the will, and the affections with the "gales of the Spirit of God" blowing upon it, which is similar to my description below. See Owen, *Hebrews*, 5:14. He also described the consent of an unregenerate will to the sin presented unto it by the mind as "a ship before the wind with all its sails displayed, without any check or stop" (*The Nature, Power, Deceit, and Prevalency of the Remainders of Indwelling Sin in Believers*, in *Works*, 6:252). Thus, my rudder illustration aligns well with Owen's conception of how the will operates differently in regenerate and unregenerate people. In an unregenerate person, there is no principle of grace in the will to prevent it from consenting to the sin presented unto it by the mind. However, in every believer, there is always a "secret reluctancy" in the will to give in to sins presented unto it by the mind—even though it may consent in particular cases—because the will has been freed and is inclined toward righteousness by the Spirit (*The Nature, Power, Deceit, and Prevalency of the Remainders of Indwelling Sin in Believers*, in *Works*, 6:253).

23. Owen wrote, "no unregenerate person doth or can answer his own convictions, or walk unto his light in obedience." See Owen, *A Discourse Concerning the Holy Spirit*, in *Works*, 3:334.

the will and inclines it toward righteousness, and implants a love for God within the affections.[24] Returning to the illustration, the captain of the ship receives knowledge of the way that he should go, a desire to go that way, and a rudder that is now free to be turned in that direction. Not only that, but the Spirit, like a constant wind blowing in the sails,[25] now inclines the ship to go that way, such that when the captain—amid momentary lapses—tries to turn back, he does not prevail, as the wind of the Spirit ultimately blows him back in the direction that he should go.[26]

Viewing the will as the rudder of a ship helps shed light on why Owen believed that the will is the principal target of regeneration.[27] The will of an unbeliever is habitually inclined toward sin in such a way that he cannot change it by his own power.[28] In regeneration, the Spirit infuses a habit of grace into the soul of the believer and frees the will, inclining it toward righteousness. Therefore, Owen says that unregenerate people are habitually inclined toward sin, whereas regenerate people are habitually inclined toward righteousness. Regenerate people do, however, retain a habitual *propensity* toward sin that they must put to death.[29]

---

24. Owen, *A Discourse Concerning the Holy Spirit*, in *Works*, 3:330–35.

25. Owen, *Hebrews*, 5:14.

26. We must also remember that a number of factors contribute to the degree to which truly regenerate people turn back toward their former sinful ways, such as providential restraints that keep them from choosing that which they sinfully desire in a particular moment.

27. Owen, *A Discourse Concerning the Holy Spirit*, in *Works*, 3:334.

28. Owen, *The Nature, Power, Deceit, and Prevalency of the Remainders of Indwelling Sin in Believers*, in *Works*, 6:190.

29. Thus, Owen makes a distinction between a habitual inclination and a habitual propensity. He explains, "We must distinguish between the *habitual frame of the heart* and the *natural propensity or habitual inclination of the law of sin in the heart*. The habitual inclination of the heart is denominated from the principle that bears chief or sovereign rule in it; and therefore in believers it is unto good, unto God, unto holiness, unto obedience. The heart is not habitually inclined unto evil by the remainders of indwelling sin; but this sin in the heart hath a constant, habitual propensity unto evil in itself or its own nature." See Owen, *The Nature, Power, Deceit, and Prevalency of the Remainders of Indwelling Sin in Believers*, in *Works*, 6:190–91 (italics original).

It is important to note one further description of the will from Owen's work. In addition to depicting the will as the ruling or governing faculty of the soul, he referred to it as "rational appetite." The will is "rational as guided by the mind, and an appetite as excited by the affections; and so in its operation or actings hath respect to both, is influenced by both."[30] In saying this, he meant that the will always chooses that which seems good to it at the time, in accordance with what the mind and the affections present unto it. He continued,

> [The will] chooseth nothing, consents to nothing, but "sub ratione boni,"—as it hath *an appearance of good*, some present good. It cannot consent to any thing under the notion or apprehension of its being evil in any kind. Good is its natural and necessary object, and therefore whatever is proposed unto it for its consent must be proposed under an appearance of being either good in itself, or good at present unto the soul, or good so circumstantiate as it is.[31]

Thus, the will is both a governing faculty and a passive, consenting faculty. It is a governing faculty in the sense that it will incline a person's soul toward whatever ruling principle resides within it, whether one of grace or one of sin. It is a passive, consenting faculty in the sense that, in accordance with whatever ruling principle directs its inclinations, it will follow that which the mind and the affections present to it as good in any particular act.[32]

Affections. The affective faculty describes the power of the soul to love and delight in particular objects. The affections are directed by the mind and governed by the ruling principle of the will. Upon

---

30. Owen, *The Nature, Power, Deceit, and Prevalency of the Remainders of Indwelling Sin in Believers*, in *Works*, 6:254.

31. Owen, *The Nature, Power, Deceit, and Prevalency of the Remainders of Indwelling Sin in Believers*, in *Works*, 6:254 (italics original).

32. Adding further complexity to this discussion is the fact that, even if the will consents to act in accordance with a particular good presented unto it by the mind and the affections, it is further limited by God's providence. If He removes the opportunity to act, then the will is prevented from doing that to which it had previously consented. See the discussion in Owen, *The Nature, Power, Deceit, and Prevalency of the Remainders of Indwelling Sin in Believers*, in *Works*, 6:261–75.

regeneration, the affections become the primary target of mortification in the Christian life.[33] Owen explained,

> Yea, after grace hath taken possession of the soul, the affections do become the principal seat of the remainders of sin;—and therefore Paul saith that this law is "in our members," Rom. 7:23; and James, that it "wars in our members," chap. 4:1,—that is, our affections. And there is no estimate to be taken of the work of mortification aright but by the affections. We may every day see persons of very eminent light, that yet visibly have unmortified hearts and conversations; their affections have not been crucified with Christ.[34]

Owen frequently described the affections as being "entangled."[35] When one encounters temptation, the affections entice the mind toward sin by stirring up frequent imaginations of the sin in the mind.[36] They also increase the will's propensity toward particular sins by frequently gaining the will's consent toward these sins and progressively carrying the soul away toward more and more sin.[37] When a love for God is implanted in the affections at regeneration, it must be cultivated through the direction of the mind and the consent of the will, and the old, sinful affections must be progressively put to death.

The body. Owen included the body as a part of the image of God in man. He wrote,

> Our whole souls, in the rectitude of all their faculties and powers, in order unto the life of God and his enjoyment, did bear his image. Nor was it confined unto the soul only; the body also, not as to its shape, figure, or natural use, but as an *essential part* of our

---

33. I will discuss mortification in greater detail below.

34. Owen, *The Nature, Power, Deceit, and Prevalency of the Remainders of Indwelling Sin in Believers*, in *Works*, 6:200. Note the direct contrast between Owen's belief that "members" in Romans 7:23 refers to the affections and Adams's belief that it refers to the physical body.

35. See, for example, Owen, *The Nature, Power, Deceit, and Prevalency of the Remainders of Indwelling Sin in Believers*, in *Works*, 6:245–51.

36. Owen, *The Nature, Power, Deceit, and Prevalency of the Remainders of Indwelling Sin in Believers*, in *Works*, 6:245.

37. Owen, *The Nature, Power, Deceit, and Prevalency of the Remainders of Indwelling Sin in Believers*, in *Works*, 6:257–58.

nature, was interested in the image of God by a participation of original righteousness.[38]

Every human act is an act of the whole person. Thus, the body participates in good and evil as the whole person participates in good and evil.[39] Owen maintained a hierarchy between the soul and the body, such that the soul is where sin begins and where restoration begins. Because of the union between body and soul, the body has an interest in the process of sanctification. Owen explained, "It is our persons that are sanctified and made holy ('Sanctify them throughout'); and although our souls are the first proper subject of the infused habit or principle of holiness, yet our bodies, as essential parts of our natures, are partakers thereof."[40]

He also seems to have closely associated the body with the sinfully disentangled affections. He explained that "body" can be a synecdoche for "the whole person as considered corrupted, and the seat of lusts and distempered affections."[41] Although sanctification does not directly change the natural, physical constitution of a person—as though it brings him from sickness to health—it affects the body by putting to death sinful passions and excesses that are so closely related to the body.

A Gracious Emphasis on the Image of God

As noted above, I suggest that Owen's understanding of nature and grace with reference to the image of God in man is consistent with his Reformed contemporaries, such that the image of God in man

---

38. Owen, *A Discourse Concerning the Holy Spirit*, in *Works*, 3:417 (italics original). Elsewhere, Owen wrote, "But, as I said, by reason of this peculiar intimate union and relation between the soul and body, there is in the whole nature a fixed aversation from a dissolution. The soul and body are naturally and necessarily unwilling to fall into a state of separation, wherein the one shall cease to be what it was, and the other knows not clearly how it shall subsist. The body claspeth about the soul, and the soul receiveth strange impressions from its embraces; the entire nature, existing in the union of them both, being unalterably averse unto a dissolution." See Owen, *A Declaration of the Glorious Mystery of the Person of Christ*, in *Works*, 1:282.

39. Owen, *A Discourse Concerning the Holy Spirit*, in *Works*, 3:420.

40. Owen, *A Discourse Concerning the Holy Spirit*, in *Works*, 3:420.

41. Owen, *Of the Mortification of Sin in Believers*, in *Works*, 6:7–8.

consists naturally of a body and a soul composed of innate faculties and supernaturally of an infused habit of grace to make him upright. The natural aspect of the image of God remains after the fall. The gracious, supernatural aspect of the image of God was lost at the fall and is regained through regeneration and sanctification.

This gracious, supernatural aspect is Owen's primary emphasis when discussing the image of God, which has led some readers of Owen to interpret him as saying that the image of God in man consists solely in the gracious, supernatural habit. This would imply that no aspect of the image of God remains in unregenerate men after the fall. Suzanne McDonald has made this case. She argues that Owen believed the image of God is completely lost in fallen men and that such a view is out of step with his Reformed predecessors and contemporaries.[42] According to Angus Stewart, however, the view that McDonald ascribes to Owen is actually widely held among the Reformed Orthodox and is the view most compatible with the major Reformed confessions.[43] Kapic, in contrast, suggests that Owen's view exists somewhere on a continuum between the image fully remaining and being completely lost.[44]

Andrew M. Leslie, however, has provided the best assessment of Owen's view. As he has shown, Owen's conception of the image of God is best read within the common understanding of nature and grace among his Reformed contemporaries. Adam was created with an uncorrupted natural constitution and a gracious habitual inclination toward righteousness. Sin caused the gracious habit to be lost, but the natural constitution remained, though it was corrupted by sin. Thus, Owen wrote that a relic of the image remained after the fall, likely referring to the natural faculties of the soul that remain.[45] How-

---

42. McDonald, "The Pneumatology of the 'Lost' Image in John Owen," 323–35.

43. Angus Stewart, "The Image of God in Man: A Reformed Reassessment (1)," *British Reformed Journal* 36 (Winter 2003): 22–31; Angus Stewart, "The Image of God in Man: A Reformed Reassessment (2)," *British Reformed Journal* 37 (Spring 2003): 18–32; Angus Stewart, "The Image of God in Man: A Reformed Reassessment (3)," *British Reformed Journal* 38 (Summer 2003): 21–34.

44. Kapic, *Communion with God*, 40.

45. Owen, *A Discourse Concerning the Holy Spirit*, in *Works*, 3:580.

ever, his emphasis in discussing the image of God was on the gracious habit that was lost. As Leslie notes, this is likely due to Owen's overall emphasis on the restoration of the image in Christ.[46]

Leslie's argument effectively explains the way that Owen discussed the image of God. For example, Owen referred to man's "universal rectitude of nature, consisting in light, power, and order, in his understanding, mind, and affections" as the "principal part" of the image of God in man at creation.[47] He continued, "And this appears… from the description which the apostle giveth us of the renovation of that image in us by the grace of Christ, Eph. 4:24, Col. 3:10."[48] Thus, Owen believed that the gracious, implanted habit is the principal part of the image of God but not the only part. However, because of this hierarchy, he sometimes referred to the gracious, implanted habit as though it were, simply, the essence of the image of God. He wrote, "There was a *quickening principle* belonging unto it; for every life is an act of a quickening principle. This in Adam was the image of God, or an habitual conformity unto God, his mind and will, wherein the holiness and righteousness of God himself was represented, Gen. 1:26, 27."[49] Here, Owen seemed to equate the habitual conformity unto God with the image of God. However, elsewhere, he acknowledged that a relic of the image remains.[50] And it seems certain that this relic of the image is our natural constitution, which includes our natural faculties. Owen wrote,

> And because these faculties are the principle and subject of all actual obedience, it is granted that there is in man a natural, remote, *passive power* to yield obedience unto God, which yet can never actually put forth itself without the *effectual* working of the grace of God, not only enabling but working in them *to will and to do*.[51]

---

46. See the insightful discussion in Leslie, *The Light of Grace*, 160–74; cf. Griffiths, *Redeem the Time*, 29–44, 86–89.

47. Owen, *A Discourse Concerning the Holy Spirit*, in *Works*, 3:101.

48. Owen, *A Discourse Concerning the Holy Spirit*, in *Works*, 3:101.

49. Owen, *A Discourse Concerning the Holy Spirit*, in *Works*, 3:285 (italics original).

50. Owen, *A Discourse Concerning the Holy Spirit*, in *Works*, 3:580.

51. Owen, *A Discourse Concerning the Holy Spirit*, in *Works*, 3:289 (italics original).

The natural aspect of the image of God in man makes him a fit subject for the gracious infusion of the supernatural aspect of the image of God. Grace was concreated in Adam with his nature, and grace restores or renovates man's fallen nature. Thus, when he discussed the image of God in man, Owen emphasized the supernatural infusion of a habit of grace both before and after the fall.[52]

Spirit-Infused Habitual Grace in Sanctification

Having discussed Owen's anthropology, I now turn to a fuller discussion of how his view of sanctification intersects with his anthropology. As stated above, Owen believed that man requires a supernatural infusion of habitual grace both before and after the fall. Man required it before the fall in order to be fully inclined unto God, and he requires it after the fall because this grace was lost at the fall and cannot be regained by his own strength. Therefore, sanctification is the gracious restoration of man's nature by the Holy Spirit, which occurs through the infusion and increase of habitual grace in the soul of man, progressively inclining all of his faculties unto God. I will discuss Owen's understanding of this work of grace in four steps. First, I will explain his distinction between imputation and infusion, which distinguishes justification from sanctification. Second, I will discuss the relationship between habits and acts. Third, I will explain Owen's understanding of the three levels of human functioning. Fourth, I will outline his view of sanctification as a progressive reordering of the faculties.

---

52. Owen believed this so strongly that he asserted that Adam had the Holy Spirit in his state of innocence. He wrote, "The Holy Spirit renews in us the image of God, the original implantation whereof was his peculiar work. And thus Adam may be said to have had the Spirit of God in his innocency. He had him in these peculiar effects of his power and goodness; and he had him according to the tenor of that covenant whereby it was possible that he should utterly lose him, as accordingly it came to pass. He had him not by especial inhabitation, for the whole world was then the temple of God. In the covenant of grace, founded in the person and on the mediation of Christ, it is otherwise. On whomsoever the Spirit of God is bestowed for the renovation of the image of God in him, he abides with him for ever." See Owen, *A Discourse Concerning the Holy Spirit*, in *Works*, 3:102–3.

Imputation and Infusion:
Distinguishing Justification and Sanctification
In question 77, the Westminster Larger Catechism asks, "Wherein do justification and sanctification differ?" It answers,

> Although sanctification be inseparably joined with justification, yet they differ, in that God in justification *imputeth* the righteousness of Christ; in sanctification his Spirit *infuseth* grace, and enableth to the exercise thereof; in the former, sin is pardoned; in the other, it is subdued; the one doth equally free all believers from the revenging wrath of God, and that perfectly in this life, that they never fall into condemnation; the other is neither equal in all, nor in this life perfect in any, but growing up to perfection.[53]

This answer espouses the classical Reformed distinction between imputation and infusion as they pertain to justification and sanctification. Such a distinction was necessary because of the Roman Catholic belief that justification occurs through the infusion of grace at baptism, which makes the person inherently righteous, on which basis God judges him to be righteous. In contrast, as R. C. Sproul explains, "The Reformers insisted that we are justified when God imputes someone else's righteousness to our account, namely, the righteousness of Christ."[54] Thus, the distinction between imputation and infusion lies at the heart of the Protestant–Roman Catholic divide over justification. The Reformers were clear that justification is a forensic declaration of righteousness based solely upon the imputed righteousness of Christ.

As the Puritans built upon the foundation laid by the Reformers, they did not abandon the idea of infused grace. Rather, they rightly located it. As question 77 of the Westminster Larger Catechism makes clear, justification occurs by imputation, while sanctification occurs by infusion. Owen's understanding of justification and sanctification

---

53. Westminster Assembly, *The Westminster Confession: The Confession of Faith, The Larger and Shorter Catechisms, The Directory for the Public Worship of God, with Associated Historical Documents* (Edinburgh: Banner of Truth, 2018), 241 (italics mine).

54. R. C. Sproul, *Are We Together?: A Protestant Analyzes Roman Catholicism* (Orlando, Fla.: Reformation Trust, 2012), 43.

was built upon this same distinction. Early on in his work *The Doctrine of Justification by Faith*, Owen asks a central question:

> Now the inquiry, on what account, or for what cause and reason, a man may be so acquitted or discharged of sin, and accepted with God, as before declared, doth necessarily issue in this:— *Whether it be any thing in ourselves, as our faith and repentance, the renovation of our natures, inherent habits of grace, and actual works of righteousness which we have done, or may do? or whether it be the obedience, righteousness, satisfaction, and merit of the Son of God our mediator, and surety of the covenant, imputed unto us?* One of these it must be,—namely, something that is our own, which, whatever may be the influence of the grace of God unto it, or causality of it, because wrought in and by us, is *inherently* our own in a proper sense; or something which, being *not our own*, not inherent in us, nor wrought by us, is yet imputed unto us, for the pardon of our sins and the acceptation of our persons as righteous, or the making of us righteous in the sight of God. Neither are these things capable of mixture or composition, Rom. 11:6. Which of these it is the duty, wisdom, and safety of a convinced sinner to rely upon and trust unto, in his appearance before God, is the sum of our present inquiry.[55]

Thus, Owen set his discussion squarely within the context of the Protestant–Roman Catholic debate over imputation and infusion in justification.[56] He sought to prove that "we have the righteousness whereby and wherewith we are justified by *imputation*; or, that our justification consists in the *non-imputation* of sin, and the *imputation of righteousness*."[57] Again, he wrote, "There is no other way whereby the original, immutable law of God may be established and fulfilled with respect unto us, but by the imputation of the perfect obedience and righteousness of Christ, who is the end of the law for righteousness unto all that do believe."[58]

---

55. Owen, *The Doctrine of Justification by Faith*, in *Works*, 5:8–9 (italics original).

56. Regarding the Roman Catholic view of justification, he wrote, "Hereon, in the whole Roman school, justification is taken for *justifaction* [sic], or the making of a man to be *inherently* righteous, by the infusion of a principle or habit of grace, who was before *inherently* and habitually unjust and unrighteous." Owen, *The Doctrine of Justification by Faith*, in *Works*, 5:124 (italics original).

57. Owen, *The Doctrine of Justification by Faith*, in *Works*, 5:163 (italics original).

58. Owen, *The Doctrine of Justification by Faith*, in *Works*, 5:250.

Though he clearly affirmed the gracious imputation of the righteousness of Christ in justification and denied the Roman Catholic doctrine of the infusion of grace in justification, Owen maintained that infused grace is operative in sanctification.[59] He explained,

> Whereas our sanctification, in the *infusion of a principle of spiritual life*, and the actings of it unto an increase in duties of holiness, righteousness, and obedience, is that whereby we are made meet for glory, and is of the same nature essentially with glory itself, whence its advances in us are said to be from "glory to glory," 2 Cor. 3:18; and glory itself is called the "grace of life," 1 Pet. 3:7: it is much more properly expressed by our being *glorified* than by being *justified*, which is a privilege quite of another nature.[60]

Therefore, there is an inherent righteousness that truly belongs to the believer, but this inherent righteousness has nothing to do with the believer's justification. Rather, this righteousness is graciously infused into the soul by the Spirit of God in regeneration and sanctification. Moreover, though it truly does belong to the believer, it is given as a gracious gift of God, which He works in the believer by His Spirit. This understanding of Spirit-infused habitual grace is central to Owen's doctrine of sanctification. He defined sanctification as

---

59. Christopher Cleveland explains that Owen relied heavily on Thomas Aquinas in his understanding of infused habits of grace in sanctification but clearly departed from him with regard to justification. He writes, "While John Owen borrowed heavily from Thomas in the development of his understanding of an infused habit of grace and its role in regeneration and sanctification, he has one major area of disagreement with Thomas over the subject. Owen, like Thomas, argues for infused habits of grace given directly to the believer by God. Unlike Thomas, however, Owen argues that these habits play no part in the justification of the believer." Cleveland, *Thomism in John Owen*, 116–17.

Kelly M. Kapic further distinguishes the views of Owen and Aquinas. He explains that, for Thomas, the goal of Christian spirituality is union with God, whereas, for Owen and the Reformed tradition, union with Christ is the starting point. See Kapic, "John Owen's Theological Spirituality," 72.

60. Owen, *The Doctrine of Justification by Faith*, in *Works*, 5:131 (italics original). Commenting on 1 Corinthians 6:11 ("But you were washed, but you were sanctified, but you were justified"), Owen wrote, "the infusion of a habit or principle of grace, or righteousness evangelical, whereby we are *inherently* righteous, by which he explains our being justified in this place, is our *sanctification*, and nothing else." Owen, *The Doctrine of Justification by Faith*, in *Works*, 5:132 (italics original).

an immediate work of the Spirit of God on the souls of believers, purifying and cleansing of their natures from the pollution and uncleanness of sin, renewing in them the image of God, and thereby enabling them, from a spiritual and habitual principle of grace, to yield obedience unto God, according unto the tenor and terms of the new covenant, by virtue of the life and death of Jesus Christ.[61]

The habitual grace infused in the soul of the believer in regeneration is the means by which the Spirit progressively sanctifies him. Sanctification, then, by definition, is a work whereby the Spirit progressively makes a man habitually holy in the whole frame of his soul, renewing the image of God in him.

Habit and Act: Distinguishing Natural and Supernatural Habits
Another significant aspect of Owen's understanding of habits is the distinction of habits from their associated acts, as well as the logical relationship between habits and acts.[62] As discussed briefly at the beginning of chapter 3, Owen believed that there exist two types of habits: natural (i.e., acquired) and supernatural (i.e., infused). Natural habits are those that can be acquired through repetitive acts of the will. In this case, the acts are antecedent to the habits. That is, the habit is acquired *through* the acts. In contrast, supernatural habits are given by God and produce the acts of the will that flow from them. Thus, supernatural habits are antecedent to their relative acts.[63]

Owen explained that natural habits may constitute a moral reformation of behavior, but that they do not constitute true holiness

---

61. Owen, *A Discourse Concerning the Holy Spirit*, in *Works*, 3:386.

62. The conflation of habits and acts is, perhaps, the greatest source of confusion in contemporary discussions of habits, even among theologians and biblical counselors. Today, the term "habit" is often used simply to refer to repetitive acts. However, as this section will show, Owen, along with others in the Puritan and Reformed tradition, consistently distinguished between habits and acts, being careful not to conflate the two.

63. Explaining the strict distinction between natural and supernatural habits, Owen wrote, "There is wrought and preserved in the minds and souls of all believers, by the Spirit of God, a supernatural principle or habit of grace and holiness, whereby they are made meet for and enabled to live unto God, and perform that obedience which he requireth and accepteth through Christ in the covenant of grace; essentially or specifically distinct from all natural habits, intellectual and moral, however or by what means soever acquired or improved." Owen, *A Discourse Concerning the Holy Spirit*, in *Works*, 3:472.

because they are acquired by natural means. He wrote, "Habits acquired by a multitude of acts, whether in things moral or artificial, are not a new nature, nor can be so called, but a readiness for acting from use and custom."[64] Thus, skillful abilities and moral dispositions can be acquired through repetitive acts of the human will, but such are not synonymous with holiness because they are acquired by the immediate agency of man and not of God.[65] What's more, these abilities and dispositions are actually sin, as they do not proceed from faith (Rom. 14:23). A habit, at its most basic level, is a governing principle, and the most fundamental governing principle of every unregenerate person is sin. Thus, every act of an unregenerate person's will is tinged with the corruption of his indwelling, habitual sinfulness. Therefore, a habitual moral disposition or skillful ability that is acquired by an unregenerate person through willful, repetitive acts can never constitute true holiness.[66]

In contrast, true holiness can only come about by an immediate act of the Holy Spirit upon the soul in the form of infused habitual grace. Such habitual grace is antecedent to all truly holy acts of the will. Therefore, supernatural habits are given, or infused, by God rather than acquired by the natural acts of man. Owen explained,

---

64. Owen, *A Discourse Concerning the Holy Spirit*, in *Works*, 3:469.

65. Owen further explained how, in such acquired habits, the acts precede the habits. He wrote, "These principles may be so excited in the exercise of natural light, and improved by education, instruction, and example, until persons, by an assiduous, diligent performance of the acts and duties of them, may attain such a readiness unto them and facility in them as is not by any outward means easily changed or diverted; and this is a moral habit. In like manner, in the duties of piety and religion, in acts of outward obedience unto God, men by the same means may so accustom themselves unto them as to have an habitual disposition unto their exercise. I doubt not but that it is so unto a high degree with many superstitious persons. But in all these things the acts do still precede the habits of the same nature and kind, which are produced by them and not otherwise." Owen, *A Discourse Concerning the Holy Spirit*, in *Works*, 3:474.

66. Here, it is helpful to remember that there is a distinction between the general habit, or governing principle of the soul, and particular habits acquired through repetitive acts. In an unregenerate person, the general habit, or governing principle, is sin (i.e., the old man, or the flesh). Such a person may acquire particular habits through repetitive acts as well. This distinction will become clearer in the below discussion of Owen's understanding of the three levels of human functioning.

> But this holiness is such a habit or principle as is antecedent unto all acts of the same kind, as we shall prove. There never was by any, nor ever can be, any act or duty of true holiness performed, where there was not in order of nature antecedently a habit of holiness in the persons by whom they were performed. Many acts and duties, for the substance of them good and approvable, may be performed without it, but no one that hath the proper form and nature of holiness can be so. And the reason is, because every act of true holiness must have something supernatural in it, from an internal renewed principle of grace; and that which hath not so, be it otherwise what it will, is no act or duty of true holiness.[67]

Owen further explained that, even though natural and supernatural habits share similar characteristics insofar as they both predispose the will toward particular acts, the origin of supernatural habits in an immediate act of God causes them to be more stable than naturally acquired habits.[68] Moreover, it has been ordained by God that, though a supernatural habit is not acquired through acts of the human will, it is "increased, strengthened, and improved" through the acts of the will that proceed from it.[69] In other words, obedience resulting from God-given faith is a means ordained by God to increase that very same faith. The acts that proceed from habitual grace are themselves a means of increasing habitual grace.[70]

The Three Levels of Human Functioning:
Principle, Operation, and Effects
Taking the two previous sections of this chapter into consideration, the complexity of human functioning can now be understood holistically. Owen believed that human functioning occurs on three levels: the principle, the operations, and the effects.[71] The *principle* is the

---

67. Owen, *A Discourse Concerning the Holy Spirit*, in *Works*, 3:474–75.

68. Owen, *A Discourse Concerning the Holy Spirit*, in *Works*, 3:475–76.

69. Owen, *A Discourse Concerning the Holy Spirit*, in *Works*, 3:476.

70. Richard Sibbes (1577–1635) described this dynamic well: "Let us remember that grace is increased, in the exercise of it, not by virtue of the exercise itself, but as Christ by his Spirit flows into the soul and brings us nearer to himself, the fountain, so instilling such comfort to the heart is further enlarged." Sibbes, *The Bruised Reed and Smoking Flax*, 97.

71. Owen, *A Discourse Concerning the Holy Spirit*, in *Works*, 3:541–44.

overall root, habit, or governing principle from which a particular act of the will flows. This is either sin or faith, the old man or the new man, the flesh or the Spirit. The *operations* are the particular lustful or righteous habits toward which the soul is inclined. The *effects* are the actual sinful or righteous acts of the soul, whether internal or external.[72] Owen explained this within the context of the opposition of the flesh and the Spirit in a regenerate person (Gal. 5:16–25). A regenerate person has remaining, indwelling sin within him. Thus, there remains in him a general propensity toward sin (i.e., the level of the principle), which is synonymous with his flesh. There also remain in him propensities of the mind and of the affections toward particular lusts (i.e., the level of the operations). And, finally, he may continue to willfully choose in accordance with the general propensity of his flesh and with the propensities of his mind and affections toward particular lusts, such that he actually sins internally in his soul and externally in his words or actions (i.e., the effects).[73] The Spirit and His infused habitual grace is a contrary governing principle that inclines the soul toward righteousness.[74] By the Spirit, a regenerate person also has various inclinations in his mind and his affections toward particular works of righteousness (i.e., the level of the operations), by which he may choose, through an act of the will, to carry out particular acts of righteousness internally in his soul or externally in his words or deeds (i.e., the effects).

This threefold approach to the levels of human functioning is significant for Owen's understanding of the process of sanctification

---

72. Owen, *A Discourse Concerning the Holy Spirit*, in *Works*, 3:541–42.

73. Note that any external sinful act would, by nature, necessarily flow from a previous internal sinful act of the will in the soul (e.g., Matt. 12:34; James 4:1–2). Furthermore, not all internal sinful acts of the will in the soul necessarily result in external, observable sinful acts.

74. Note again the distinction that Owen made between a *propensity* and an *inclination*. An unregenerate person has an *inclination* toward sin. A regenerate person has a remaining *propensity* toward sin but an *inclination* toward righteousness. For Owen, an inclination is stronger than a propensity. See Owen, *The Nature, Power, Deceit, and Prevalency of the Remainders of Indwelling Sin in Believers*, in *Works*, 6:190–91.

as it pertains to mortification and vivification.[75] Both must occur on all three levels. Mortification must seek to restrain actual sins of the will—both internal and external—it must weaken the habitual propensities of the mind and the affections toward particular sins, and, as the ultimate end of this work, it must put to death the flesh, that is, the remaining principle, or habit, of sin within us. Simultaneously, in vivification, the believer must strengthen the principle, or habit, of grace infused by the Spirit through frequent operations of the mind and the affections toward righteousness, which lead to internal and external righteous acts of the will.

The Reordering of the Faculties

It is difficult to avoid the conclusion that Owen understood the faculties of the soul to have a proper order. In the garden, the faculties were "all in perfect harmony and union," such that

> the mind and reason were in perfect subjection and subordination to God and his will; the will answered, in its choice of good, the discovery made of it by the mind; the affections constantly and evenly followed the understanding and will. The mind's subjection to God was the spring of the orderly and harmonious motion of the soul and all the wheels in it.[76]

If this is the picture of the image of God in unfallen man, and if sanctification is the progressive restoration of that image, then sanctification will necessarily result in a progressive reordering of the faculties. According to the three levels of human functioning, in sanctification, the Spirit will progressively strengthen the habit, or principle, of grace in the soul of the believer such that the mind rightly perceives the good, the affections rightly desire the good, and the will chooses the good, with regard to both internal and external actions. The renewed faculties are progressively enabled to rightly apprehend, by faith, the most glorious object: the exalted Christ. Owen explained, "If we are

---

75. Owen, *A Discourse Concerning the Holy Spirit*, in *Works*, 3:543–44. I will discuss mortification and vivification further in the last section of this chapter.

76. Owen, *The Nature, Power, Deceit, and Prevalency of the Remainders of Indwelling Sin in Believers*, in *Works*, 6:173.

spiritually renewed, all the faculties of our souls are enabled by grace to exert their respective powers towards this glorious object."[77]

Upon being confirmed as perfect and complete image bearers of God in glorification, Christians will have their faculties rightly and unchangeably ordered and oriented toward one another, just as Christ does in His human nature. Returning to the discussion of the previous chapter, Christ, the perfect image bearer, serves as the pattern into which we are being conformed in sanctification. He also perfectly displayed the process by which we are sanctified. And on the day when we are glorified, we will have completed the process, such that we both see Him with our eyes and image Him in our natures, with a glorified soul and body like His. Owen wrote, "In heaven, when we are come to our centre, that state of rest and blessedness which our nature is ultimately capable of, nothing but one infinite, invariable object of our minds and affections, received by vision, can render that state uninterrupted and unchangeable."[78] Our glorified nature will include a soul with rightly ordered faculties like Christ's and a body like His, which rightly functions in accordance with and not contrary to that soul as we behold our Lord and Savior face-to-face.

Grace and Duty

Having established that the faculties of the soul are renewed in regeneration through an infusion of habitual grace and progressively reordered in sanctification through an increase of habitual grace, I must now discuss the relationship between grace and duty. If sanctification is a work of grace by the Spirit, wherein lies human duty and responsibility? Where is the soul passive, and where is the soul active, in sanctification? Owen asserted that the Spirit's work of infusing and increasing habitual grace does not negate nor undermine the Christian's duty to actively pursue holiness. I will support this claim in three steps. First, I will examine Owen's understanding of the relationship between grace and duty theologically by considering the passive and active aspects of sanctification. Second, I will discuss

---

77. Owen, *A Declaration of the Glorious Mystery of the Person of Christ*, in *Works*, 1:320.
78. Owen, *A Declaration of the Glorious Mystery of the Person of Christ*, in *Works*, 1:320.

it practically by focusing on the means of grace as the ordinary conduit through which habitual grace is increased. Third, I will discuss it experientially by explaining how habitual grace serves as a fundamental motivator toward Christian activity in sanctification.

Grace and Duty Theologically Considered:
Passivity and Activity in Sanctification

As I discussed in chapter 3, the Creator–creature distinction requires that divine action precede human action. Therefore, all Christian duty must arise from a prior act of God, who is Himself pure act. Such a causal relationship does not, however, destroy human agency. The human will remains free and always chooses that which it judges to be good, yet such choices always accord with the providence of God.[79] Thus, the Holy Spirit's work of infusing and increasing habitual grace within the soul of the believer does not undermine the believer's free agency and responsibility to act—rather, it works in accordance with them.

Like many of his contemporaries, Owen employed causal distinctions in order to explain such a dynamic.[80] Regarding regeneration and sanctification—and salvation in general—he distinguished between the originating (or supreme) cause, the procuring cause, the efficient cause, and the instrumental cause.[81] The Father is the originating cause of every work of grace in the believer. Owen explained,

---

79. Owen, *A Display of Arminianism*, in *Works*, 10:119.

80. Like Aquinas, as well as many of his own Reformed contemporaries, Owen employed Aristotle's fourfold causality in order to describe the process of change. The four causes are (1) the material cause, (2) the formal cause, (3) the final cause, and (4) the efficient cause. To this the Reformed scholastics consistently added an additional cause that maintained a subordinate relationship to the efficient cause: the instrumental cause. See T. Theo J. Pleizier and Maarten Wisse, "'As the Philosopher Says': Aristotle," in *Introduction to Reformed Scholasticism*, ed. Willem J. van Asselt, trans. Albert Gootjes, Reformed Historical-Theological Studies (Grand Rapids: Reformation Heritage Books, 2011), 39–40. The efficient cause and the instrumental cause are relevant to this discussion. Furthermore, Owen utilized causal distinctions to serve his own purposes, and he did not remain bound by Aristotle's terminology or conceptualization. As will be seen, he also discussed a supreme, or originating, cause as well as a procuring cause.

81. Owen, *A Discourse Concerning the Holy Spirit*, in *Works*, 3:158–59, 503, 506, 523; *A Treatise of the Dominion of Sin and Grace*, in *Works*, 7:552–54.

"He is the peculiar fountain of them all. His love, his grace, his wisdom, his goodness, his counsel, his will, are their supreme cause and spring."[82] To Him belongs the "supreme purpose, design, contrivance, and disposal" of the whole work of redemption.[83] The procuring cause of our holiness is the mediatorial work of Christ the Son.[84] The Holy Spirit is the immediate, internal, efficient cause of the work of grace in the believer.[85] The instrumental cause is the dutiful acts of faith by the believers themselves.[86] Owen explained the relationship between these distinct causes in a discussion of Hosea 14:1–8, writing,

> Although God will repair our spiritual decays and heal our backslidings freely, yet he will do it so, or in such a way, as wherein he may communicate grace to us, to the praise of his own glory. Therefore are these duties prescribed unto us in order thereunto; for although they are not the procuring cause of the love and grace from whence alone we are healed, yet they are required, in the method of the dispensation of grace, to precede the effect of them. Nor have we anywhere a more illustrious instance and testimony of the consistency and harmony which is between sovereign grace and the diligent discharge of our duty than we have in this place; for as God promiseth that he would heal their backslidings out of his free love, verse 4, and would do it by the communication of effectual grace, verse 5, so he enjoins them all these duties in order thereunto.[87]

To be restored from backsliding, the believer requires the originating cause of God's promise of free grace, the effectual cause of the bestowal of that grace, and the instrumental cause of the performance of his holy duties through the use of their Spirit-inclined natural

---

82. Owen, *A Discourse Concerning the Holy Spirit*, in *Works*, 3:199.

83. Owen, *A Discourse Concerning the Holy Spirit*, in *Works*, 3:158.

84. Owen, *A Discourse Concerning the Holy Spirit*, in *Works*, 3:506; *A Treatise of the Dominion of Sin and Grace*, in *Works*, 7:553.

85. Owen, *A Discourse Concerning the Holy Spirit*, in *Works*, 3:523; *A Treatise of the Dominion of Sin and Grace*, in *Works*, 7:554. Notice that, in using the supreme, procuring, and efficient causes, Owen maintained the trinitarian shape of salvation as discussed with regard to the trinitarian order of operation in chapter 3.

86. Owen, *A Discourse Concerning the Holy Spirit*, in *Works*, 3:446; *A Treatise of the Dominion of Sin and Grace*, in *Works*, 7:554.

87. Owen, *Meditations and Discourses Concerning the Glory of Christ*, in *Works*, 1:456–57.

faculties. Note as well that, as Owen made clear, such duties do not constitute the procuring cause, which can only be the mediatorial work of Christ.

Philip Craig, in his excellent comparison of Owen's soteriology with that of the seventeenth-century antinomians, shows that Owen's causal distinctions enabled him to adequately refute antinomianism. He explains that the seventeenth-century antinomians argued that the operations of the Holy Spirit are immediate and instantaneous and do not occur indirectly through means nor through the progress of time.[88] In contrast, Owen argued that the Spirit works through means over time, thereby preserving the primacy and efficacy of the work of the Spirit while also accounting for the necessary instrumental causality of the Christian's dutiful use of means.[89] The antinomian approach required one to passively await the work of the Spirit, whereas Owen's approach required one to actively use one's faculties to work in accordance with the prior gracious work of the Spirit in one's soul.[90]

Sanctification, then, can be considered passively and actively.[91] Passively, man is worked upon by the Spirit through the infusion and increase of habitual grace. Actively, man works by the power of the Spirit through the actual performance of holy duties. All this work is concurrent and simultaneous. As a person is passively moved by the Spirit, he actively moves in accordance with the Spirit.[92] Owen explained,

> The inquiry is, what believers themselves, who have received this principle of spiritual life and are habitually sanctified, can do as to actual duties by virtue thereof, without a new immediate assistance and working of the Holy Spirit in them; and I say, they can no more do any thing that is spiritually good, without the particular concurrence and assistance of the grace of God unto every act thereof,

---

88. Philip A. Craig, *The Bond of Grace and Duty in the Soteriology of John Owen* (Cape Coral, Fla.: Founders Press, 2020), 51.

89. Craig, *The Bond of Grace and Duty*, 77, 82.

90. Craig, *The Bond of Grace and Duty*, 85.

91. Michael Allen, *Sanctification*, New Studies in Dogmatics (Grand Rapids: Zondervan, 2017), 253–54.

92. Craig explains, "The Holy Spirit renews human faculties in regeneration, so that He is able to act through them in sanctification, without overriding human agency." See *The Bond of Grace and Duty*, 86–87.

than a man can naturally act, or move, or do any thing in an absolute independency of God, his power and providence.[93]

The believer does not simply need habitual grace to begin his spiritual life—rather, for every holy act, he needs concurrent gracious assistance from the Spirit. It is not as though the Spirit begins the work, and the man carries it forward. The Spirit begins the work and carries the man forward as he acts out of the Spirit's gracious supplies.[94]

Grace and Duty Practically Considered:
The Ordinary Means of Grace

The prominence of the ordinary means of grace is a key feature of Puritan theology, in general, and of Owen's theology, in particular.[95] For Owen, the ordinary means of grace are the practical ways in which holiness is increased in the believer. They are the place in which grace and duty practically meet in Christian living. In short, they are the channels through which God ordinarily communicates His grace unto our souls. The hearing of the preached Word of God, for example, is the ordinary means through which faith is ingenerated in the souls of the lost, whereupon they are converted (Rom. 10:18).[96]

---

93. Owen, *A Discourse Concerning the Holy Spirit*, in *Works*, 3:530.

94. Michael Allen puts it well: "The passivity of the regenerated soul bespeaks God's action, which can in this case be called infusion, meaning transformation from without itself. But this passivity kick-starts a life of energy and activity. Thus, we can speak of an infusion of habits, which lead to innumerable obedient actions. But grace does not simply jump-start a life of energy and activity. Sanctifying grace changes the person, not merely the aggregation of their actions. Grace transforms the very character of the person, leading not only to increasing action in a holy direction but to growth of the very self." See Allen, *Sanctification*, 254.

95. Craig, *The Bond of Grace and Duty*, 88; Ferguson, *John Owen on the Christian Life*, 184; Packer, *A Quest for Godliness*, 199; John W. Tweeddale, "Living on Things Above: John Owen on Spiritual-Mindedness," in *The Beauty and Glory of Christian Living*, ed. Joel R. Beeke (Grand Rapids: Reformation Heritage Books, 2014), 37.

96. Owen, *A Discourse Concerning the Holy Spirit*, in *Works*, 3:230, 306. In addition to preaching, Owen also included as ordinary means of grace "prayer, meditation, mourning, reading and hearing of the Word, in all ordinances of divine worship, private and public, in diligent obedience" (*A Declaration of the Glorious Mystery of the Person of Christ*, in *Works*, 1:319). Furthermore, as Ferguson explains, Owen viewed every duty of the Christian life as a means of grace (*John Owen on the Christian Life*, 184). However, as I will discuss below, Owen viewed the sacraments of baptism and the Lord's Supper as peculiar means of grace

Thus, in preparation for regeneration, it is the duty of unbelievers to outwardly attend unto the preaching of the Word of God and the other external means of grace, that the Holy Spirit may work faith in them.[97] Furthermore, the outward attendance unto the means of grace is a reflection of the desire of God's people to grow in their sanctification.[98]

The practical, outward attendance unto the ordinary means of grace, however, can never be confused with the habitual, inward sanctification of the believer. As Ferguson explains, "The bare use of

that are set apart from the other gospel ordinances due to their special signification of covenant promises (*Two Short Catechisms*, in *Works*, 1:490–91).

It should also be noted that, like many of his Puritan contemporaries, Owen prioritized the public means of grace over the private means of grace and, thus, public, corporate worship over private worship with one's family or in one's closet. As McGraw explains, Owen believed that God's instituted corporate worship facilitates "two-way traffic between heaven and earth. Public worship is not the only means of holding communion with [God], but it is the greatest means of doing so." See McGraw, *A Heavenly Directory*, 138. This is consistent with the famous sermon on Psalm 87:2 preached by Owen's friend and copastor David Clarkson (1622–1686), entitled "Public Worship to be Preferred before Private," in *The Practical Works of David Clarkson* (Edinburgh: James Nichol, 1865), 3:187–209.

Furthermore, also like his Puritan contemporaries, Owen placed a great deal of significance on the Lord's Day as a day of sacred rest that is set aside for holy pursuits. He viewed it as a means of preserving the public and private worship of God, as a means of preserving the church's gospel witness in the world, and as a means of abundantly providing God's gracious resources to His people as "the sacred repository of all sanctifying ordinances" (*Hebrews*, 2:263–64). Sibbes summarized the Puritan emphasis on attending unto the means of grace on the Lord's Day, writing, "Therefore keep the soul open for entertainment of the Holy Ghost, for he will bring in continually fresh forces to subdue corruption, and this most of all on the Lord's day," Sibbes, *The Bruised Reed and Smoking Flax*, 97.

97. Owen, *A Discourse Concerning the Holy Spirit*, in *Works*, 3:230. The topic of "preparationism," specifically in Puritan theology, has been much debated. Jay Adams himself cited preparationism as a reason why the Puritans ought to be avoided. See Jay E. Adams, "Reflections on the History of Biblical Counseling," in *Practical Theology and the Ministry of the Church, 1952–1984: Essays in Honor of Edmund P. Clowney*, ed. Harvie M. Conn (Phillipsburg, N.J.: P&R, 1990), 203–18; Adams, "Biblical Counseling and Practical Calvinism," 492; Jay E. Adams, "Grace Alone," *Institute for Nouthetic Studies* (blog), March 11, 2011, https://nouthetic.org/grace-alone/; Fraser, *Developments in Biblical Counseling*, 114–15. However, for works explaining what the Puritans meant by preparation for grace and why this teaching has been misunderstood, see Craig, *The Bond of Grace and Duty*; Cor Harinck, "Preparationism as Taught by the Puritans," *Puritan Reformed Journal* 2, no. 2 (July 2010): 159–71; Joel R. Beeke and Paul M. Smalley, *Prepared by Grace, for Grace: The Puritans on God's Ordinary Way of Leading Sinners to Christ* (Grand Rapids: Reformation Heritage Books, 2013).

98. Craig, *The Bond of Grace and Duty*, 91.

means does not *guarantee* the end—they are not mechanical (*ex opera operato*) in nature. Rather they are given as *covenant* pledges."[99] The believer must use the means by faith, trusting that God will use the means for the end that He has promised.[100] Thus, it is through the ordinary means that the Spirit produces faith *in* the believer, and it is through the ordinary means that faith is expressed *by* the believer. The ordinary means of grace poignantly reveal that the Christian is bound to Christ in both duty and dependance. He is dutifully bound to obey Christ's command to use the means of grace, but he is dependently bound to Christ in order to use the means effectively. As J. Stephen Yuille writes, Christians "must have their affections stirred to perform spiritual duties properly so that their affections might be stirred."[101] Summarizing the work of Gavin J. McGrath,[102] Yuille describes the Christian's dutiful use of the ordinary means of grace as "instrumental causes, deriving value only as a consequence of the work of the Holy Spirit."[103] Duty is thus grounded in and made effective by grace. In other words, the act of dutifully using the means must proceed from the habit of grace that is worked in the believer by the Spirit, and the Spirit graciously uses the believer's active participation in the means to habitually conform him unto the image of Christ.

A helpful example of Owen's understanding of the relationship between grace and duty in the use of the ordinary means of grace can be seen in his exposition of Hebrews 6:1a ("Therefore, leaving the discussion of the elementary principles of Christ, let us go on to perfection"). He noted the significance of the passive φερώμεθα, translated as "let us go on." Owen explained, "It is of a passive signification, denoting the effect, 'Let us be acted, carried on;' but it

---

99. Ferguson, *John Owen on the Christian Life*, 184 (italics original).

100. Note how the centrality of faith here aligns with the emphasis of Pierre, "Trust in the Lord with All Your Heart"; Pierre, *The Dynamic Heart in Daily Life*.

101. J. Stephen Yuille, *Puritan Spirituality: The Fear of God in the Affective Theology of George Swinnock*, Studies in Christian History and Thought (Eugene, Ore.: Wipf and Stock, 2008), 186.

102. Gavin J. McGrath, *Grace and Duty in Puritan Spirituality*, Grove Spirituality Series 37 (Cambridge: Grove Books, 1991).

103. Yuille, *Puritan Spirituality*, 188.

includes the active use of means for the producing [of] that effect."[104] Thus, the believer actively uses the means by faith, trusting that he is being and will be passively worked upon by the Spirit in order to produce the intended effect of the means. Owen prescribed five principles according to which the Christian should dutifully approach the ordinary means of grace. First, the believer must diligently utilize the best means toward achieving Christian maturity or perfection.[105] This means that worldly means cannot produce holy ends; only the means of grace can.[106] Second, the believer must intently exercise his mind as he uses the ordinary means of grace.[107] The Spirit does not work through the means apart from the engagement of the mind.[108] Third, the believer must also actively engage his will and his affections in the dutiful use of the means of grace.[109] We must dutifully meditate on that which is presented in the means, love that which is presented in the means, and seek to conform our wills unto it, with the hope that "the holy gales of the Spirit of God" will breathe upon us.[110] Fourth, the believer must diligently practice what he comes to know through the means, for "doing what we know is the great key

---

104. Owen, *Hebrews*, 5:13.

105. Owen, *Hebrews*, 5:13.

106. Note the significance of this argument for biblical counseling over against secular models. The goal of biblical counseling is to promote holiness. No purely secular methodology can achieve this end because holiness can only be achieved through God's appointed means of grace. This will be further discussed in chapter 7.

107. Owen, *Hebrews*, 5:13.

108. See also Paul's words on the importance of the use of the mind in worship: "For if I pray in a tongue, my spirit prays, but my understanding is unfruitful. What is the conclusion then? I will pray with the spirit, and I will also pray with the understanding. I will sing with the spirit, and I will also sing with the understanding. Otherwise, if you bless with the spirit, how will he who occupies the place of the uninformed say 'Amen' at your giving of thanks, since he does not understand what you say? For you indeed give thanks well, but the other is not edified. I thank my God I speak with tongues more than you all; yet in the church I would rather speak five words with my understanding, that I may teach others also, than ten thousand words in a tongue" (1 Cor. 14:14–19). Owen mentioned 1 Corinthians 14:15 and the importance of understanding in *The Nature, Power, Deceit, and Prevalency of the Remainders of Indwelling Sin in Believers*, in Works, 6:233.

109. Owen, *Hebrews*, 5:14.

110. Owen, *Hebrews*, 5:14.

to give us an entrance into knowing what we do not."[111] Finally, the believer must use the means toward the right end, which is "to arrive at the measure of our perfection appointed unto us in Jesus Christ."[112] It is through the use of the means of grace in this way, and no other, that we can achieve this end.[113]

The sacraments are a peculiar example of the relationship between grace and duty in Christian living. Owen described the sacraments of baptism and the Lord's Supper as "the principal mysteries of our religion, as to its external form and administration,—the sacred rites whereby all the grace, mercy, and privileges of the gospel are sealed and confirmed unto them who are in a due manner made partakers of them."[114] The sacraments are signs of the covenant that visibly set forth the Christ of the covenant. Baptism is "an holy action, appointed of Christ, whereby being sprinkled with water in the name of the whole Trinity, by a lawful minister of the church, we are admitted into the family of God, and have the benefits of the blood of Christ confirmed unto us," and it is for "all to whom the promise of the covenant is made; that is, to believers, and to their seed."[115] Unlike

---

111. Owen, *Hebrews*, 5:14.

112. Owen, *Hebrews*, 5:14.

113. Owen elsewhere wrote, "There is not any thing in the whole course of our obedience wherein the continual exercise of faith and spiritual wisdom, with diligence and watchfulness, is more indispensably required than it is unto the due use and improvement of gospel privileges and ordinances; for there is no other part of our duty whereon our giving glory to God and the eternal concern of our own souls do more eminently depend. And he is a spiritually thriving Christian who knows how duly to improve gospel institutions of worship, and doth so accordingly; for they are the only ordinary outward means whereby the Lord Christ communicates of his grace unto us, and whereby we immediately return love, praise, thanks, and obedience unto him; in which spiritual intercourse the actings of our spiritual life principally do consist, and whereon, by consequence, its growth doth depend. It is therefore certain that our growth or decay in holiness, our steadfastness in or apostasy from profession, are greatly influenced by the use or abuse of these privileges." See Owen, *The Nature of Apostasy*, in *Works*, 7:250.

114. Owen, *A Discourse Concerning Evangelical Love, Church Peace, and Unity*, in *Works*, 15:168. For an excellent analysis of Owen's understanding of the sacraments, see Ferguson, *John Owen on the Christian Life*, 211–24.

115. Owen, *Two Short Catechisms*, in *Works*, 1:491. A discussion of Owen's pedobaptist convictions and their relationship to his covenant theology is not pertinent to my overall argument, nor is a credobaptist refutation of these convictions. For an overview of

the Lord's Supper, baptism is a singular, initiatory rite rather than an ongoing, confirmatory rite of the covenant. Thus, as Ferguson explains, its significance is not tied to the time of its administration.[116] Rather, baptism serves as a token and a pledge of one's forgiveness of sins and union with Christ.[117] A Christian looks back on his baptism and takes hold of the promise set forth in it, "as it is a token of our initiation and implanting into Christ"[118] and a "seal of that promise which gives pardon of all to believers."[119]

The Lord's Supper is "an earthly encounter with the heavenly Christ."[120] It is "an holy action instituted and appointed by Christ, to set forth his death, and communicate unto us spiritually his body and blood by faith, being represented by bread and wine, blessed by his word, and prayer, broken, poured out, and received of believers," and it is for those "who by faith have an holy interest in Christ."[121] In the Lord's Supper, true believers act by faith in Christ, spiritually participate in His body and blood, and have His abundant sanctifying grace communicated unto them. In a published sermon that he preached

---

Owen's beliefs on pedobaptism, see Ferguson, *John Owen on the Christian Life*, 215–20; Lee Gatiss, "From Life's First Cry: John Owen on Infant Baptism and Infant Salvation," in *The Ashgate Research Companion to John Owen's Theology*, ed. Kelly M. Kapic and Mark Jones, Ashgate Research Companions (New York: Routledge, 2015), 271–81. For helpful credobaptist approaches to covenant theology, see Nehemiah Coxe and John Owen, *Covenant Theology from Adam to Christ*, ed. Ronald D. Miller, James M. Renihan, and Francisco Orozco (Palmdale, Calif.: Reformed Baptist Academic Press, 2005); Pascal Denault, *The Distinctiveness of Baptist Covenant Theology: A Comparison between Seventeenth-Century Particular Baptist and Paedobaptist Federalism*, rev. ed. (Birmingham, Ala.: Solid Ground Christian Books, 2017); Samuel Renihan, *The Mystery of Christ, His Covenant, and His Kingdom* (Cape Coral, Fla.: Founders Press, 2019).

116. Ferguson, *John Owen on the Christian Life*, 216.

117. Ferguson, *John Owen on the Christian Life*, 216.

118. Owen, *A Discourse Concerning the Holy Spirit*, in *Works*, 3:561.

119. Owen, *Two Short Catechisms*, in *Works*, 1:491.

120. Beeke and Jones, *A Puritan Theology*, 743.

121. Owen, *Two Short Catechisms*, in *Works*, 1:491–92. Owen had a very pastoral approach to the Lord's Supper, which is evident in his *Sacramental Discourses*, published posthumously in 1760. These are found in *Works*, 9:517–621, and have been introduced and republished by Jon D. Payne in *John Owen on the Lord's Supper* (Edinburgh: Banner of Truth, 2004).

to his congregation on the occasion of taking the Lord's Supper, Owen stated,

> Now, brethren, the end of this ordinance is, to lift up Christ *in representation*: as he was lifted up really on the cross, and as in the whole preaching of the gospel Christ is evidently crucified before our eyes, so more especially in the administration of this ordinance. Do we see, then, wherein the special acting of faith in this ordinance does consist? God forbid we should neglect the stirring up our hearts unto the particular acting of faith in Jesus Christ, who herein is lifted up before us. That which we are to endeavour in this ordinance is, to get a view by faith,—faith working by thoughts, by meditation, acting by love,—a view of Christ as lifted up; that is, as bearing our iniquities in his own body on the tree. What did Christ do on the tree? what was he lifted up for, if it was not to bear our sins? Out of his love and zeal to the glory of God, and out of compassion to the souls of men, Christ bore the guilt and punishment of sin, and made expiation for it. O that God in this ordinance would give our souls a view of him! I shall give it to myself and to you in charge at this time,—if we have a view of Christ by faith as lifted up, our hearts will be drawn nearer to him. If we find not our hearts in any manner drawn nearer to him, it is much to be feared we have not had a view of him as bearing our iniquities. Take, therefore, this one remembrance as to the acting of faith in the administration of this ordinance,—labour to have it fixed upon Christ as bearing sin, making atonement for it, with his heart full of love to accomplish a cause in righteousness and truth.[122]

This sacrament is a visible presentation of Christ to be received by His people in faith. The faith engendered in the believer by the Spirit leads the believer to obedient participation in the sacrament by this faith, through which the Spirit, in turn, graciously increases the habit of faith in the believer. As Owen explained in the quote above, the believer is commanded in the ordinance to receive Christ in faith,

---

122. Owen, *Sacramental Discourses*, in *Works*, 9:593 (italics original). Notice Owen's strong emphasis on seeing Christ in the sacrament with eyes of faith. In the discourse preceding this one in his published works, he stated that the Roman Catholic doctrine of transubstantiation came from men who could not see Christ with eyes of faith. Therefore, they, "finding nothing of the light and power of it in their own souls, gave birth to transubstantiation; that they might do that with their mouths and teeth which they could not do with their souls" (*Sacramental Discourses*, in *Works*, 9:591).

but this must be done with the belief that it is Christ Himself, by His Spirit, who enables the believer to receive Him. The sacrament tightly holds together the bond of grace and duty.

Within the Lord's Supper is a visible representation of what is intended by all the ordinances of divine worship: that the believer would delight in Christ Himself. Owen wrote,

> This alone is that which they seek after, cleave unto, and are satisfied withal. They make use of the streams, but only as means of communication with the spring. When men are really renewed in the spirit of their minds it is so. Their regard unto ordinances and duties of divine worship is, as they are appointed of God a blessed means of communion and intercourse between himself in Christ and their souls. By them doth Christ communicate of his love and grace unto us; in and by them do we act faith and love on him.[123]

As in the parable of the man who found treasure in the field and bought the field, thus delighting in the treasure, the means of grace are the avenue through which we delight in Christ.[124]

The final subjects I will discuss regarding the means of grace are mortification and vivification. These terms essentially describe the process by which the believer puts to death the principle of indwelling sin and stirs up the principle of habitual grace through the use of the ordinary means of grace. Mortification occurs through the gracious work of the Holy Spirit upon the responsible, dutiful believer. In *The Mortification of Sin in Believers*, Owen explained,

> He doth not so work our mortification in us as not to keep it still an act of our *obedience*. The Holy Ghost works in us and upon us, as we are fit to be wrought in and upon; that is, so as to preserve our own liberty and free obedience. He works upon our understandings, wills, consciences, and affections, agreeably to their own natures he works *in us* and *with us*, not *against us* or *without us*; so that his assistance is an encouragement as to the facilitating of the work, and no occasion of neglect as to the work itself.[125]

---

123. Owen, *The Grace and Duty of Being Spiritually Minded*, in *Works*, 7:431–32.

124. Owen, *The Grace and Duty of Being Spiritually Minded*, in *Works*, 7:432.

125. Owen, *Of the Mortification of Sin in Believers*, in *Works*, 6:20 (italics original).

Moreover, Owen emphasized that the mortification of particular sins must be pursued through universal obedience. He wrote, "Without sincerity and diligence in a universality of obedience, there is no mortification of any one perplexing lust to be obtained."[126] By this he meant that one cannot hope to mortify his sin and become habitually inclined toward righteousness by picking and choosing which of God's commands to obey. All of the means of grace must be sincerely employed by faith if one hopes to put his sin to death. The Spirit grows Christians in habitual, universal righteousness through the means of dutiful, universal obedience. As Craig has summarized, "Mortification is both a grace and a duty."[127] It is an end to be dutifully pursued, but it can only be effectually pursued through the gracious enablement of the Holy Spirit, which stirs up and increases the influence of the habit of grace that is infused in the soul of the believer at regeneration.

Grace and Duty Experientially Considered:
Grace Motivates Obedience

In the experience of the believer, the promise of grace powerfully motivates dutiful obedience. Not only in our theology but also in our experience, we must hold together the promises of God and the commands of God. Owen explained,

> And we may here divert a little, to consider what ought to be the frame of our minds in the pursuit of holiness with respect unto these things,—namely, what regard we ought to have unto the *command* on the one hand, and to the *promise* on the other,—to our own *duty*, and to the *grace* of God. Some would separate these things, as inconsistent. A command they suppose leaves no room for a promise, at least not such a promise as wherein God should take on himself to work in us what the command requires of us; and a promise they think takes off all the influencing authority of the command. "If holiness be our *duty*, there is no room for *grace* in this matter; and if it be an effect of *grace*, there is no place for *duty*." But all these arguings are a fruit of the wisdom of the flesh before mentioned, and we have before disproved them. The "wisdom that is from above" teacheth us other things. It is true, our works and

---

126. Owen, *Of the Mortification of Sin in Believers*, in *Works*, 6:40.
127. Craig, *The Bond of Grace and Duty*, 196.

grace are opposed in the matter of justification, as utterly inconsistent; if it be of works it is not of grace, and if it be of grace it is not of works, as our apostle argues, Rom. 11:6. [But] our duty and God's grace are nowhere opposed in the matter of sanctification, yea, the one doth absolutely suppose the other. Neither can we perform our duty herein without the grace of God; nor doth God give us this grace unto any other end but that we may rightly perform our duty. He that shall deny either that God commands us to be holy in a way of duty, or promiseth to work holiness in us in a way of grace, may with as much modesty reject the whole Bible.[128]

Owen helpfully explained the different ways in which believers are to consider the command and the promise in their daily lives. Regarding the command, believers must: (1) be affected with the authority of the command; (2) understand "the reasonableness, the equity, and the advantage" of the command; and (3) come to love and delight in the command.[129] Regarding the promise, believers must: (1) constantly recognize our own inability to keep the command in and of ourselves; (2) adore the undeserved grace that has come to rescue us from our inability; (3) act by faith through prayer, with the expectation that God will graciously enable us to obey; and (4) remember not only the promises of God in general but also the promises of God for us in the face of particular temptations and sins.[130]

Owen made clear that obedience in the Christian life is motivated by the glorious truth that God supplies what He requires. By His Spirit He has planted the seed of faith within His children—the principle, or habit, of grace that inclines His people toward righteousness—and by the same Spirit He will increasingly, habitually conform them unto the image of Christ. Thus, we obey with faith in the promise that He who began a good work in us "will complete it until the day of Jesus Christ" (Phil. 1:6). We work out our salvation with fear and trembling because we believe that God is already at work in us "both to will and to do for His good pleasure" (Phil. 2:12–13).

---

128. Owen, *A Discourse Concerning the Holy Spirit*, in *Works*, 3:384.
129. Owen, *A Discourse Concerning the Holy Spirit*, in *Works*, 3:384–85.
130. Owen, *A Discourse Concerning the Holy Spirit*, in *Works*, 3:385.

Conclusion

This chapter has concluded my examination of John Owen's theology of Spirit-infused habitual grace in sanctification. I have located this doctrine within Owen's doctrine of God, his Christology, and his anthropology in order to provide a robust understanding of the Spirit's work of grace in sanctification. This book did not begin with John Owen, however. Rather, it began with a discussion of habituation and sanctification in the biblical counseling movement, after which it moved to Owen's theology in an attempt to correct the movement's understanding of habituation. In the final two chapters, I will explain why the recovery of the doctrine of Spirit-infused habitual grace in sanctification is so important—particularly in the way Owen formulated and employed it—and how this doctrine may be practically applied to counseling and to the overall ministry of the Word in modern times.

Chapter 6

Anthropological Considerations
for Soul Care

In these two final chapters, I seek to apply the major contours of John Owen's theology of Spirit-infused habitual grace to relevant areas of modern soul care. I will focus on the biblical counseling movement, but, because this movement has developed in conversation with other approaches to soul care and Christian formation, I will interact with resources from outside of the movement as necessary. In this chapter, I will discuss four aspects of Owen's theology of Spirit-infused habitual grace in sanctification that ought to lead counselors to reconsider the practical implications of their anthropological commitments.

First, Owen rightly located the power of sin in the soul rather than the body (where Adams located it), and he formulated an appropriate theology of habituation that properly relates the soul with the external context of the body and its environment. Second, Owen correctly framed the faculties of the soul in man—in both his unfallen and fallen states—which is fundamental to the development of a biblical theology of sanctification. Third, Owen clearly distinguished between natural and supernatural habits, a distinction that is often missed in discussions of habituation in biblical counseling literature and in evangelical literature at large. Fourth, Owen's conception of the three levels of human functioning helps to clarify the methodological target of counseling. In all of this, I seek to propose principles for pneumatologically grounded counseling—in other words, principles for an approach to counseling that is consciously grounded in a robust understanding of the work of the Holy Spirit in the sanctification of believers.

The Priority of the Soul in Relation to the Body and Its Environment

In this section, I will discuss, first, how Owen's right emphasis on the priority of the soul corrects Jay Adams's assertion that the power of indwelling sin is located in the physical body. Second, I will discuss how Owen's emphasis on the priority of the habituation of the soul, or the heart, in relation to external environmental factors corrects and develops similar themes in biblical counseling and evangelical literature on Christian formation.

The Priority of the Soul over the Body

As discussed in chapter 1, Jay Adams's methodological emphasis in counseling arose primarily from one fundamental feature of his theology: his understanding of "the flesh" (σαρξ), or "the old man" (παλαιος ανθρωπος). According to Adams, Paul's use of these terms refers to the physical body, which is "plunged into sinful practices and habits as the result of Adam's fall."[1] Sanctification, then, is the process by which the regenerate inner man dehabituates and rehabituates his sinfully habituated body. The second generation of biblical counselors rightly rejected Adams's understanding of the flesh as well as its methodological implications.[2] However, few have taken up the task of reformulating an appropriate theology of habituation without repeating Adams's mistakes.[3]

Owen, however, appropriately used the concept of habituation to explain the strength of sin's grip on fallen man and the power of the Spirit to overcome it. For Adams, the believer must address the sinful inclinations that remain in the physical body. But for Owen, the believer's ongoing battle against sin results from sin's powerful

---

1. Adams, *A Theology of Christian Counseling*, 160n1.

2. See Welch, "How Theology Shapes Ministry."

3. Recent literature from within the biblical counseling movement that has addressed habituation includes: Emlet, "Practice Makes Perfect?"; Mesimer, "Habits and the Heart"; Mesimer, "Rehabilitating Habituation"; Gifford, "The Role of Habits in Spiritual Maturity from the Perspective of the English Puritans"; Gifford, "Jay Adams' Teaching of Habituation"; Gifford, *Heart and Habits*. I will discuss these authors below.

influence upon the soul or the heart.[4] It is because a habit of indwelling sin remains in the soul and continues to influence its faculties that Christians must engage in the process of progressive sanctification by the power of the Spirit.

Owen also used the concept of habituation to clarify the difference between sin's power in the unbeliever and its power in the believer. He wrote,

> The habitual inclination of the heart is denominated from the principle that bears chief or sovereign rule in it; and therefore in believers it is unto good, unto God, unto holiness, unto obedience. The heart is not habitually inclined unto evil by the remainders of indwelling sin; but this sin in the heart hath a constant, habitual propensity unto evil in itself or its own nature.[5]

Thus, a significant distinction between believers and unbelievers is the manner in which sin exercises power over the faculties of their souls. The faculties of an unbeliever's soul are habitually inclined toward sin, whereas the faculties of a believer's soul are habitually inclined toward righteousness. Though a true believer retains a habitual *propensity* toward sin in his soul, he is not habitually *inclined* toward sin in the way that he was as an unbeliever. This change in the ruling habitual inclination of the soul is wrought by the Spirit, who infuses a habit of grace in the soul and progressively increases its influence over the soul's faculties.

This aspect of Owen's theology of sanctification corrects Adams's errors and addresses the relative disregard for habituation among the second generation of biblical counselors. Habit is important for understanding sanctification, but it must be applied to the depth of human functioning. Sanctification does not merely reprogram the physical body; it reforms the soul, beginning in its innermost parts and moving outward. The habitual frame of the heart must be

---

4. Owen, *The Nature, Power, Deceit, and Prevalency of the Remainders of Indwelling Sin in Believers*, in *Works*, 6:170.

5. Owen, *The Nature, Power, Deceit, and Prevalency of the Remainders of Indwelling Sin in Believers*, in *Works*, 6:190–91.

progressively changed, and this must begin with the faculties of the soul and move outwardly to one's bodily behavior.

Furthermore, Owen's distinction between the habit of indwelling sin and the habit of infused grace connects two major theological concepts that are important for Christians to understand as they pursue sanctification: restraining grace/renewing grace and law/gospel. Restraining grace is a work whereby the Spirit prevents someone from committing a sin that he has already conceived in his mind by convincing him of the impossibility, inconvenience, unprofitableness, or unacceptability of committing that sin.[6] In this work, the Spirit uses such external means as physical or social barriers to prevent the person from committing a sin that he would, given other circumstances, readily commit. Restraining grace keeps the habit of sin from producing its outward effects, and, though it does not constitute true holiness, Christians should be thankful for the ways that the Spirit uses external means to restrain our indwelling sin. Renewing grace is the habitual increase of the Spirit's gracious work, such that someone is prevented from sinning due to his increasingly fervent pursuit of righteousness.[7] The believer should thank God for the ways in which he has been kept from sin simply because the Spirit has pulled him out of sin through habitually setting his mind, affections, and will on that which is holy.

Biblical counseling benefits from this distinction, as the counselor can help the counselee distinguish between true, inward holiness and simple, outward restraint. For example, a man who is addicted to pornography should be thankful for the outward restraints that can keep him from pursuing his sin, such as accountability and filtering software. However, he must know that such restraints do not constitute true holiness and that he needs to combine them with engagement in the means of grace as he pursues the Spirit's sanctifying work. Only this will strengthen his inclination toward righteousness and away

---

6. Owen, *The Nature, Power, Deceit, and Prevalency of the Remainders of Indwelling Sin in Believers*, in *Works*, 6:270–74.

7. Owen, *The Nature, Power, Deceit, and Prevalency of the Remainders of Indwelling Sin in Believers*, in *Works*, 6:270, 275–77.

from his lustful pursuits. The external restraints might keep his eyes from looking upon that which is impure, but they will not in and of themselves increase his internal, habitual holiness.

Regarding law and gospel, Owen explained that "the law guides, directs, commands, all things that are against the interest and rule of sin. It judgeth and condemneth both the things that promote it and the persons that do them."[8] The gospel, on the other hand,

> is the means and instrument of God for the communication of internal spiritual strength unto believers. By it do they receive supplies of the Spirit or aids of grace for the subduing of sin and the destruction of its dominion. By it they may say they can do all things, through Him that enables them.[9]

The Christian uses the law as a means of bringing to light the operations and effects of the remaining habitual sin within him, and he can rely on the grace that is promised in the gospel to put that habit of sin to death and habitually walk in righteousness through the power of the Spirit.[10] In this way, Christians can confidently evaluate

---

8. Owen, *A Treatise of the Dominion of Sin and Grace*, in *Works*, 7:547.

9. Owen, *A Treatise of the Dominion of Sin and Grace*, in *Works*, 7:547.

10. In the Reformed understanding of the threefold use of the law, this has been historically termed the "didactic use of the law." For a helpful overview of this use of the law, see Beeke and Jones, *A Puritan Theology*, 555–71; Joel R. Beeke, *Puritan Reformed Spirituality: A Practical Theological Study from Our Reformed and Puritan Heritage* (Darlington, England: Evangelical Press, 2006), 101–24. For a practical exposition on how to make use of law and gospel, see Joel R. Beeke and Michael P. V. Barrett, *A Radical, Comprehensive Call to Holiness* (Fearn, Scotland: Christian Focus, 2021), 177–91.

Though practical expositions of the Ten Commandments have been a characteristic feature of historic Puritan and Reformed spirituality, biblical counselors have seldom used such expositions for counseling. This is likely due to the fact that, though the biblical counseling movement has had a Calvinistic bent from its inception, there has not been a widespread embrace of the other major emphases of the Reformed tradition within the church at large. For example, historic Reformed orthodoxy holds that the Ten Commandments continue to be morally binding upon all people, including Christians. However, the majority of evangelical theologians do not. Rather, they believe that the commandments are morally binding only insofar as the principles contained within them are repeated in the New Testament. Sinclair Ferguson refers to this approach as "exegetical antinomianism" in *The Whole Christ: Legalism, Antinomianism, and Gospel Assurance—Why the Marrow Controversy Still Matters* (Wheaton, Ill.: Crossway, 2016), 142–43. Beeke and Meyers note that this approach results in "agile circumlocutions to retain the Decalogue's 'principles' while relegating its form to a past era of redemptive history" in *Reformed Piety: Covenantal*

their hearts and their actions according to the law, as every sin that is thereby exposed can be put to death and replaced with righteousness by the power of the gospel. They can do this because the Spirit has infused an internal habit of grace within them, one which He will inevitably increase unto its perfection (Phil. 1:6).

The Soul and Its External Environment

A prominent concept in biblical counseling literature and other modern evangelical literature is the influence of external factors on the soul in Christian formation. Its prominence in the biblical counseling movement can be traced back to David Powlison, who is credited with developing the model proposed by Lane and Tripp in *How People Change*.[11] The influence of one's environment is also a key component of the models proposed by Emlet,[12] Pierre,[13] and Gifford.[14] In all of these models, the person is viewed as a responsible responder to his environment, and the way that he responds to his environment influences his heart. His Spirit-empowered, faithful responses grow him in righteousness, while his sinful responses lead him more and more into unrighteousness.

Outside of the biblical counseling movement, James K. A. Smith and Dru Johnson have produced extensive philosophical works devoted to Christian formation and environmental influence. Both focus on formation as it pertains to habit. Smith's *Cultural Liturgies* trilogy is an

---

and Experiential (Darlington, England: Evangelical Press, 2019), 12. This is the approach taken by Jay Adams, who departs from his own tradition and strongly denies the ongoing, binding nature of the Ten Commandments in *Keeping the Sabbath Today?* (Stanley, N.C.: Timeless Texts, 2008). An exception to this within the biblical counseling movement is Elyse Fitzpatrick, who, in several of her works, affirms that the Ten Commandments remain binding and useful for Christians. See Fitzpatrick, *Idols of the Heart*, 50–53; Elyse M. Fitzpatrick and Dennis E. Johnson, *Counsel from the Cross: Connecting Broken People to the Love of Christ* (Wheaton, Ill.: Crossway, 2012), 83–85. Pierre also refers to the Ten Commandments as God's "revealed will for how human beings ought to function" in *The Dynamic Heart in Daily Life*, 112. In addition, Lane and Tripp provide a brief, practical exposition of the Ten Commandments in *How People Change*, 135–38.

    11. See Powlison's unpaginated foreword in Lane and Tripp, *How People Change*.

    12. See Emlet, "Understanding the Influences on the Human Heart."

    13. See Pierre, *The Dynamic Heart in Daily Life*.

    14. See Gifford, *Heart and Habit*.

analysis of how human affections are formed through habitual cultural practices and how the church can counteract this cultural influence through its own formative practices.[15] Whereas Smith approaches habitual formation primarily with reference to the affections, Johnson does so primarily with reference to the intellect. He focuses on how ritualistic practices are a means of acquiring knowledge.[16] These authors are important not only because their work is scholarly and substantive but also because it has been increasingly referenced and relied upon in biblical counseling literature.[17]

The emphases of the above-mentioned authors overlap with those of Owen in two areas. One area is that all of these approaches to Christian formation rightly acknowledge that the enticements of the world work together with our indwelling sin. Pierre explains that we all have trajectories of influence by which we are, in part, passively influenced by our environment.[18] In other words, like Smith's cultural liturgies, our environment tends to "recruit our unconscious drives and desires through embodied stories that fuel our imagination."[19]

---

15. See Smith, *Desiring the Kingdom*; James K. A. Smith, *Cultural Liturgies*, vol. 2, *Imagining the Kingdom: How Worship Works* (Grand Rapids: Baker Academic, 2013); James K. A. Smith, *Cultural Liturgies*, vol. 3, *Awaiting the King: Reforming Public Theology* (Grand Rapids: Baker Academic, 2017). Smith has also written a popular-level work that summarizes his overall approach in this series—see James K. A. Smith, *You Are What You Love: The Spiritual Power of Habit* (Grand Rapids: Brazos Press, 2016).

16. See Dru Johnson, *Biblical Knowing: A Scriptural Epistemology of Error* (Eugene, Ore.: Cascade Books, 2013); Dru Johnson, *Scripture's Knowing: A Companion to Biblical Epistemology*, Cascade Companions (Eugene, Ore.: Cascade Books, 2015); Dru Johnson, *Knowledge by Ritual: A Biblical Prolegomenon to Sacramental Theology*, Journal of Theological Interpretation Supplements 13 (Winona Lake, Ind.: Eisenbrauns, 2016); Dru Johnson, *Human Rites: The Power of Rituals, Habits, and Sacraments* (Grand Rapids: Eerdmans, 2019).

17. See Gifford, *Heart and Habit*, 18; Greg E. Gifford, "A Theological Understanding of the Effects of Addictive Habits in Cultivating Addictive Desires," *Midwestern Journal of Theology* 19, no. 1 (Spring 2020): 55; Emlet, "Practice Makes Perfect?"; Mesimer, "Habits and the Heart"; Mesimer, "Rehabilitating Habituation." Popular works from outside of the biblical counseling movement have also begun to take a similar approach to Christian formation. See, for example, Tish Harrison Warren, *Liturgy of the Ordinary: Sacred Practices in Everyday Life* (Downers Grove, Ill.: IVP Books, 2016); Tony Reinke, *12 Ways Your Phone Is Changing You* (Wheaton, Ill.: Crossway, 2017); Justin Whitmel Earley, *The Common Rule: Habits of Purpose for an Age of Distraction* (Downers Grove, Ill.: IVP Books, 2019).

18. Pierre, *The Dynamic Heart in Daily Life*, 89–90.

19. Smith, *Imagining the Kingdom*, 15.

Our environment presents an opportunity for the deep, sinful desires of our hearts to be further conformed to the pattern of this world. Owen similarly understood that the one who does not discern the allurements of the world stands on the brink of ruin.[20] This is not simply because the things of this world are so enticing but also because our indwelling habit of sin stands at the ready to act upon that which the world presents to it. He likened indwelling sin to traitors in a castle, writing,

> If a castle or fort be ever so strong and well fortified, yet if there be a treacherous party within, that is ready to betray it on every opportunity, there is no preserving it from the enemy. There are traitors in our hearts, ready to take part, to close, and side with every temptation, and to give up all to them; yea, to solicit and bribe temptations to do the work, as traitors incite an enemy.[21]

The heart tends to respond to the world's daily enticements in such a way that reveals and fosters its underlying corruption.[22]

A second area of overlap is that these authors recognize one's responsibility to respond rightly to the influences of his environment. This is clear in Lane and Tripp,[23] Emlet,[24] Pierre,[25] and Gifford.[26] It is also clear in Smith, who instructs Christians to be aware of the secular liturgies that form their affections and to counter such formation through Christian liturgies.[27] Similarly, Johnson explains that people develop rituals based upon their environment, and he encourages them to examine what their rituals are, what they mean, and whether or not they should change them.[28] Thus, all of these authors stress

---

20. Owen, *Of Temptation*, in *Works*, 6:96.

21. Owen, *Of Temptation*, in *Works*, 6:104–5.

22. Pierre illustrates this with the metaphor of frozen, polluted water. The stench of the water goes unnoticed until the environment heats up and melts the water. Then, its pollution becomes evident. See Pierre, *The Dynamic Heart in Daily Life*, 62.

23. Lane and Tripp, *How People Change*, 83.

24. Emlet, "Understanding the Influences on the Human Heart," 52.

25. Pierre, *The Dynamic Heart in Daily Life*, 90.

26. Gifford, *Heart and Habit*, 82–84.

27. Smith, *You Are What You Love*, 57–58.

28. Johnson, *Human Rites*, 8–9.

personal responsibility amid worldly influences, which, as I have already established, is a key emphasis in Owen's work.

However, with regard to rightly relating the soul to its external environment, the proposals of Smith and Johnson require one significant correction. Both authors place an undue emphasis on the habituation of the body, whereas Owen emphasized the habituation of the soul. Johnson argues that "knowing—including reason and interpretation—is fundamentally an embodied act."[29] Habits are formed in the body through ritualistic practices that shape our thinking.[30] Johnson believes that the body is the key to change. Describing how he came to this understanding, he explains,

> I could see how my pre-programmed reactions to the triumphs and foolishness of my kids held them captive and became a grid through which we all processed the world. When I realized how my embodied life shaped me intellectually, emotionally, and communally, I re-evaluated everything I did with my body—which means exactly that: I re-evaluated everything I did, every ritual.[31]

He later writes, "Our rituals represent an embodied parable based on our story of the world. Our body is the stage, and our ritual movements perform as actors. If this is correct, then to understand our thoughts, we simply decode the symbols of our outward actions."[32] According to this approach, the methodological target for change is the bodily rituals that habituate a person toward certain ends.

Smith, meanwhile, identifies habits as an embodied orientation toward the world:

> Only an appreciation of this embodied know-how, this visceral knowledge, can enable us to understand how habits are acquired. And such habits are central to a liturgical anthropology. As we've just noted, our inclinations to construe and constitute the world are themselves habits—dispositional inclinations to perceive the world in a certain way, against the background of a specific horizon. Furthermore, at the heart of a liturgical anthropology is an

---

29. Johnson, *Knowledge by Ritual*, 90.
30. Johnson, *Knowledge by Ritual*, 112.
31. Johnson, *Human Rites*, 2.
32. Johnson, *Human Rites*, 16.

appreciation for the centrality of habit in guiding and generating our action. Insofar as virtue (and vice) is at the center of a Christian account of action, we are on the terrain of habits…if human persons are conceived of as fundamentally thinking things, then "habit" will always be some sort of intellectual accomplishment—the outcome of thinking. Habit will be thought to originate as an act of the intellect. But this regularly proves itself both wrong and inadequate…. The acquisition of a habit happens on a register that eludes and exceeds the intellect. Nonetheless, it is still an acquisition, an embodied orientation that is acquired, that we learn.[33]

Habits are precognitive, animalistic instincts formed through embodied practices.[34] Although Smith ultimately locates the habits in the heart, he claims that these habits are nonetheless noncognitive and that they are formed through embodied practices. He writes,

Different kinds of material practices infuse noncognitive dispositions and skills in us through ritual and repetition precisely because our hearts (site of habits) are closely tethered to our bodies. The senses are portals to the heart, and thus the body is a channel to our core dispositions and identity. Over time, rituals and practices—often in tandem with aesthetic phenomena like pictures and stories—mold and shape our precognitive dispositions to the world by training our desires. It's as if our appendages function as a conduit to our adaptive unconscious: the motions and rhythms of embodied routines train our minds and hearts so that we develop habits—sort of attitudinal reflexes—that make us tend to act in certain ways toward certain ends.[35]

Precognitive habits formed through embodied practices are the "fulcrum" through which the affections are shaped.[36] Again, the methodological target for change is embodied practices.

---

33. Smith, *Imagining the Kingdom*, 57.

34. Smith, *Desiring the Kingdom*, 56. Smith states in a footnote (56n34) that the reflection upon one's dispositions toward the world is important. However, he also argues that such reflection happens after the dispositions have already been developed and that it is sporadic and unsustainable.

35. Smith, *Desiring the Kingdom*, 58–59.

36. Smith, *Desiring the Kingdom*, 55–56.

Johnson's and Smith's approaches to the body are reminiscent of Adams's view of the flesh as the sinfully habituated body.[37] The key difference is that Adams's relation of the habit to the body was a theological conclusion based upon an exegetical understanding of "the flesh," whereas Johnson and Smith draw their conclusions from neuroscience and philosophical reflection. That said, the result regarding the relationship of habit and sanctification is the same. Sanctification essentially becomes a process of reprogramming the body through dehabituation and rehabituation. As Adams wrote,

> The body has been programmed by one's sinful nature to sin. At conversion that programming does not automatically disappear, so that there is an absolutely fresh start. Quite to the contrary—it carries over into the new life, making the body with its desires an enemy within.... The body, as well as the rest of the person, has been set free from sin's dominion. But the body is still viewed as a "body of sin." In other words, it is a body that, apart from changes made by sanctification (in which new habits replace old ones), still persists in indulging its desires.[38]

Like Smith and Johnson, Adams viewed bodily practices as the methodological target of sanctification. Such an approach bears little practical difference from a secular understanding of habit-acquisition.

For Owen, Christian habit-formation was not synonymous with frequent, embodied practices. The body is certainly a part of what it means to be created in the image of God, and it is an important part of human functioning. But the soul is where true, holy habituation occurs. He wrote, "It is our persons that are sanctified and made holy ('Sanctify them throughout'); and although our souls are the first proper subject of the infused habit or principle of holiness, yet our bodies, as essential parts of our natures, are partakers thereof."[39] Habit-formation in the body is a benefit of what the Spirit does in the soul. Furthermore, as the soul empowered by the Spirit acts

---

37. In particular, Johnson's references to the "habit-body" closely resemble Adams's references to the "sin-habituated body" in *A Theology of Christian Counseling*, 143, 160n1; *Winning the War Within*, 43; *Sanctification and Counseling*, 213.

38. Adams, *Winning the War Within*, 40–41.

39. Owen, *A Discourse Concerning the Holy Spirit*, in *Works*, 3:420.

through the body in obedience, the Spirit increases habitual grace in the soul. Thus, habit-formation is not a simple process of replacing one set of embodied practices with another. It is a Spirit-empowered reformation of the soul. Without this understanding, discussions of habit-formation lose their supernatural focus and become mechanical. They fail to focus on the wonder of what Christ has promised to do and is doing in the soul by His Spirit, and they result in checklists of behaviors that a person needs to stop doing and start doing.[40] If you want to change yourself, you simply change your embodied practices and your environment. Though such considerations are an important component of sanctification, Owen rightly asserted that the methodological target is much deeper. We must consciously aim at this target through an examination of the heart and of sin's internal influence upon it.

The Faculties of the Soul

Although Jay Adams emphasized the need for the heart—the innermost part of man—to be renewed by the gracious work of the Holy Spirit in order for proper human functioning to be progressively achieved, he did not articulate a comprehensive understanding of the functions of the heart. Any discussion of interior human functioning in his work focused primarily on the mind exerting cognitive effort to identify sinful habits and replace them with righteous habits. In sanctification, the believer studies, in order to know what is right, and practices, in order to establish a habit of doing what is right, all the while paying careful attention to orient his choices toward commands rather than desires.[41] While Adams's description generally approximates the process of sanctification, it fails to articulate the complexity of human functioning and the work of the Spirit in sanctifying the faculties. Furthermore, it leads to a counseling methodology that

---

40. This was one of Edward Welch's key criticisms of Adams. He writes of Adams's approach, "Counseling will be similar to a consultation with a physician. What is important is the right diagnosis (the habit that must be broken) and the proper prescription (the habit that must be substituted)," in "How Theology Shapes Ministry," 22.

41. Adams, *A Theology of Christian Counseling*, 241–48.

unhelpfully de-emphasizes interior human functioning and overemphasizes external behavior.

In contrast, as I discussed in chapter 5, a thorough articulation of interior human functioning was central to Owen's doctrine of sanctification. He believed that the soul possesses three faculties: the mind, the will, and the affections. Sanctification properly reorders the faculties such that they function in relation to one another according to God's original design.[42] As the believer is progressively enabled by the Spirit to behold Christ by faith in all his faculties, he is prepared to perfectly behold Christ by sight in his glorified state, when his faculties will be perfectly ordered just like Christ's.[43] In this way, man's natural, interior constitution (i.e., his faculties) is renewed by grace such that he regains what was lost in the garden: a rightly ordered nature that is graciously inclined toward righteousness. However, the last state will be greater than the first because he will be confirmed in his righteousness, never to lose it as it was lost in the garden. Owen, therefore, appropriately related sanctification to anthropology and set it within a redemptive-historical framework. He developed a robust theology of man's inner life regarding both its natural constitution and its gracious influences in each stage of redemption history (i.e., creation, fall, redemption, restoration).

Similarly, several writers within the segment of biblical counselors who emphasize heart motivation have sought to describe the complexity of man's inner life, including Fitzpatrick,[44] Emlet,[45] and Pierre.[46] These three use the same threefold model of the faculties as Owen.[47] One area of modern soul care literature that needs correction is an overemphasis on one faculty to the detriment of the

---

42. Owen, *A Declaration of the Glorious Mystery of the Person of Christ*, in *Works*, 1:320; *The Nature, Power, Deceit, and Prevalency of the Remainders of Indwelling Sin in Believers*, in *Works*, 6:173.

43. Owen, *A Declaration of the Glorious Mystery of the Person of Christ*, in *Works*, 1:320.

44. Fitzpatrick, *Idols of the Heart*, 93–97.

45. Emlet, "Understanding the Influences on the Human Heart."

46. Pierre, *The Dynamic Heart in Daily Life*.

47. See also A. Craig Troxel, *With All Your Heart: Orienting Your Mind, Desires, and Will toward Christ* (Wheaton, Ill.: Crossway, 2020).

others. While this error is not widely evident in biblical counseling literature, it is evident in discussions of habit in evangelical literature more broadly.

The error is particularly evident in both Smith and Johnson. Smith emphasizes the affections over against the intellect. One of his central arguments is that humans are primarily affective beings rather than cognitive beings. He writes,

> the way we inhabit the world is not primarily as thinkers, or even believers, but as more affective, embodied creatures who make our way in the world more by feeling our way around it…. One might say that in our everyday, mundane being-in-the-world, we don't lead with our head, so to speak; we lead with our heart and hands.[48]

Thus, Smith relates Christian formation primarily to embodied practices/habits and to the affections.[49]

Johnson, in contrast, elevates the role of the intellect. In his approach, the practice of rituals is the primary means by which humans come to know things. He writes,

> The Hebrew Bible and Christian Scriptures presume a thoroughly ritualed life for the sake of knowing correctly…. Among other goals, Israel's rituals were intended to bring Israelites to know something. The Hebrew Bible portrays Israelites as logically separated from knowing that which they need to know apart from their participation in its specified rituals. For their part, the Christian Scriptures presume that ritual knowing remains the norm.[50]

Furthermore, Johnson, like Smith, explains the importance of habit in forming who we are as human beings. One important reason for this, he argues, is the well-documented plasticity of the human brain. Repetitive practices have a formative effect on the structures of the human brain. Johnson concludes, "The implications of this combination—habit and plasticity—are profound. If correct, it means that as humans, we do not get to choose whether our thinking is shaped by

---

48. Smith, *Desiring the Kingdom*, 47. Smith himself recognizes the irony of writing a book that is full of cognitive content in order to argue for the primacy of the affections. See Smith, *Imagining the Kingdom*, xii.

49. See also Smith, *Desiring the Kingdom*, 55–63.

50. Johnson, *Scripture's Knowing*, 66.

ritual or not. Rather, we must assess which ritualized practices we ought to participate in and hence, allow to shape our plastic habit-bodies."[51] Johnson relates Christian formation primarily to embodied rituals/habits and the intellect.

As discussed above, Owen portrayed sanctification as a habitual restoration of all of the faculties of the soul, particularly as it pertains to their ability to perceive Christ with eyes of faith. He wrote, "If we are spiritually renewed, all the faculties of our souls are enabled by grace to exert their respective powers towards this glorious object [i.e., Christ]."[52] Furthermore, a perfect reordering of the faculties in their apprehension of Christ is the final goal of sanctification.[53] Therefore, sanctification in the here and now involves the restoration of all of the faculties through faith in Christ.[54] An example of how this restoration occurs can be seen in Owen's directions for spiritual-mindedness based upon Romans 8:6. He explained that to be spiritually minded is "to have the mind changed and renewed by a principle of spiritual life and light, so as to be continually acted and influenced thereby unto thoughts and meditations of spiritual things, from the affections cleaving unto them with delight and satisfaction."[55] The sanctification of the affections through spiritual-mindedness results in a life of willful obedience: "And every affection is originally sanctified according unto the use it is to be of in the life of holiness and obedience."[56] This is the scriptural process by which the Christian grows in holiness: he intentionally directs his mind toward the things of God in order to increase his affections for God, resulting in willful obedience to God. It is a holy

---

51. Johnson, *Knowledge by Ritual*, 112.

52. Owen, *A Declaration of the Glorious Mystery of the Person of Christ*, in *Works*, 1:320.

53. Owen, *A Declaration of the Glorious Mystery of the Person of Christ*, in *Works*, 1:320.

54. The restoration of all of the faculties through faith in Christ is also a key assertion of Pierre in *The Dynamic Heart in Daily Life* and "'Trust in the Lord with All Your Heart.'"

55. Owen, *The Grace and Duty of Being Spiritually Minded*, in *Works*, 7:270. Further describing the relationship between the mind and the affections, he wrote, "Spiritual affections, whereby the soul adheres unto spiritual things, taking in such a savour and relish of them as wherein it finds rest and satisfaction, is the peculiar spring and substance of our being spiritually minded." *The Grace and Duty of Being Spiritually Minded*, in *Works*, 7:395.

56. Owen, *The Grace and Duty of Being Spiritually Minded*, in *Works*, 7:419.

engagement of all the faculties, not just the intellect or the affections.[57] While the intellect may be logically prioritized in relation to the will and the affections, it is so only as it guides and directs the other faculties, and it is not prioritized to the detriment of the other faculties.

In light of this, counselors must recognize that their task will always have a cognitive emphasis, as the other faculties will necessarily be limited by the amount of light that the mind has received. However, the communication of cognitive content for the enlightenment of the mind is not the end point of counseling. Rather, it is a means whereby the mind can be directed toward the truth, the affections raised for it, and the will progressively inclined to choose in accordance with it. Thus, though the affections will be sinfully entangled if the believer passively allows himself to be drawn away by the world, they will not be disentangled through this same passivity. Disentangling the affections and strengthening the will's inclination toward righteousness will only occur through the active engagement of the mind. Every faculty, in its proper order and relation to the others, must be cultivated in righteousness.

Natural and Supernatural Habits

Perhaps the clearest area of confusion in modern discussions of habit among biblical counselors and others outside of the biblical counseling movement is the conflation of natural and supernatural habits. Owen applied a distinction between natural and supernatural habits that was widely used among Puritan and Reformed Orthodox theologians. Natural habits are those that can be acquired by utilizing natural effort to perform repetitive acts. Supernatural habits,

---

57. Beeke states that "meditation must enter three doors: the door of the understanding, the door of the heart and affections, and the door of practical living," in Beeke, *Puritan Reformed Spirituality*, 75. For a helpful study of Puritan meditation, see also David W. Saxton, *God's Battle Plan for the Mind: The Puritan Practice of Biblical Meditation* (Grand Rapids: Reformation Heritage Books, 2015). Smith's de-emphasis of the mind is particularly detrimental to Christian formation. As shown above, the mind must engage with the truth in order to truly stir holy affections. Smith's discussion of cultural liturgies is accurate regarding how the world can shape us somewhat unconsciously, but true sanctification requires conscious, cognitive effort.

however, cannot be acquired through repetitive acts. Rather, they must be supernaturally infused by the Holy Spirit. Three authors in particular from within the biblical counseling movement have sought to restore habituation to counseling: Michael Emlet, Brian Mesimer, and Greg Gifford. Although they are to be commended for their efforts, each author fails to rightly or consistently distinguish between natural and supernatural habits.

Michael Emlet

Michael Emlet's 2013 article "Practice Makes Perfect? Exploring the Relationship between Knowledge, Desire, and Habit" was the first substantial treatment of habit within the biblical counseling movement since Welch's and Schwab's critiques of Adams in 2002 and 2003, respectively.[58] Emlet's article is an extended interaction with James K. A. Smith's *Desiring the Kingdom*, a work that he described as the most important book he had read in several years.[59] As I discussed above, Smith's major premise in his work is that

> the way we inhabit the world is not primarily as thinkers, or even believers, but as more affective, embodied creatures who make our way in the world more by feeling our way around it…. One might say that in our everyday, mundane being-in-the-world, we don't lead with our head, so to speak; we lead with our heart and hands.[60]

Thus, Smith emphasizes the centrality of desire—or the affections—in human functioning over against cognition. Humans act primarily based upon what they love, and what they love is significantly influenced by what they do.[61] In his interaction with Smith, Emlet considers how Smith's proposal might affect counseling. One of his conclusions is that counselors must remember that the primary problem counselees face is rarely a lack of information but, rather, a lack of desire and an

---

58. Mesimer and Gifford have both noted this as well. See Mesimer, "Rehabilitating Habituation," 54; Gifford, "Jay Adams' Teaching of Habituation," 137.

59. Emlet, "Practice Makes Perfect?," 48.

60. Smith, *Desiring the Kingdom*, 47.

61. James Sire has critiqued Smith's view as an oversimplification of the relationship between cognition, affection, and volition. See James W. Sire, *Naming the Elephant: Worldview as a Concept*, 2nd ed. (Downers Grove, Ill.: IVP Academic, 2015), 65.

unwillingness to engage in those practices that might increase their desire.[62] Counselors must view their counselees as habitual creatures whose habits significantly affect their desires. Examining counselees' habitual practices will help discern why they lack holy desires, and prescribing biblical practices will help increase their holy desires.[63]

Appropriating Smith's proposal for counseling is problematic—particularly for those who counsel within the Reformed tradition—because he discusses habit merely in an acquired, natural sense. His approach, therefore, differs little from that of Aristotle, who viewed habits, or virtue, as something that could simply be acquired through repetitive practice.[64] Such habit-acquisition can occur, but it is not true holiness. Truly holy habituation can only occur through the Spirit's supernatural infusion and increase of a habit of grace in the soul of the believer. Michael Allen has noted the deficiency in Smith's work, explaining that "his approach cannot be adopted by a Reformed theologian, however, without a good bit of work being done to ask how divine involvement in cultural practices, both inside and outside the church, and granting of infused habits will fill out his discussion of human formation."[65] Emlet's appropriation of Smith's proposal, then, does not properly correct Adams's view of habituation. Rather, it repackages dehabituation and rehabituation by stressing desire more than Adams did.

In contrast, Owen set Spirit-infused habitual grace at the center of his theology of regeneration and sanctification. Regeneration "consists in a new, spiritual, supernatural, vital principle or habit of grace, infused into the soul, the mind, will, and affections, by the power of the Holy Spirit, disposing and enabling them in whom it is unto spiritual, supernatural, vital acts of faith and obedience."[66] Furthermore, "in the sanctification of believers, the Holy Ghost doth work in them,

---

62. Emlet, "Practice Makes Perfect?," 45–46.

63. Emlet does acknowledge the importance of cognitive engagement in biblical practices in order to increase desires. See Emlet, "Practice Makes Perfect?," 45.

64. Aristotle, *Aristotle's Nicomachean Ethics*, trans. Robert C. Bartlett and Susan D. Collins (Chicago: University of Chicago Press, 2011), 2.1 (1103b 14).

65. Allen, *Sanctification*, 248n36.

66. Owen, *A Discourse Concerning the Holy Spirit*, in *Works*, 3:329.

in their whole souls, their minds, wills, and affections, a gracious, supernatural habit, principle, and disposition of living unto God; wherein the substance or essence, the life and being, of holiness doth consist."[67] Without this emphasis on Spirit-infused habitual grace, the Christian runs the risk of losing his consistent dependence on the ongoing work of the Spirit in the reformation of the whole soul. Smith places a great deal of emphasis on habit-acquisition, but because his emphasis on habit lacks an account of the Spirit's work in habituation, it ultimately differs little from secular accounts of habituation.[68]

Brian Mesimer

Brian Mesimer notes the absence of habits in recent discussions on theology and practice within the biblical counseling movement and suggests that counselors revisit the topic: "If the Bible emphasizes habitual actions toward holiness, then it is imperative that counselors fully grasp this emphasis for the benefit of those under our care."[69] After summarizing the discussion of habits within the biblical counseling movement and providing several biblical texts that suggest the importance of habits, Mesimer concludes that understanding habituation requires an appropriate balance of the divine and the human in sanctification. He writes,

> Sanctification involves human effort that is powered and directed by God's underlying workings. God gives us an inner heart disposition that exists prior to the practice of habituation, and the practice of properly motivated habits serves to further cooperate with God's

---

67. Owen, *A Discourse Concerning the Holy Spirit*, in *Works*, 3:468–69.

68. Smith does refer to the work of the Spirit (*You Are What You Love*, 66–69, 89). However, like Adams, he does not state that the Spirit actually does the work of habituation. A similar critique may be leveled against Dru Johnson, who, though he discusses habit extensively, makes no mention of the Spirit's involvement in habituation in his book on sacramental theology. Johnson's one mention of the Holy Spirit's work in the sacraments is a footnoted quotation of the Heidelberg Catechism. See Johnson, *Knowledge by Ritual*, 260n10.

69. Mesimer, "Rehabilitating Habituation," 55. Mesimer also completed a master's thesis at Reformed Theological Seminary titled "Habits and the Heart." However, because his later article in the *Journal of Biblical Counseling* includes the main conclusions from his thesis as well as several revisions and updates to them, I will primarily focus on this article in the present discussion.

initial work in us. Efforts to change behavior that do not arise from God's work in us and through us are guaranteed to fail. But the command remains: work. Live out, over time, in practices and by habit, all that it means to be saved.[70]

Drawing on historical sources, including Aristotle, Thomas Aquinas, John Calvin, and John Owen, Mesimer explains that Adams was too imprecise in his discussion of habituation. Whereas Adams used the term "habits" to refer to repetitive behaviors, the term historically referred to an inward disposition.[71]

Mesimer explains the benefits that biblical counselors may reap by adopting the historic understanding of the term:

> The benefit of this shift becomes immediately clear: we no longer speak of behavioral actions as habits only, but of the change of the whole soul toward godly dispositions as a *habitus*. Part of what made Adams's conceptualization of habit unappealing was its seeming emphasis on individual actions, or what would usually be called a habit. Yet a true *habitus* is the stable state of being that produces individual actions. Using this kind of language makes habit talk more consonant with the Bible's emphasis on the heart. A heart that has stable desires toward good or ill would necessarily evince consistent behavior patterns. Seen from this perspective, Adams's major (but not novel) claim therefore is that individual actions can influence, form, and shape this habitual state. Moving toward the older, fuller conception of *habitus* would resolve multiple problematic emphases in the habituation debate while promising a new way forward in integrating biblical motivation into Adams's view of habituation.[72]

Here, Mesimer provides an important corrective to Adams's view and approximates the intention of my work. Furthermore, he goes on to helpfully explain the historic distinction between acquired and infused habits.[73] In all of this, he provides a sound theology of habituation for biblical counseling.

---

70. Mesimer, "Rehabilitating Habituation," 66–67.
71. Mesimer, "Rehabilitating Habituation," 68.
72. Mesimer, "Rehabilitating Habituation," 68 (italics original).
73. Mesimer, "Rehabilitating Habituation," 68–73.

However, a problem arises when Mesimer proposes a counseling methodology based upon this theology of habituation. Although his theology of habituation locates the habits in the soul and specifies that these habits are infused by the Spirit, his methodology consistently relates habits to the body. He writes,

> The biblical counselor must focus on both body and soul in the counseling room because both body and soul are stricken with sin. In the case of someone struggling with a habitual sin pattern, this means simultaneously focusing on changing behaviors while also discussing the heart idols and personal history that provide the context for this sin.[74]

Summarizing this approach to sanctification, he states, "Sanctification requires both habit-oriented action and heart-piercing insight."[75] He also makes assertions that seem to explicitly locate habit in the body, such as, "Certain problems require more heart work, while others require more habitual work."[76] Ultimately, his methodology is a balancing act between focusing on the counselees' bodily practices (i.e., habits) and focusing on their inward heart motivations.[77] Thus, he ends up making the same mistake of which he accused Adams: referring to habits as individual actions rather than a stable disposition of the heart.

Although Mesimer does well to engage the historic understanding of habits—particularly in distinguishing between naturally acquired habits and Spirit-infused habits of grace—he merely uses this understanding to emphasize the importance of addressing bodily practices in conjunction with heart motivation. Thus, theologically, he acknowledges the significance of supernaturally infused habits, but, methodologically, he discusses habits in a natural, acquired sense. The biblical counseling movement needs a methodology that consistently arises from a theology of infused habits and accounts for

---

74. Mesimer, "Rehabilitating Habituation," 73.

75. Mesimer, "Rehabilitating Habituation," 74.

76. Mesimer, "Rehabilitating Habituation," 74.

77. This is further evidenced by his relation of habit to issues with clear bodily components, such as sexual sin, addictions, mild anxiety, and slothfulness. See Mesimer, "Rehabilitating Habituation," 74–75.

how these infused habits operate upon the functions of the heart and result in outward works.[78]

Greg Gifford

Greg Gifford has noted the appropriate reorientation brought about by Powlison's emphasis on desire and human motivation.[79] But he has also sought to defend Adams's view of habituation by appealing to the discussion of habits among the English Puritans. He argues that the "English Puritans demonstrated an understanding similar to that of Adams' perspective of habits as learned behavior through frequent practice."[80] He further states that the Puritans used the term "habit" to "describe frequent practice that leads to automaticity."[81] He rightly notes the important distinction among the Puritans between habit and act: that a habit both disposes one toward the acts that accord with it and is increased by the acts that accord with it.[82]

To his credit, Gifford recognizes that the biblical counseling movement has failed to properly ground its understanding of habituation in the work of the Spirit. Unfortunately, however, he misrepresents the Puritan distinction between natural (i.e., acquired) and supernatural (i.e., infused) habits, which leads him to faulty conclusions. He asserts that "[John] Owen says that the Spirit creates both 'natural habits' and 'infused habits' within the believer."[83] He elsewhere writes, "the English Puritans clearly stated that supernatural and natural habits advanced spiritual maturity."[84]

Gifford's misrepresentation of the distinction between supernatural and natural habits seems to lie in his strict identification of natural

---

78. As I will discuss in the next chapter, such a methodology must combine a proper understanding of Spirit-infused habitual grace with a proper understanding of the Spirit's use of the ordinary means of grace.

79. Gifford, "The Role of Habits in Spiritual Maturity from the Perspective of the English Puritans," 21.

80. Gifford, "Jay Adams' Teaching of Habituation," 139.

81. Gifford, "Jay Adams' Teaching of Habituation," 139.

82. Gifford, "Jay Adams' Teaching of Habituation," 140.

83. Gifford, "Jay Adams' Teaching of Habituation," 145.

84. Gifford, "The Role of Habits in Spiritual Maturity from the Perspective of the English Puritans," 3. This statement is taken from the thesis of his dissertation.

habits with the moral responses of man and of supernatural habits with Spirit-infused dispositions. He suggests that the Puritans viewed repentance as a natural habit, and he apparently draws this conclusion from the fact that the Puritans spoke of repentance as a duty. Thus, if it is a duty, Gifford concludes, then it must be a natural habit.[85]

The Puritans, however, maintained a strict distinction between naturally acquired habits and supernaturally infused habits. Natural habits "can be acquired by a multitude of acts, whether in things moral or artificial."[86] In the case of such naturally acquired habits, the acts precede the habits, such that the habits are acquired through repetitive actions.[87] Any person, whether regenerate or unregenerate, can acquire such habits. A supernaturally infused habit, however, is the result of the Spirit's work alone. In this case, the habit precedes all of the acts that flow from it. Owen explained, "There never was by any, nor ever can be, any act or duty of true holiness performed, where there was not in order of nature antecedently a habit of holiness in the persons by whom they were performed."[88] All holy acts proceed from a Spirit-infused habit of grace that the Spirit works upon the souls of believers, producing outward acts of holiness.[89] The Puritans

---

85. Gifford, "The Role of Habits in Spiritual Maturity from the Perspective of the English Puritans," 117. In another publication, Gifford makes conflicting statements regarding John Owen's distinction between natural and supernatural habits. On the one hand, he suggests that natural habits can promote holiness: "John Owen emphatically taught that these habits—both infused and the natural habits—promote holiness and the sanctity of the church through union with Christ." However, he also writes, "John Owen helps differentiate between morality and habits of genuine holiness," and, "infused habits of the Spirit must be present for the work of holy habits." See Gifford, "John Owen's Perspective on the Effects of Habits," 65, 69. It seems safe to conclude that such statements stem from Gifford's identification of natural habits as the moral responses of man and of supernatural habits as dispositions infused by the Spirit. Gifford continues to employ this distinction in his most recent work, *Heart and Habit*, 20–21. However, as I will explain below, Owen believed that natural habits are categorically distinct from supernatural habits and cannot promote true holiness.

86. Owen, *A Discourse Concerning the Holy Spirit*, in *Works*, 3:469.

87. Owen, *A Discourse Concerning the Holy Spirit*, in *Works*, 3:474.

88. Owen, *A Discourse Concerning the Holy Spirit*, in *Works*, 3:474.

89. Owen, *A Discourse Concerning the Holy Spirit*, in *Works*, 3:468–69. Note also Stephen Charnock's distinction between natural (i.e., moral virtue) and supernatural habits: "Moral virtue is gained by human industry, natural strength, frequent exercises; it is made

clearly believed that supernatural habits were of a wholly different category than natural habits. The former was holy, while the latter had nothing to do with holiness.

Gifford's misrepresentation of natural and supernatural habits leads him to prematurely conclude that the Puritan understanding of habits supports that of Adams.[90] The Puritans—and particularly John Owen—viewed holy habituation as a work that is begun by the Spirit's infusion of a habit of grace within the believer at regeneration. This work is continued through sanctification as the Spirit progressively increases the operations of the habit upon the faculties of the soul, thereby fostering an inward inclination toward righteousness that leads to outward acts of righteousness. In this way, the Puritans discussed habituation at a deeper level than did Adams, and they much more vividly portrayed the Spirit-dependent nature of sanctification.

Summary and Conclusion

Although Emlet, Mesimer, and Gifford do well to resurrect the discussion of habit in biblical counseling, each of their proposals suffers to some degree from a lack of clarity in applying the distinction

---

up of habits, engendered by frequent acts. But regeneration is an habit infused, which grows not upon the stock of nature, nor is it brought forth by the strength of nature; for man being flesh, cannot prepare himself to it. That may be the fruit of education, example, philosophy; this is of the Spirit; that is a fruit of God's common grace, this of his special grace; that grows upon the stock of self-love, not from the root of faith, and a divine affection; that is like a wild flower in the field, brought forth by the strength of nature; this like a flower in the garden, transplanted from heaven, derived from Christ, set and watered by the Spirit. And therefore the other being but the work of nature, cannot bear the characters of excellency, which the affections planted by the Spirit do. That is the product of reason, this of the Spirit; that is the awakening of natural light, this the breaking out of spiritual light and love upon it; that is the excitation of an old principle, this the infusion of a new; that a rising from sleep by the jog of conscience, this a rising from death by the breath of the Spirit, working a deep contrition, and making all new." See Stephen Charnock, *A Discourse of the Nature of Regeneration,* in *The Works of Stephen Charnock* (Edinburgh: Banner of Truth, 1997), 3:132–33.

90. He completely accepts Adams's view, writing, "I believe that Adams' teaching on habituation is what it should be, as even a cursory glance at the Scriptures and the English Puritans demonstrates. What Jay Adams taught in regard to the importance of cultivating habits through frequent action was criticized as behavioristic, but it is consistent with biblical and historical teaching." See Gifford, "Jay Adams' Teaching of Habituation," 146.

between natural and supernatural habits. Mesimer comes closest to the historic view held by Owen. His articulation of habituation is correct theologically, but it loses clarity when moving to method-ological application and ends up practically equating habituation with repetitive bodily actions. Bodily action is, indeed, necessary to a right understanding of habituation. However, such bodily actions only contribute to inward, habitual holiness if they are the right actions (i.e., according to God's law and His prescribed means of grace) and if they themselves proceed from an antecedent inward habit of holi-ness. Thus, the counselor should not merely seek to strike a balance between "heart work" and "habitual work," as Mesimer suggests.[91] Rather, the counselor must promote holy habituation through Spirit-engendered, faithful obedience. The soul is habitually reformed by Spirit-produced faith, and that faith results in holy actions that the Spirit uses, in turn, to increase faith. Therefore, the counselor must prescribe the right actions and discourage the wrong actions, but he must do so as he simultaneously helps the counselee engage in these actions with self-conscious faith in Christ and His promises. Such an understanding of holy habituation helps keep counseling Spirit depen-dent. Furthermore, it centers the focus of habituation on the heart rather than the bodily actions. The habituation does not occur in the bodily actions. Habituation begins in the heart as the Spirit increases faith, and it results outwardly in bodily actions.

The Three Levels of Human Functioning

Owen's understanding of the three levels of human functioning pro-vides a fuller experiential framework for sanctification. In human functioning, Owen distinguished between the principle, the opera-tions, and the effects.[92] The work of mortification and vivification must occur at every level. Adams's methodological focus was on the effects: the behavioral results of indwelling sin. The focus on heart motivation that accompanied the "idols of the heart" motif led Powlison and his followers to focus on the operations: the particular

---

91. Mesimer, "Rehabilitating Habituation," 74.
92. Owen, *A Discourse Concerning the Holy Spirit*, in *Works*, 3:541–42.

thoughts, desires, and inclinations that lead one to sin. Owen took the methodological target one step deeper: the overall habit of remaining sin in the believer. Understanding a habit as an underlying principle that inclines the soul in a particular direction reminds us that we are not merely trying to put to death particular thoughts, desires, and inclinations. Rather, we are holistically seeking to become a different type of person, one who thinks, desires, wills, and acts righteously rather than sinfully. Furthermore, Owen's distinction between indwelling sin as a habitual *propensity* and infused habitual grace as a stronger, indwelling *inclination* means that the believer should have confidence that the Spirit will increase his habitual inclination toward righteousness and enable him to overcome his remaining habitual propensity toward sin.[93]

Distinguishing between the habit (i.e., the underlying, inclining principle of the soul) and the act (i.e., the actual operations and effects of the habit in the soul and in outward behavior) as Owen did properly connects two overarching themes of Christian experience: union/communion and command/promise. Regarding union and communion, in uniting a person to Christ, the Spirit implants a habit of grace in the soul, inclining him toward righteousness. Communion increases as that habit influences the operations of the soul and its effects. Though communion can wax and wane, union does not, which means that the habit of grace in the soul can never be lost, though its influence may be diminished.[94] Thus, when a true believer's communion with God has declined due to sin in his heart and his actions, the underlying habit of grace remains. Even if it is like a small spark, the Spirit can fan that spark into a flame, thereby renewing one's efforts toward obedience in the operations of his soul and in his outward actions.

---

93. Owen, *The Nature, Power, Deceit, and Prevalency of the Remainders of Indwelling Sin in Believers*, in *Works*, 6:190–92.

94. Habitual grace is an important component of Owen's theology of perseverance. Because obedience is twofold—habitual and actual—a believer may outwardly oppose God through acts of disobedience while inwardly delighting in God through the habit of grace infused within his soul. See *The Doctrine of the Saints' Perseverance Explained and Confirmed*, in *Works*, 11:442.

With respect to command and promise, the command regards one's actual obedience to God, while the promise regards the work of the Spirit whereby He increases habitual grace to enable one to keep the commands.[95] Commands must be obeyed in the operations of the soul and in the outward effects, but they must be obeyed with self-conscious faith in the promise that God is already at work in the deepest part of one's being. Because the Spirit is already at work, inwardly and habitually inclining a believer toward righteousness, the believer can obey in his mind, affections, will, and actions with faith in the promise that the Spirit will use such obedience to further increase his holiness.

Furthermore, Owen's understanding of the three levels of human functioning is a helpful evaluative tool for the counselor. The goal of the Spirit's work of sanctification is universal holiness.[96] Thus, as Adams emphasized, counselors must urge holiness in one's outward behaviors. As Powlison and others have emphasized, counselors must also urge holiness in the operations of the heart. However, for Owen, counselors must go a step further and urge counselees to mortify the overall power of indwelling sin and to increase the overall habitual inclination toward righteousness in the soul, thereby becoming, from the depth of the soul, the type of person who walks in righteousness.

---

95. Owen, *A Discourse Concerning the Holy Spirit*, in *Works*, 3:384.
96. Owen, *A Discourse Concerning the Holy Spirit*, in *Works*, 3:389.

Chapter 7

Soteriological Considerations
for Soul Care

In this final chapter, I continue to apply the main contours of Owen's theology of Spirit-infused habitual grace in sanctification to soul care. Here, I will examine four aspects of Owen's theology that ought to lead counselors to reconsider the practical implications of their soteriological commitments. First, Owen's theology of the means of grace helps clarify the resources available to the counselor and the context in which counseling should occur. Second, the christological shape of Owen's theology of sanctification helps clarify the *telos* of the task of counseling and Christian formation. Third, the way in which Owen grounds his theology of sanctification in the doctrine of God leads counselors toward greater humility. Fourth, Owen's theology of Spirit-infused habitual grace accounts well for the scriptural commands for humans—who have complex natures—to imitate the simple, purely actual God.

The Means of Grace and the Method of Soul Care

For Owen, the ordinary means of grace were the connective tissue between a habit of grace and its associated acts in sanctification. It is through the means of grace that the Spirit infuses the habit of grace in regeneration and increases the influence of this habit of grace upon the soul in sanctification. The Christian obediently acts by using the means of grace in faith, trusting that the Spirit of Christ, by the means of grace, will increase the habit of grace in his soul, thus inclining him further and further toward righteousness. In this section, I will discuss two areas in which Owen's theology of infused habitual grace and the means of grace can benefit biblical counseling. First, I will explain how Owen's understanding of the means of grace can strengthen the biblical counseling movement's argument for the sufficiency of Scripture. Second, I will discuss how Owen's understanding of the means of grace can sharpen the biblical counseling movement's approach to soul care in relation to pastoral ministry. These two emphases—the sufficiency of Scripture and pastoral counseling in the church—have remained central within the biblical counseling movement from the beginning of Jay Adams's ministry until now, and I wish to bolster them through the influence of the wisdom of John Owen.

The Means of Grace and the Sufficiency of Scripture
The basic tenet of the biblical counseling movement is that the ordinary means of grace are the only sufficient means through which people may deal with their deepest problems. Jay Adams wrote in *Competent to Counsel*,

> The Holy Spirit ordinarily effects his characterological work in the lives of believers through the means of grace. He uses the ministry of the Word, the sacraments, prayer and the fellowship of God's people as the principal vehicles through which he brings about such changes. How can counseling that is removed from the means of grace expect to effect the permanent changes that come only by growth in grace?[1]

Lambert states that the sufficiency of Scripture is "the doctrine on which the biblical counseling movement will succeed or fail."[2] Powlison,[3] Lambert,[4] Pierre,[5] and others[6] have offered helpful

---

1. Adams, *Competent to Counsel*, 21–22.

2. Heath Lambert, *A Theology of Biblical Counseling: The Doctrinal Foundations of Counseling Ministry* (Grand Rapids: Zondervan, 2016), 37.

3. David Powlison, "The Sufficiency of Scripture to Diagnose and Cure Souls," *Journal of Biblical Counseling* 23, no. 2 (Spring 2005): 2–14; David Powlison, "Cure of Souls (and the Modern Psychotherapies)," *Journal of Biblical Counseling* 25, no. 2 (Spring 2007): 5–36.

4. Lambert, *A Theology of Biblical Counseling*, 35–64.

5. Jeremy Pierre, "Scripture Is Sufficient, but to Do What?," in *Scripture and Counseling: God's Word for Life in a Broken World*, ed. Bob Kellemen and Jeff Forrey (Grand Rapids: Zondervan, 2014), 94–108.

6. Robert D. Jones, Kristin L. Kellen, and Rob Green, *The Gospel for Disordered Lives:*

doctrinal and practical expositions of the sufficiency of Scripture that I do not intend to rehearse here. Rather, I seek to add to their arguments by viewing man's need for the Scriptures through two lenses that are central to Owen's theology. First, I will revisit Owen's belief that sanctification is a process wherein grace restores, or perfects, nature. Second, I will discuss God's ordained means of grace as the ordinary way by which God does this work and explain the significance of this concept in Scripture and for counseling.

Grace restores nature. As I discussed in chapter 5, Owen held the common Reformed belief that grace restores nature. Grace restores, renovates, and renews what was lost in our natures due to the fall.[7] The Spirit accomplishes this by infusing a restorative habit of grace in the soul at regeneration and increasing that habitual grace in the soul in sanctification.[8] What this means is that God's purpose for man in regeneration and sanctification is to graciously and progressively restore his natural functioning as he approaches perfection. The habit infused by the Spirit in regeneration will, by the power of the Spirit and through faith in Christ, progressively incline the faculties of the soul toward righteousness until the day when we are perfect, when we see Him face-to-face and are like Him, being fully conformed into His image. This is the work in which pastors and counselors participate—therefore, the goal of all pastoral ministry and all counseling that calls itself Christian or biblical ought to be the perfection of the saints.[9]

An Introduction to Christ-Centered Biblical Counseling (Nashville: B&H Academic, 2021), 37–47; Steve Viars and Rob Green, "The Sufficiency of Scripture," in *Christ-Centered Biblical Counseling: Changing Lives with God's Changeless Truth*, ed. James MacDonald, Bob Kellemen, and Steve Viars (Eugene, Ore.: Harvest House, 2013), 89–105; Paul Tautges and Steve Viars, "Sufficient for Life and Godliness," in *Scripture and Counseling: God's Word for Life in a Broken World*, ed. Bob Kellemen and Jeff Forrey (Grand Rapids: Zondervan, 2014), 47–61; Heath Lambert et al., *Sufficiency: Historic Essays on the Sufficiency of Scripture* (Jacksonville, Fla.: Association of Certified Biblical Counselors, 2016).

7. Owen, *A Discourse Concerning the Holy Spirit*, in *Works*, 3:9, 102, 212, 244, 282, 285–86, 382, 418, 446, 455, 469, 580, 629. See also Ferguson, *John Owen on the Christian Life*, 218–19.

8. Owen, *A Discourse Concerning the Holy Spirit*, in *Works*, 3:329, 468–69.

9. The KJV translates Ephesians 4:11–12, "And he gave some, apostles; and some, prophets; and some, evangelists; and some, pastors and teachers; for the perfecting of the

The ordinary means of grace. Sanctification is a supernatural work performed by the Spirit. As Owen makes clear, this gracious work by which God restores our nature cannot occur through natural means. This is evident in Owen's contrast between supernaturally infused habits and naturally acquired habits. He wrote, "Habits acquired by a multitude of acts, whether in things moral or artificial, are not a new nature, nor can be so called, but a readiness for acting from use and custom."[10] Furthermore,

> There is wrought and preserved in the minds and souls of all believers, by the Spirit of God, a supernatural principle or habit of grace and holiness, whereby they are made meet for and enabled to live unto God, and perform that obedience which he requireth and accepteth through Christ in the covenant of grace; essentially or specifically distinct from all natural habits, intellectual and moral, however or by what means soever acquired or improved.[11]

Thus, Christians depend upon the Spirit to work habitual holiness within them; this is not a work that they can accomplish through their own natural effort. Furthermore, it is not a work that happens through just any means. There are particular means ordained by God to achieve this end. Owen explained, "The whole that God requireth of us in the gospel in a way of duty is, that we should be holy, and abide in the use of those means whereby holiness may be attained and improved in us."[12] If the means of grace ordained by God are what the Spirit uses to increase our habitual holiness, then we must ask where it is that we find these means of grace. Owen answered, "The end wherefore God granted his word unto the church was, that thereby it might be instructed in his mind and will as to what concerns the worship and obedience that he requireth of us, and which is accepted with him. This the whole Scripture itself everywhere declares and

---

saints." I will discuss in the next section the significance of this translation for pastoral ministry over against the more modern rendering of verse 12 as "to equip the saints" (e.g., ESV).

10. Owen, *A Discourse Concerning the Holy Spirit*, in *Works*, 3:469.

11. Owen, *A Discourse Concerning the Holy Spirit*, in *Works*, 3:472.

12. Owen, *A Discourse Concerning the Holy Spirit*, in *Works*, 3:377.

speaks out unto all that do receive it."[13] To the question of whether there are any other means whereby men might grow in faith and achieve holiness and obedience in this life, he answered,

> All our faith, all our obedience in this life, whatever may be obtained or attained unto therein, it all belongs unto our walking with God in the covenant of grace, wherein God dwells with men, and they are his people, and God himself is with them to be their God. Other ways of communion with him, of obedience unto him, of enjoyment of him, on this side heaven and glory, he hath not appointed nor revealed.[14]

The purpose of soul care is to help a person grow in holiness. The purpose of the Word is to tell us how we might grow in holiness. And the Spirit uses this Word—and no other means—in order to internally and habitually conform us unto the way of holiness revealed therein.

Owen, like the biblical counseling movement, clearly had a high view of Scripture's ability to teach us what holiness looks like and of the Spirit's ability to use Scripture to graciously grow us in holiness. Scripture is the source in which we discover the means of grace, and it is a means of grace itself. To see the advantage of this view of Scripture for biblical counseling, observe the contrast between Owen's view and that of a counselor and Christian psychologist outside of the biblical counseling movement. Consider how Eric Johnson describes Scripture:

> The Bible gives us many general soul care principles, goals and means. But it does not contain, on the one hand, higher-order theoretical statements regarding, for example, cognitive, emotional and volitional aspects of the soul, the structure of the personality or psychospiritual abnormality, or, on the other hand, lower-order detailed, step-wise treatment strategies for applying the gospel and remediating sin and biological and psychological damage. Such

---

13. Owen, *A Brief Instruction in the Worship of God and Discipline of the Churches of the New Testament*, in *Works*, 15:450.

14. Owen, *A Brief Instruction in the Worship of God and Discipline of the Churches of the New Testament*, in *Works*, 15:454. This and the previous quote come from Owen's catechism on instituted worship. However, though Owen makes these statements in a context that pertains to Scripture's strict regulation of public worship, the statements themselves clearly speak to the entirety of the Christian life.

higher- and lower-order discourse is the fruit of scientific reflection and research.[15]

Johnson continues by explaining that, though the Bible states in general terms that sin arises from the heart, "it nowhere describes the components that make up the heart, how the heart is related to the memory, emotion and reasoning subsystems, how original sin develops into specific sins, or how genetics and social experiences influence these processes."[16] He concludes, "While the Bible is sufficient for salvation, doctrine and morality, the phenomena of Scripture itself force upon us the conclusion that it was not God's design to have the Bible answer directly all the concerns of psychologists or counselors for all places in all times, containing everything that would be of value to soul care in the future."[17] If this is the case, then psychologists and counselors who work in the area of soul care must be concerned with the wrong things.[18] As I have shown from Owen, sanctification is the purpose of soul care; sanctification is a gracious, progressive, and habitual renovation of our souls by the Spirit; and the means that the Spirit uses to accomplish this is obedience to the Scriptures. There is certainly more that can be learned and refined regarding how the Spirit does this work through the Scriptures, but do Owen and the tradition of Puritan and Reformed spirituality not show us just how rich the mines of Scripture are? It would behoove biblical counselors

---

15. Johnson, *Foundations for Soul Care*, 184–85.

16. Johnson, *Foundations for Soul Care*, 185.

17. Johnson, *Foundations for Soul Care*, 185. Note also how Johnson's definition of the sufficiency of Scripture for soul care implies the necessity of resources outside of Scripture in "abnormal" cases: "The sufficiency of the Bible regarding psychology and soul care means that the Bible is the Christian community's foundational psychology and soul care text, because it amply communicates enough about the nature of God, human beings and divine salvation that no other text is necessary for normal Christians to thrive psychospiritually." *Foundations for Soul Care*, 188.

18. In writing this, I do not mean to imply that extrabiblical resources offer nothing of value for understanding and helping people. However, the topic under discussion, in Johnson's own words, is "soul care." Scripture clearly defines what a soul is; it is Scripture alone that can tell us how a soul may be healed of its fundamental brokenness; and it is the Spirit alone who can perform the work of renovating the soul. Thus, my point is that the sanctifying work of God by the Spirit of God through the Word of God should be the overarching concern of Christians who are involved in the work of soul care.

to continue emphasizing the Spirit's work through Scripture in soul care and to follow Owen's lead in mining Scripture for all of its worthy jewels for holy living.

Soul Care and the Centrality of the Pastoral Ministry

Jay Adams made the following statement as he spoke to students at the Rosemead School of Psychology:

> This program has no reason for existence. Not only can you not integrate pagan thought and biblical teaching, but what you are trying to do is to train people to attempt the work of the church without ordination, outside the church. That is distorting God's order of things. Counseling may not be set up as a life calling on a free-lance basis; all such counseling ought to be done as a function of the church, utilizing its authority and resources.[19]

Adams was certainly unafraid of controversy, and his strong belief in counseling as a work of the church has remained a consistent feature of the biblical counseling movement.[20] One area of interest within the movement is the relationship between pastoral counseling and lay counseling in the church. In this section, I will provide insight from John Owen regarding how the ministry of pastors in soul care is fundamentally distinct from the ministry of church members, focusing specifically on Ephesians 4:11–16.

Ephesians 4:11–16 is an oft-referenced text in biblical counseling literature. Typically, authors reference this passage to support the idea that pastors should equip lay members of the church to counsel others, such that the church becomes a community of care. Powlison summarized what has become the standard approach to this text: "God has given certain people as gifts to the rest in doing the ministry

---

19. Quoted in Adams, *A Theology of Christian Counseling*, 276.

20. A few examples that prove this ongoing emphasis are David Powlison, *Speaking Truth in Love: Counsel in Community* (Greensboro, N.C.: New Growth Press, 2005); Robert W. Kellemen, *Equipping Counselors for Your Church: The 4E Ministry Training Strategy* (Phillipsburg, N.J.: P&R, 2011); Bob Kellemen and Kevin Carson, eds., *Biblical Counseling and the Church: God's Care through God's People* (Grand Rapids: Zondervan, 2015); Jeremy Pierre and Deepak Reju, *The Pastor and Counseling: The Basics of Shepherding Members in Need* (Wheaton, Ill.: Crossway, 2015); T. Dale Johnson Jr., *The Church as a Culture of Care: Finding Hope in Biblical Community* (Greensboro, N.C.: New Growth Press, 2021).

of his Word (Eph. 4:11). Their task is to equip everyone else within the body, so that all of us will do the work of ministry (4:12–13), learn to avoid the world's lies (4:14), do our part with words and gifts (4:15–16), and change our thinking, motives, and lifestyle (4:17–6:9), participating in Christ's victory over darkness (6:10–20)."[21] This may be termed a "pastor as equipping" approach to pastoral ministry, and it is the prominent view of pastoral ministry within the biblical counseling movement.[22] This view, however, departs from an older view that may be termed a "pastor as perfecting" approach to pastoral ministry.

The shift in the prominent view of this passage is related to two issues in the text, one semantic and the other syntactical. The semantic issue is that the older rendering of καταρτισμος as "perfecting" in verse 12 shifted in the twentieth century to the newer rendering of "equipping."[23] The syntactical issue is the function of the three prepositional phrases in verse 12, "For the perfecting of the saints (πρὸς τὸν καταρτισμὸν τῶν ἁγίων), for the work of the ministry (εἰς ἔργον διακονίας), for the edifying of the body of Christ (εἰς οἰκοδομὴν τοῦ σώματος τοῦ Χριστοῦ)" (KJV). In the KJV, the three phrases all refer back to the gifted ministers. Newer translations, however, tend to render the second and third phrases as subordinate to and resulting from the first phrase (e.g., the NKJV, "for the equipping of the saints for the work of ministry, for the edifying of the body of Christ"). Several

---

21. David Powlison, *Seeing with New Eyes: Counseling and the Human Condition through the Lens of Scripture*, Resources for Changing Lives (Phillipsburg, N.J.: P&R, 2003), 260n1.

22. See, for example, Rob Green and Steve Viars, "The Biblical Counseling Ministry of the Local Church," in *Christ-Centered Biblical Counseling: Changing Lives with God's Changeless Truth*, ed. James MacDonald, Bob Kellemen, and Steve Viars (Eugene, Ore.: Harvest House, 2013), 228–30; Brad Bigney and Steve Viars, "A Church of Biblical Counseling," in *Biblical Counseling and the Church: God's Care through God's People*, ed. Bob Kellemen and Kevin Carson (Grand Rapids: Zondervan, 2015), 20–33; Jones, Kellen, and Green, *The Gospel for Disordered Lives*, 27–28; Johnson, *The Church as a Culture of Care*.

23. For a translational history, see Richard C. Barcellos, "The Christian Ministry in the Church: Its Reasons, Duration and Goal, and Practical Effects (Ephesians 4:11–16), with Special Emphasis on Verse 12," *The Confessional Presbyterian* 11 (2015): 54–56.

modern scholars have argued for a return to the older rendering, particularly regarding the translation of καταρτισμὸν.[24]

Unsurprisingly, Owen favored what has now become the older rendering, and this passage was foundational to his understanding of pastoral ministry. Harkening back to my explanation of Owen's distinctions between gifts and grace (chapter 3),[25] one could say that the newer view of pastoral ministry sees the pastor primarily as a cultivator of spiritual gifts among his people, whereas the older view—the one held by Owen—sees the pastor primarily as a cultivator of holiness through the Spirit's increase of habitual grace in his people. Notice the intricate connection between the pastoral office, the means of grace, and the perfection of grace in the saints in the following quote from one of Owen's several discussions of Ephesians 4:11–16:

> The thing aimed at is, the bringing of all the saints and disciples of Christ, the whole church, to that measure and perfection of grace which Christ hath assigned to them in this world, that they may be meet for himself to receive in glory. The means whereby this is to be done and effected is, the faithful, regular, and effectual discharge of the work of the ministry; unto which the administration of all his ordinances and institutions doth confessedly belong. That this work may be discharged in an orderly manner to the end mentioned, he has granted unto his church the offices mentioned, to be executed by persons variously called thereunto, according to his mind and will.[26]

Owen's belief that the perfecting of the saints could not occur according to God's ordained, ordinary means apart from the work of the pastor was so strong that his first instruction to churches without a

---

24. Barcellos, "The Christian Ministry in the Church"; Henry P. Hamann, "The Translation of Ephesians 4:12—A Necessary Revision," *Concordia Journal* 14, no. 1 (1988): 42–49; T. David Gordon, "'Equipping' Ministry in Ephesians 4?," *Journal of the Evangelical Theological Society* 37, no. 1 (March 1994): 69–78; John Jefferson Davis, "Ephesians 4:12 Once More: 'Equipping the Saints for the Work of Ministry?,'" *Evangelical Review of Theology* 24, no. 2 (April 2000): 57–65; Sydney Page, "Whose Ministry? A Re-Appraisal of Ephesians 4:12," *Novum Testamentum* 47, no. 1 (January 2005): 26–46.

25. See Owen, *A Discourse of Spiritual Gifts*, in *Works*, 4:428–38.

26. Owen, *A Discourse Concerning Liturgies, and Their Imposition*, in *Works*, 15:11.

pastor was to lawfully obtain a pastor as quickly as possible.[27] The saints demonstrate their desire for holiness by urgently seeking a holy and gifted man to labor for their perfection.[28]

The emphasis on lay ministry within the biblical counseling movement runs the risk of unhelpfully de-emphasizing pastoral ministry. Christians must know that they need not only the fellowship and love of their fellow church members but also the ministry of their pastors, which the Spirit uses to bring about their perfection, their habitual holiness. Pastors must recognize this as well—they are not delegators of ministry but doers of ministry.

Finally, it is not the members of the church who will give an account for the souls of the congregation; it is the pastors (Heb. 13:17). The "pastor as equipping" approach tends to pass off pastoral responsibilities to "equipped lay counselors" or "equipped lay small group leaders." These people will not give an account for the souls of the congregation as will the pastors. Pastors have the primary responsibility of seeing to the saints' perfection, and on the day of judgment, they will give an account not for how well they delegated their ministry to lay leaders but for how faithfully they labored for the perfection of the saints in holiness.

The Christological Shape of Sanctification

Without Spirit-infused habitual grace, it is difficult to account for Christ's sanctification in His human nature and to understand how His sanctification can be a paradigm for ours. Understanding Christ's sanctification is difficult because it raises the question of how a sinless

---

27. Owen, *The True Nature of a Gospel Church and Its Government*, in *Works*, 16:79–80.

28. This emphasis on the pastor's duty to labor for the perfection of the saints does not mean that members should not minister the Word to one another. The pastor labors for their perfection so that they will speak the truth in love (Eph. 4:15). However, this comes about not because they have been "equipped" to do so through the cultivation of ministerial gifts but because they have grown more toward perfection through habitual holiness. Furthermore, this emphasis does not undermine the pastor's responsibility to seek and cultivate gifted members of his congregation. But his primary aim in doing so will be to put men in the pastorate to labor for the perfection of the saints alongside him or in another congregation.

person can be sanctified. Yet, Christ truly did grow in His human capacity to glorify the Father, as is evidenced by Luke 2:52. A Spirit-infused habit of grace that inclined Christ's human faculties toward righteousness and filled them up according to the measure of their receptivity is what best accounts for this.[29] Otherwise, it is difficult to explain exactly what increased in Christ and how the Spirit works similarly in Christians. The Spirit, through the infusion and increase of this habit, enabled Christ in His human nature to live righteously to God in all of His faculties and in His response to His environment. This immediately kept Him, in His human nature, from responding sinfully to His human environment and from giving in to temptation. Thus, He serves as the model for the Christian life whom we are to follow. We must seek to have the Spirit inwardly, habitually renovate our souls to be like His. Thus, Owen's theology of Spirit-infused habitual grace connects Christ's sanctification and ours more effectively than biblical counseling literature has done thus far.

Understanding the christological shape of sanctification is practically advantageous for biblical counseling in many ways—I will discuss two particularly relevant advantages here. First, it helps clarify the nature of temptation. Christ was tempted in every way, yet without sin (Heb. 4:15). He could truly experience temptation by having worldly objects presented to His faculties and perfectly responding to them in righteousness, both in the faculties of His soul and in His outward actions. Thus, Christ's temptations always originated in external sources and never in the internal source of His own soul. Christians, however, experience temptation from external sources as well as from the flesh, or habit of indwelling sin, that continues to reside in their souls. Contemplating Christ's sanctification can help Christians determine whether their temptation originates externally, internally, or both. William Perkins (1558–1602) explained,

> The cogitation or motion of the heart is of three sorts. The first is some glancing or sudden thought suggested to the mind by Satan which suddenly vanishes away and is not received by the mind. This is no sin. For it was in Christ when He was tempted by the

---

29. Owen, *A Discourse Concerning the Holy Spirit*, in *Works*, 3:169.

devil (Matt. 4:1, 3). The second is a more permanent thought or motion, the which as it were tickles and inveighs the mind with some inward joy. The third is a cogitation drawing from the will and affection full assent to sin.[30]

It is quite difficult to determine one's culpability amidst temptation. Counselors encounter both the person whose conscience is too easily pricked and the person whose conscience is not easily pricked enough. In the face of temptation, counselors can help both people by teaching them to ask, "Could Christ's soul have responded to this temptation in the way that my soul did?" If not, then the person has sinned; if so, then the person has not sinned. If one's internal responses to outward temptation could not have been present in Christ, then his conscience should be pricked, and he must confess and repent. If they could have been present in Christ because the mind did not actively receive and delight in what was presented unto it, then one should not let his conscience condemn him.

The second practical advantage is closely related to the first and pertains to ethical questions surrounding sinful desires. Because Christ was perfectly habitually inclined toward righteousness, no sinful desire could ever arise from within Him. Our sanctification is to be patterned after His, and, thus, we should strive to put to death any sinful desires that might arise within us. Recent discussions among evangelicals, however, have sought to limit sin to outward effects and remove one's culpability for the inward desires that lead to such effects. This has been particularly evident in discussions regarding same-sex attraction. Eric Johnson, for example, writes,

> Guilt is not imputed to those who have a sinful desire pass through their consciousness, so long as they do not intentionally pursue the desire; so it should be viewed as an internal temptation. But to succumb to such a temptation with action is personal sin, and it can eventually become a vice through repetition. All of that is to say, having SSA [same-sex attraction] by itself fits the category of weakness,

---

30. William Perkins, *A Golden Chain*, in *The Works of William Perkins*, ed. Joel R. Beeke and Derek W. H. Thomas, vol. 6, ed. Joel R. Beeke and Greg A. Salazar (Grand Rapids: Reformation Heritage Books, 2018), 149.

whereas consenting to and pursuing one's SSA would constitute personal sin, together warranting the designation of fault.[31]

At best, Johnson's statement lacks clarity; at worst, it excuses sin and actually misleads people who struggle with sexual sin rather than helping them. According to Owen's portrayal of Christ's sanctification as the pattern for ours, anything present within us that could not have been present within Christ's human nature is sin. No inward, sinful desire ever arose from within Christ's soul. So, any inward, sinful desire that might arise from within our souls must be sin. Anything within us that does not arise from an inward, Spirit-infused habit of grace is sin. As Owen wrote, "Internal conformity unto [Christ's] habitual grace and holiness" is "the fundamental design of the Christian life."[32] No inward desire for something contrary to God's law ever arose from within Christ's soul, and we should strive to mortify any such desire that might arise within our own souls because it is sinful and contrary to our conformity to the image of God in Christ.

Although counselors should have compassion for those who experience same-sex attraction and other such temptations, they should help these counselees delineate between unwanted, passing thoughts and actively received thoughts that delight the soul, even if just for a moment. The former are not sinful because they originate in an external source; the latter are sinful because they originate in an inward habit of indwelling sin.[33] By making such distinctions, the counselor can actually give hope to the counselee: by the power of the Spirit, the habit of indwelling sin can be progressively mortified such that its ability to affect the operations of the soul are diminished,

---

31. Eric L. Johnson, *God and Soul Care: The Therapeutic Resources of the Christian Faith* (Downers Grove, Ill.: IVP Academic, 2017), 295.

32. Owen, *A Declaration of the Glorious Mystery of the Person of Christ*, in *Works*, 1:169–70.

33. It should also be noted that the complexity of the soul and the limited capacity of our perception sometimes make it impossible for us to know whether a passing thought has arisen from an external temptation or from an internal habit of indwelling sin. In such cases, as in all things, a person should rest in the abundant forgiveness available in Christ and the hope that, in the eternal state, it will be unmistakably clear that none of our thoughts have arisen from indwelling sin because indwelling sin will be no more, and all of our thoughts, desires, and choices will be holy.

and the operations of the habit of grace can be increased such that one is further and further inclined toward righteousness. Conformity unto the image of God in Christ means that sinful desires are put to death because there were no sinful desires in Christ. Thus, those who struggle with same-sex attraction should have hope as they look to Christ and see nothing of the kind within Him, and they should trust that they are being conformed unto His image by the same Spirit that worked in Him.[34]

The Doctrine of God, Sanctification, and Humility in Soul Care
Owen's theology of Spirit-infused habitual grace in sanctification arises out of his doctrine of God. His understanding of trinitarian relations and operations led him to view the Spirit as the "immediate operator of all divine works that outwardly are of God."[35] Furthermore, his understanding of divine simplicity led him to conclude that humans completely depend upon God in both creation and redemption.[36] As I discussed in chapter 3, Owen's doctrine of divine simplicity includes four fundamental claims: (1) God is not composed of parts because, otherwise, He would be dependent upon something other than Himself, thus undermining His aseity; (2) because God is not composed of parts, His existence is His essence; (3) because God is not composed of parts, all of His attributes must be the same as one another and the same as His essence; and (4) everything that is composed of parts maintains some degree of potentiality, but a simple being has no potentiality—therefore, God must be pure and simple act.[37] The other attributes of God are directly related to the claims of divine simplicity. All that is in God is God (simplicity), and all that God is must be what He is in all places (omnipresence) and at all times (eternality). God is everywhere (omnipresence), and there is no place wherein He is not present in all of His divine perfection (simplicity).

---

34. We may take this same approach with all manner of deep-seated, sinful desires, such as other forms of sexual immorality, drunkenness, substance abuse, gambling, etc.

35. Owen, *A Discourse Concerning the Holy Spirit*, in *Works*, 3:57.

36. Owen, *A Display of Arminianism*, in *Works*, 10:118–19.

37. Owen, *The Mystery of the Gospel Vindicated and Socinianism Examined*, in *Works*, 12:71–72.

God is timeless (eternality), and there is no time in which God is not present in all of His divine perfection (simplicity). God is uncaused (aseity), and there is no motion that did not first originate in the eternal, pure actuality of God in all of His divine perfection (simplicity).[38]

Practically considered, divine simplicity reminds us that we are completely and utterly dependent upon God in both creation and redemption. There is nothing that we add to God. Everything that is true of His nature would be true of Him even if we and the entire created order never existed. All that we are and have we receive from Him. Our very existence and every individual act of our wills are governed by His creation and providence (Acts 17:25).[39] By nature, we are completely dependent upon God to exist and to act; by grace, we are completely dependent upon God to act for good, for "all spiritual acts well-pleasing unto God, as faith, repentance, obedience, are supernatural."[40] Simplicity, then, reminds counselors of their complete and utter dependence upon God in all that they do. It reminds counselors of what is happening in the counseling process. A creature who is dependent upon God (the counselor) is, by a free act of his will, subservient to the providence of God, acting as a means to help another creature who is dependent upon God (the counselee) to be sanctified. In this counseling, the independent God is present in all of His divine perfection, using the ministry of the Word by His Spirit to habitually conform the counselee to the image of Christ. He is not

---

38. Samuel D. Renihan explains, "Divine aseity and divine simplicity therefore are mutually reinforcing, and they stand and fall together. Simplicity affirms that God is not composed, and therefore not caused. As an uncaused being, God exists *a se*, in and of himself." *Deity and Decree* (Self-published, 2020), 38. James Dolezal likewise writes, "Without simplicity, God must be dependent on something other than His divinity for some aspects of his being, and thus He cannot be *a se* and independent. Without simplicity, God is open to the acquisition of being in addition to His essence and thus not immutable. Without simplicity, it is not clear why God could not experience temporal change and thus fail to be timelessly eternal. Without simplicity, it is impossible that God be in every way infinite as there must be parts in Him, and parts by definition must be finite. Moreover, that which is built of parts cannot be infinite since the finite cannot aggregately yield the infinite. Many more such arguments could be arranged." *All That Is in God*, 135–36.

39. For a discussion of the relationship between human free will and the providence of God, see Owen, *A Display of Arminianism*, in *Works*, 10:119–20.

40. Owen, *A Display of Arminianism*, in *Works*, 10:122.

responding to and being moved by the creatures. They are not in a give-and-take relationship to Him. Rather, He Himself is the prior act antecedent to all the acts of the creatures. This should instill humility in the counselor and cause him to turn and give glory to God in response to both his successes and failures. If the counselee is going to grow in sanctification, then this will happen through the Spirit's increase of habitual grace within him. The counselor's efforts are merely a means that the Spirit uses to do His work.

Conformity unto God

Owen's theology of Spirit-infused habitual grace in sanctification helps clarify the way in which divine and human virtue (i.e., habitual perfection) are analogous. Humans think and speak about God through analogical reasoning and language. As Renihan explains, "Analogical knowledge and language attribute one thing to God in a way that corresponds with divine being and attribute the same thing to the creature in a way that corresponds with creaturely being."[41] God is incomprehensible and ineffable, which means that He cannot be completely known by humans. He can, however, be known truly, through analogous reasoning and language. As Beeke and Smalley explain, this means that when God reveals Himself in Scripture in a way that portrays Him in some creaturely fashion, we must interpret it such that it does not compromise all that we know must be true of God and his perfections. For example, if God is described as powerful, we must reason from what is true of earthly power to what must be true of divine power. We cannot allow what we know about the limitations of earthly power to somehow limit our conception of the divine power. "We must constantly transpose earthly concepts into a higher key of the divine nature."[42]

Such is the case with human and divine virtue. Virtue, in a scriptural sense, is moral excellence or perfection. It is synonymous with habitual holiness, a perfect inclination toward that which is righteous

---

41. Renihan, *Deity and Decree*, 25.

42. Joel R. Beeke and Paul M. Smalley, *Reformed Systematic Theology*, vol. 1, *Revelation and God* (Wheaton, Ill.: Crossway, 2019), 535.

and good. God is said to be virtuous in Scripture (Phil. 4:8; 1 Peter 2:9; 2 Peter 1:3),[43] indicating His perfect and habitual inclination in His very being toward that which is good. Divine simplicity requires that divine virtue be singular, such that all of God's virtues, or perfections, are synonymous with and inseparable from one another. His love is His justice, and His justice is His love. His love is always just, and His justice is always loving. The same goes for His power, goodness, and wisdom.[44] In many places, Scripture commands humans to be like God in our pursuit of virtue:[45]

---

43. The word used in these texts is ἀρέτη, which is also translated as "praises" or "excellencies." The differing translations indicate the same concept of moral purity, excellence, or goodness. See also 2 Peter 1:5.

44. Dolezal elucidates well the way that divine virtue should be understood: "Those virtues that are predicated of creatures accidentally are predicated of God substantively. Divine simplicity maintains that God *just is* the love by which he loves, *just is* the kindness by which he is merciful and gracious, *just is* the perfect justice and consuming fire of holiness by which he demonstrates wrath against sin, and so forth. God's love, mercy, vindicative justice, and the like are not non-God constituents making him to be what he otherwise would not have been. Such virtues are not passions in God because they are not states of being into which God is moved on account of some causal action befalling him. In God no process of undergoing actualizes his virtues. It is a profoundly misguided accusation to charge that impassible love, mercy, kindness, and self-vindicating justice are made less genuine or intense simply because they do not come about in God through a process of change enacted within him by the creature. Nothing could be further from the truth. In God such virtues are infinitely *more* lively and dynamic than in their passionate creaturely counterparts inasmuch as they are nothing but the unbounded fullness of God's act of being itself." James E. Dolezal, "Strong Impassibility," in *Divine Impassibility: Four Views of God's Emotions and Suffering*, ed. Robert J. Matz and A. Chadwick Thornhill, Spectrum Multiview Books (Downers Grove, Ill.: InterVarsity Press, 2019), 27–28 (italics original).

45. It is important to note that Owen wrote against the concept of moral virtue in *Truth and Innocence Vindicated*, in *Works*, 13:411–15. However, he clearly had in mind the type of moral virtue that is detached from the gracious work of the Spirit. He opposed the idea of moral reformation apart from the Spirit's enabling. However, taking grace and virtue together, he wrote, "No man living ever distinguished between grace and virtue any otherwise than the cause and the effect are to be, or may be, distinguished; much less was any person ever so brutish as to fancy an inconsistency between them: for, take grace in one sense, and it is the efficient cause of this virtue, or of these virtues, which are the effects of it; and in another, they are all graces themselves, for that which is wrought in us by grace is grace, as that which is born of the Spirit is spirit." *Truth and Innocence Vindicated*, in *Works*, 13:415. Elsewhere, he showed that his concern regarding virtue was that it be rightly viewed as a fruit of regeneration rather than the cause of it. See *A Discourse Concerning the Holy Spirit*, in *Works*, 3:217–23.

"Therefore you shall be perfect, just as your Father in heaven is perfect" (Matt. 5:48); "Therefore be merciful, just as your Father also is merciful" (Luke 6:36); "The glory which You gave Me I have given them, that they may be one just as We are one" (John 17:22); "Therefore be imitators of God as dear children" (Eph. 5:1); "as He who called you is holy, you also be holy in all your conduct" (1 Peter 1:15); as "partakers of the divine nature," we are to "add to [our] faith virtue, to virtue knowledge, to knowledge self-control, to self-control perseverance, to perseverance godliness, to godliness brotherly kindness, and to brotherly kindness love" (2 Peter 1:4–7).

We cannot possess these virtues in the way that God possesses them, for He possesses them in infinite perfection. He possesses them as His very essence. However, Scripture uses analogous language to reveal to us the humanly perfection that we ought to pursue. By the power of the Spirit, we ought to become habitually inclined toward that which is good and righteous. God's virtues cannot be separated from one another—analogously, neither can human virtues. The singularity of the "fruit" of the Spirit (Gal. 5:22) indicates that "the various aspects of the fruit of the Spirit are interconnected."[46] This is further evidenced by the multifaceted description of love in 1 Corinthians 13. As Mark Jones explains,

> Love is often love because it is patient kindness. In Galatians 5, Paul is saying that our love must be joyful love, patient love, peaceful love, faithful love, gentle love, and so forth. Our patience is joyful patience. In this way, when we manifest the fruit of the Spirit, we model in some sense God's simplicity.... The Spirit-filled life represents an analogy of how God is all that he is in his simple, undivided essence.[47]

As William Ames (1576–1633) explained, virtue is not a "mean between two extremes."[48] One does not pursue mercy by striking a balance between love and justice. Rather, the simplicity of virtue requires that, as one becomes truly loving or truly just, one also becomes,

---

46. Mark Jones, *God Is: A Devotional Guide to the Attributes of God* (Wheaton, Ill.: Crossway, 2020), 35. See also Beeke and Smalley, *Reformed Systematic Theology,* 1:635–36.

47. Jones, *God Is,* 35–36.

48. William Ames, *The Marrow of Theology,* trans. John Dykstra Eusden (Grand Rapids: Baker Books, 1997), 230–31.

in proportion, truly merciful. For all of the virtues are ultimately different descriptions of the same, perfect quality: an overall, increasing, habitual holiness. Thus, the work of God, through His Spirit, to grow us in holiness is a holistic work.

The simplicity of human virtue provides counselors with both a goal and an evaluative tool in their task. As discussed above, the goal of counseling is the promotion of universal holiness. Problem-oriented counseling tends to lose sight of the fact that the goal of the ministry of the Word is the "perfecting of the saints" (Eph. 4:12 KJV). The Spirit's work of infusing and increasing habitual grace in regeneration and sanctification should make the counselor confident that the Spirit's work of grace in one area of a person's life will affect other areas of his life. The simplicity of human virtue also provides counselors with an evaluative tool, such that, if they perceive a major area of concern—an area in which the counselee lacks Christian virtue or habitual holiness—then they ought to suppose that there are likely other areas of concern to be discussed. For example, it should not surprise us if a person who lacks self-control also lacks patience, kindness, and gentleness. Conversely, as we see a person grow in true self-control, we should expect to see him grow in patience, kindness, and gentleness.

Conclusion

The biblical counseling movement is not monolithic. Two divergent models of sanctification have emerged over time, the incompatibility of which has become increasingly clear. The one, grounded in the pioneering work of Jay Adams, sees behavioral habits as the primary methodological target for change. The other, following the thoughtful reflection of David Powlison, sees the heart—including its thoughts, desires, and motivations—as the methodological target. In this work, I have not sought to provide a middle way between these two models. Adams's understanding of human change arises from a theological understanding of "the flesh" as the sinfully habituated body. This is an erroneous conclusion that has significantly weakened his counseling methodology. The shift toward heart motivation by Powlison and his followers represented a positive development and a return to a more premodern approach to soul care, one closer to that of the Puritans.

In seeking to carry forward this development, I have returned in this work to the old paths of Puritan and Reformed spirituality in order to retrieve a theological concept that I suggest strengthens the dominant understanding of sanctification among biblical counselors today: Spirit-infused habitual grace. Specifically, I have focused on Spirit-infused habitual grace in John Owen's theology of sanctification. Although this concept was prevalent among Owen's fellow Puritans, it is one in which Owen explicitly and consistently grounded his understanding of the work of the Spirit in sanctification.

In chapters 1 and 2, I set the stage for my discussion of Owen by providing an overview of the two divergent models of sanctification within the biblical counseling movement and by showing how each has understood the concept of habituation and its relation to sanctification. In chapter 3, I grounded Owen's theology of Spirit-infused habitual grace in his doctrine of God, specifically his trinitarian theology and his theology of divine simplicity. In chapter 4, I discussed Owen's understanding of the Spirit's work in the human nature of Christ, which he viewed as the paradigm for the Spirit's work in the members of Christ's body. In chapter 5, I concluded my main discussion of Owen's theology by outlining the major contours of his anthropology and the Spirit's work of infusing and increasing habitual grace in man. In chapters 6 and 7, I practically applied Owen's theology of Spirit-infused habitual grace by highlighting areas in which this theological concept overlaps with, departs from, and develops major themes within biblical counseling and modern soul care.

My overall goal in this work has been to provide a historically informed, pneumatologically grounded theology of sanctification for the biblical counseling movement. Furthermore, the flavor of the work is intended to be one of warm, experiential theological reflection. Paul says in Philippians 1:9–10 that our growth in knowledge and discernment should enable us to approve what is excellent. My hope is that the theological reflection and practical application I have provided here will constitute one more resource that helps Christians approve what is excellent—to put to the test in their own lives that which I have proposed and to see its usefulness for faithful living. To the extent that this work promotes such results, it has been successful.

Much work has been done in recent decades to retrieve the theological, practical, and experiential riches found within Puritan works, especially the works of John Owen. However, I suggest three key areas in which Puritan theology can be further mined, specifically for the benefit of biblical counseling. The first area is the Puritan theology of worship and its relationship to counseling. As I have shown in this work, the Puritans emphasized a constant reflection on the supernatural work of the Spirit through means. Puritan public worship was the high point of the Spirit's work, and I suggest that we explore this high, supernaturally focused view of public worship and the way in which a high view of the Spirit's work through the means of Word-centered counseling would naturally flow from it. The second area is the Puritan view of the pastorate. As I discussed earlier in this work, the Puritans held to a view of Ephesians 4:11–16 that understood pastors as those who labor for the perfection of the saints, rather than those who equip the saints for works of ministry. Richard Baxter's well-known practice of pastoral visitation is one example of how this conviction may have influenced pastoral practice.[1] It would be helpful to study how pastoral visitation may have differed from daily, holy conversation between lay Christians. Such a study could help clarify the difference between what modern biblical counselors typically refer to as formal counseling and informal counseling. This leads me to one last area, which I have just mentioned: holy conversation. Joanne Jung has written two fascinating studies of the Puritan practice of holy conversation,[2] and the biblical counseling movement ought to consider how this practice may correct and develop current emphases among biblical counselors, specifically regarding how counseling relates to the use of small groups in church life.

May the Lord bless the work I have presented here to be used by His church, that the saints might better perceive Christ with eyes of faith and be further conformed unto His image on their way to seeing Him face-to-face. Amen.

---

1. Richard Baxter, *The Reformed Pastor* (Edinburgh: Banner of Truth, 1974).

2. Joanne J. Jung, *Godly Conversation: Rediscovering the Puritan Practice of Conference* (Grand Rapids: Reformation Heritage Books, 2011); Joanne J. Jung, *The Lost Discipline of Conversation: Surprising Lessons in Spiritual Formation Drawn from the English Puritans* (Grand Rapids: Zondervan, 2018).

Bibliography

Adams, Jay E. "Biblical Counseling and Practical Calvinism." In *The Practical Calvinist: An Introduction to the Presbyterian and Reformed Heritage*, edited by Peter A. Lillback, 484–94. Fearn, Scotland: Christian Focus, 2002.

———. "Change Them…Into What?" *Journal of Biblical Counseling* 13, no. 2 (Winter 1995): 13–17.

———. *The Christian Counselor's Manual: The Practice of Nouthetic Counseling*. Grand Rapids: Zondervan, 1973.

———. *Competent to Counsel: Introduction to Nouthetic Counseling*. Grand Rapids: Zondervan, 1970.

———. "Counseling and the Heart." *Institute for Nouthetic Studies* (blog), June 17, 2011. https://nouthetic.org/counseling-and-the-heart/.

———. *Galatians, Ephesians, Colossians, Philemon*. The Christian Counselor's Commentary. Hackettstown, N.J.: Timeless Texts, 1994.

———. "Grace Alone." *Institute for Nouthetic Studies* (blog), March 11, 2011. https://nouthetic.org/grace-alone/.

———. "Heart Idols?" *Institute for Nouthetic Studies* (blog), August 6, 2014. https://nouthetic.org/heart-idols/.

———. "The Heart of the Matter." *Institute for Nouthetic Studies* (blog), May 7, 2012. https://nouthetic.org/the-heart-of-the-matter/.

———. *Keeping the Sabbath Today?* Stanley, N.C.: Timeless Texts, 2008.

———. *Lectures on Counseling*. Grand Rapids: Baker, 1978.

———. "Reflections on the History of Biblical Counseling." In *Practical Theology and the Ministry of the Church, 1952–1984: Essays in Honor of Edmund P. Clowney*, edited by Harvie M. Conn, 203–18. Phillipsburg, N.J.: P&R, 1990.

————. *Romans, Philippians, I Thessalonians, II Thessalonians*. The Christian Counselor's Commentary. Hackettstown, N.J.: Timeless Texts, 1995.

————. *Sanctification and Counseling: Growing by Grace*. Memphis: Institute for Nouthetic Studies, 2020.

————. *A Theology of Christian Counseling: More than Redemption*. Grand Rapids: Zondervan, 1979.

————. "What Alternative?" In *The Biblical Counseling Movement after Adams*, by Heath Lambert, 165–70. Wheaton, Ill.: Crossway, 2012.

————. *Winning the War Within: A Biblical Strategy for Spiritual Warfare*. Woodruff, S.C.: Timeless Texts, 1994.

Allen, Michael. *Sanctification*. New Studies in Dogmatics. Grand Rapids: Zondervan, 2017.

Allison, Gregg R. "The *Corpus Theologicum* of the Church and Presumptive Authority." In *Revisioning, Renewing, Rediscovering the Triune Center: Essays in Honor of Stanley J. Grenz*, edited by Derek J. Tidball, Brian S. Harris, and Jason S. Sexton, 319–39. Eugene, Ore.: Cascade Books, 2014.

————. *Historical Theology: An Introduction to Christian Doctrine*. Grand Rapids: Zondervan, 2011.

Ames, William. *The Marrow of Theology*. Translated by John Dykstra Eusden. Grand Rapids: Baker Books, 1997.

Aristotle. *Aristotle's Nicomachean Ethics*. Translated by Robert C. Bartlett and Susan D. Collins. Chicago: University of Chicago Press, 2011.

Asselt, Willem J. van. "Covenant Theology as Relational Theology: The Contributions of Johannes Cocceius (1603–1669) and John Owen (1618–1683) to a Living Reformed Theology." In *The Ashgate Research Companion to John Owen's Theology*, edited by Kelly M. Kapic and Mark Jones, 65–84. Ashgate Research Companions. New York: Routledge, 2015.

Ayres, Lewis. *Augustine and the Trinity*. New York, Cambridge University Press, 2010.

Barcellos, Richard C. "The Christian Ministry in the Church: Its Reasons, Duration and Goal, and Practical Effects (Ephesians 4:11–16), with Special Emphasis on Verse 12." *The Confessional Presbyterian* 11 (2015): 54–68.

————. "Guest Post: No Communion and No Christ? Part 3." *Petty France* (blog), April 8, 2020. https://pettyfrance.wordpress.com/2020/04/08/guest-post-no-communion-and-no-christ-part-3/.

————. "John Owen and New Covenant Theology: Owen on the Old and New Covenants and the Functions of the Decalogue in Redemptive History in Historical and Contemporary Perspective." *Reformed Baptist Theological Review* 1, no. 2 (July 2004): 12–46.

Barrett, Matthew, and Michael A. G. Haykin. *Owen on the Christian Life: Living for the Glory of God in Christ*. Theologians on the Christian Life. Wheaton, Ill.: Crossway, 2015.

Bavinck, Herman. *Essays on Religion, Science, and Society*. Edited by John Bolt. Translated by Harry Boonstra and Gerrit Sheeres. Grand Rapids: Baker Academic, 2003–2008.

————. *Reformed Dogmatics*. Edited by John Bolt. Translated by John Vriend. 4 vols. Grand Rapids: Baker Academic, 2003–2008.

Baxter, Richard. *The Reformed Pastor*. Edinburgh: Banner of Truth, 1974.

Beeke, Joel R. *Puritan Reformed Spirituality: A Practical Theological Study from Our Reformed and Puritan Heritage*. Darlington, England: Evangelical Press, 2006.

————. *Puritan Reformed Theology: Historical, Experiential, and Practical Studies for the Whole of Life*. Grand Rapids: Reformation Heritage Books, 2020.

Beeke, Joel R., and Michael P. V. Barrett. *A Radical, Comprehensive Call to Holiness*. Fearn, Scotland: Christian Focus, 2021.

Beeke, Joel R., and Mark Jones. *A Puritan Theology: Doctrine for Life*. Grand Rapids: Reformation Heritage Books, 2012.

Beeke, Joel R., and Stephen G. Myers. *Reformed Piety: Covenantal and Experiential*. Darlington, England: Evangelical Press, 2019.

Beeke, Joel R., and Paul M. Smalley. *Prepared by Grace, for Grace: The Puritans on God's Ordinary Way of Leading Sinners to Christ*. Grand Rapids: Reformation Heritage Books, 2013.

————. *Reformed Systematic Theology*. Vol. 1, *Revelation and God*. Wheaton, Ill.: Crossway, 2019.

Belt, Henk van den. "*Vocatio* as Regeneration: John Owen's Concept of Effectual Calling." In *John Owen between Orthodoxy and Modernity*, edited by Willem van Vlastuin and Kelly M. Kapic, 148–63. Studies in Reformed Theology 39. Boston: Brill, 2019.

Bigney, Brad, and Steve Viars. "A Church of Biblical Counseling." In *Biblical Counseling and the Church: God's Care through God's People*, edited by Bob Kellemen and Kevin Carson, 20–33. Grand Rapids: Zondervan, 2015.

Bolt, John. "Herman Bavinck on Natural Law and Two Kingdoms: Some Further Reflections." *The Bavinck Review* 4 (2013): 64–93.

Bray, Gerald. *God Has Spoken: A History of Christian Theology*. Wheaton, Ill.: Crossway, 2014.

Calvin, John. *Commentaries on the Book of Jeremiah and Lamentations*. Translated by John Owen. Calvin's Commentaries. Edinburgh: Calvin Translation Society, 1855.

————. *Institutes of the Christian Religion*. Edited by John T. McNeill. Translated by Ford Lewis Battles. Philadelphia: Westminster, 1960.

Caughey, Christopher Earl. "Puritan Responses to Antinomianism in the Context of Reformed Covenant Theology: 1630–1696." PhD diss., Trinity College Dublin, 2013.

Charnock, Stephen. *The Works of Stephen Charnock*. 5 vols. Edinburgh: Banner of Truth, 1997.

Claunch, Kyle David. "The Son and the Spirit: The Promise of Spirit Christology in Traditional Trinitarian and Christological Perspective." PhD diss., The Southern Baptist Theological Seminary, 2017.

————. "What God Hath Done Together: Defending the Historic Doctrine of the Inseparable Operations of the Trinity." *Journal of the Evangelical Theological Society* 56, no. 4 (December 2013): 781–800.

Clarkson, David. *The Practical Works of David Clarkson*. Vol. 3. Edinburgh: James Nichol, 1865.

Cleveland, Christopher. *Thomism in John Owen*. Burlington, Vt.: Ashgate, 2013.

Coxe, Nehemiah. *A Discourse of the Covenants That God Made with Men before the Law*. London: John Darby, 1681.

Coxe, Nehemiah, and John Owen. *Covenant Theology from Adam to Christ*. Edited by Ronald D. Miller, James M. Renihan, and Francisco Orozco. Palmdale, Calif.: Reformed Baptist Academic Press, 2005.

Craig, Philip A. *The Bond of Grace and Duty in the Soteriology of John Owen*. Cape Coral, Fla.: Founders Press, 2020.

Crisp, Oliver D. *Divinity and Humanity: The Incarnation Reconsidered*. Current Issues in Theology 5. New York: Cambridge University Press, 2007.

————. "John Owen on Spirit Christology." *Journal of Reformed Theology* 5, no. 1 (January 2011): 5–25.

————. *Revisioning Christology: Theology in the Reformed Tradition*. New York: Routledge, 2011.

Daniels, Richard W. *The Christology of John Owen*. Grand Rapids: Reformation Heritage Books, 2004.

Davis, John Jefferson. "Ephesians 4:12 Once More: 'Equipping the Saints for the Work of Ministry?'" *Evangelical Review of Theology* 24, no. 2 (April 2000): 57–65.

Deckard, Mark A. *Helpful Truth in Past Places: The Puritan Practice of Biblical Counseling*. Fearn, Scotland: Mentor, 2010.

Denault, Pascal. *The Distinctiveness of Baptist Covenant Theology: A Comparison between Seventeenth-Century Particular Baptist and Paedobaptist Federalism*. Rev. ed. Birmingham, Ala.: Solid Ground Christian Books, 2017.

Dolezal, James E. *All That Is in God: Evangelical Theology and the Challenge of Classical Christian Theism*. Grand Rapids: Reformation Heritage Books, 2017.

———. "Strong Impassibility." In *Divine Impassibility: Four Views of God's Emotions and Suffering*, edited by Robert J. Matz and A. Chadwick Thornhill, 13–36. Spectrum Multiview Books. Downers Grove, Ill.: InterVarsity Press, 2019.

Earley, Justin Whitmel. *The Common Rule: Habits of Purpose for an Age of Distraction*. Downers Grove, Ill.: IVP Books, 2019.

Emlet, Michael R. *CrossTalk: Where Life & Scripture Meet*. Greensboro, N.C.: New Growth Press, 2009.

———. "Practice Makes Perfect? Exploring the Relationship between Knowledge, Desire, and Habit." *Journal of Biblical Counseling* 27, no. 1 (2013): 26–48.

———. *Saints, Sufferers, and Sinners: Loving Others as God Loves Us*. Greensboro, N.C.: New Growth Press, 2021.

———. "Understanding the Influences on the Human Heart." *Journal of Biblical Counseling* 20, no. 2 (Winter 2002): 47–52.

Eveson, Philip. "The Inner or Psychological Life of Christ." In *The Forgotten Christ: Exploring the Majesty and Mystery of God Incarnate*, edited by Stephen Clark, 191–231. Nottingham, England: InterVarsity Press, 2007.

Eyrich, Howard, and Elyse Fitzpatrick. "The Diagnosis and Treatment of Idols of the Heart." In *Christ-Centered Biblical Counseling: Changing Lives with God's Changeless Truth*, edited by James MacDonald, Bob Kellemen, and Steve Viars, 339–50. Eugene, Ore.: Harvest House, 2013.

Ferguson, Sinclair B. "John Owen and the Doctrine of the Holy Spirit." In *John Owen: The Man and His Theology: Papers Read at the Conference of the John Owen Centre for Theological Study, September 2000*, edited by Robert W. Oliver, 101–30. Phillipsburg, N.J.: P&R, 2002.

———. "John Owen and the Doctrine of the Person of Christ." In *John Owen: The Man and His Theology: Papers Read at the Conference of the John Owen Centre for Theological Study, September 2000*, edited by Robert W. Oliver, 69–100. Phillipsburg, N.J.: P&R, 2002.

———. *John Owen on the Christian Life*. Edinburgh: Banner of Truth, 1987.

———. *The Whole Christ: Legalism, Antinomianism, and Gospel Assurance—Why the Marrow Controversy Still Matters*. Wheaton, Ill.: Crossway, 2016.

Fesko, J. V. "Aquinas's Doctrine of Justification and Infused Habits in Reformed Soteriology." In *Aquinas among the Protestants*, edited by Manfred Svensson and David VanDrunen, 249–65. Hoboken, N.J.: Wiley-Blackwell, 2017.

———. "John Owen on Union with Christ and Justification." *Themelios* 37, no. 1 (April 2012): 7–19.

———. *The Spirit of the Age: The 19th-Century Debate over the Holy Spirit and the Westminster Confession*. Grand Rapids: Reformation Heritage Books, 2017.

Fitzpatrick, Elyse. *Idols of the Heart: Learning to Long for God Alone*. Phillipsburg, N.J.: P&R, 2001.

Fitzpatrick, Elyse M., and Dennis E. Johnson. *Counsel from the Cross: Connecting Broken People to the Love of Christ*. Wheaton, Ill.: Crossway, 2012.

Fraser, J. Cameron. *Developments in Biblical Counseling*. Grand Rapids: Reformation Heritage Books, 2015.

Gatiss, Lee. "From Life's First Cry: John Owen on Infant Baptism and Infant Salvation." In *The Ashgate Research Companion to John Owen's Theology*, edited by Kelly M. Kapic and Mark Jones, 271–81. Ashgate Research Companions. New York: Routledge, 2015.

Gifford, Greg E. *Heart and Habits: How We Change for Good*. The Woodlands, Tex.: Kress Biblical Resources, 2021.

———. "Jay Adams' Teaching of Habituation: Critiqued, Revisited, and Supported." In *Whole Counsel: The Public and Private Ministries of the Word: Essays in Honor of Jay E. Adams*, edited by Donn R. Arms and Dave Swavely, 129–46. Memphis: Institute for Nouthetic Studies, 2020.

———. "John Owen's Perspective on the Effects of Habits: Habits Promote the Sanctity of the Church." *The Journal of Biblical Soul Care* 3, no. 1 (Fall 2019): 53–69.

———. "The Role of Habits in Spiritual Maturity from the Perspective of the English Puritans." PhD diss., Southwestern Baptist Theological Seminary, 2018.

———. "A Theological Understanding of the Effects of Addictive Habits in Cultivating Addictive Desires." *Midwestern Journal of Theology* 19, no. 1 (Spring 2020): 45–57.

Gleason, Randall C. *John Calvin and John Owen on Mortification: A Comparative Study in Reformed Spirituality*. Studies in Church History 3. New York: Peter Lang, 1995.

Goodwin, Thomas. *The Works of Thomas Goodwin*. Vol. 6. Grand Rapids: Reformation Heritage Books, 2006.

Gordon, T. David. "'Equipping' Ministry in Ephesians 4?" *Journal of the Evangelical Theological Society* 37, no. 1 (March 1994): 69–78.

Green, Rob, and Steve Viars. "The Biblical Counseling Ministry of the Local Church." In *Christ-Centered Biblical Counseling: Changing Lives with God's Changeless Truth*, edited by James MacDonald, Bob Kellemen, and Steve Viars, 225–37. Eugene, Ore.: Harvest House, 2013.

Gregory Nazianzen. "To Cledonius the Priest Against Apollinarius (Epistle 101)." In *A Select Library of Nicene and Post-Nicene Fathers of the Christian Church*. Series 2, vol. 7, *Cyril of Jerusalem, Gregory Nazianzen*, edited by Philip Schaff and Henry Wace, 439–43. New York: Christian Literature, 1894.

Griffiths, Steve. *Redeem the Time: Sin in the Writings of John Owen*. Fearn, Scotland: Mentor, 2001.

Grillmeier, Aloys. *Christ in Christian Tradition*. Vol. 1, *From the Apostolic Age to Chalcedon (451)*, translated by John Bowden. Atlanta: Westminster John Knox Press, 1975.

Hamann, Henry P. "The Translation of Ephesians 4:12 — A Necessary Revision." *Concordia Journal* 14, no. 1 (1988): 42–49.

Hamilton, James M., Jr. *God's Indwelling Presence: The Holy Spirit in the Old and New Testaments*. New American Commentary Studies in Bible and Theology. Nashville: B&H, 2006.

Harinck, Cor. "Preparationism as Taught by the Puritans." *Puritan Reformed Journal*, 2 no. 2 (July 2010): 159–71.

Helm, Paul. *Human Nature from Calvin to Edwards*. Grand Rapids: Reformation Heritage Books, 2018.

———. "Nature and Grace." In *Aquinas among the Protestants*, edited by Manfred Svensson and David VanDrunen, 229–47. Hoboken, N.J.: Wiley-Blackwell, 2017.

———. *Reforming Free Will: A Conversation on the History of Reformed Views on Compatibilism (1500–1800)*. Reformed Exegetical and Doctrinal Studies. Fearn, Scotland: Mentor, 2020.

Holifield, E. Brooks. *A History of Pastoral Care in America: From Salvation to Self-Realization*. Nashville: Abingdon Press, 1983.

Johnson, Dru. *Biblical Knowing: A Scriptural Epistemology of Error*. Eugene, Ore.: Cascade Books, 2013.

———. *Human Rites: The Power of Rituals, Habits, and Sacraments*. Grand Rapids: Eerdmans, 2019.

———. *Knowledge by Ritual: A Biblical Prolegomenon to Sacramental Theology*. Journal of Theological Interpretation Supplements 13. Winona Lake, Ind.: Eisenbrauns, 2016.

———. *Scripture's Knowing: A Companion to Biblical Epistemology*. Cascade Companions. Eugene, Ore.: Cascade Books, 2015.

Johnson, Eric L. *Foundations for Soul Care: A Christian Psychology Proposal*. Downers Grove, Ill.: InterVarsity Press, 2007.

———. *God and Soul Care: The Therapeutic Resources of the Christian Faith*. Downers Grove, Ill.: IVP Academic, 2017.

Johnson, T. Dale, Jr. *The Church as a Culture of Care: Finding Hope in Biblical Community*. Greensboro, N.C.: New Growth Press, 2021.

Jones, Mark. *God Is: A Devotional Guide to the Attributes of God*. Wheaton, Ill.: Crossway, 2020.

Jones, Robert D. "Biblical Counseling: An Opportunity for Problem-Based Evangelism." *Journal of Biblical Counseling* 31, no. 1 (2017): 75–92.

Jones, Robert D., Kristin L. Kellen, and Rob Green. *The Gospel for Disordered Lives: An Introduction to Christ-Centered Biblical Counseling*. Nashville: B&H Academic, 2021.

Jung, Joanne J. *Godly Conversation: Rediscovering the Puritan Practice of Conference*. Grand Rapids: Reformation Heritage Books, 2011.

———. *The Lost Discipline of Conversation: Surprising Lessons in Spiritual Formation Drawn from the English Puritans*. Grand Rapids: Zondervan, 2018.

Junius, Franciscus. *The Mosaic Polity*. Edited by Andrew M. McGinnis. Translated by Todd M. Rester. Sources in Early Modern Economics, Ethics, and Law. Grand Rapids: CLP Academic, 2015.

Kapic, Kelly M. *Communion with God: The Divine and the Human in the Theology of John Owen*. Grand Rapids: Baker Academic, 2007.

———. "John Owen's Theological Spirituality: Navigating Perceived Threats in a Changing World." In *John Owen between Orthodoxy and Modernity*, edited by Willem van Vlastuin and Kelly M. Kapic, 55–82. Studies in Reformed Theology 39. Boston: Brill, 2019.

Kay, Brian K. *Trinitarian Spirituality: John Owen and the Doctrine of God in Western Devotion*. Studies in Christian History and Thought. Eugene, Ore.: Wipf and Stock, 2008.

Kellemen, Bob, and Kevin Carson, eds. *Biblical Counseling and the Church: God's Care through God's People*. Grand Rapids: Zondervan, 2015.

———. *Equipping Counselors for Your Church: The 4E Ministry Training Strategy*. Phillipsburg, N.J.: P&R, 2011.

Keller, Timothy. "Puritan Resources for Biblical Counseling." *Journal of Pastoral Practice* 9, no. 3 (1988): 11–44.

Lambert, Heath. *The Biblical Counseling Movement after Adams*. Wheaton, Ill.: Crossway, 2012.

———. *A Theology of Biblical Counseling: The Doctrinal Foundations of Counseling Ministry*. Grand Rapids: Zondervan, 2016.

Lambert, Heath, Wayne Mack, Doug Bookman, and David Powlison. *Sufficiency: Historic Essays on the Sufficiency of Scripture*. Jacksonville, Fla.: Association of Certified Biblical Counselors, 2016.

Lane, Timothy S., and Paul David Tripp. "How Christ Changes Us by His Grace." *Journal of Biblical Counseling* 23, no. 2 (Spring 2005): 15–21.

———. *How People Change*. Greensboro, N.C.: New Growth Press, 2008.

Lelek, Jeremy. *Biblical Counseling Basics: Roots, Beliefs, and Future*. Greensboro, N.C.: New Growth Press, 2018.

Leslie, Andrew M. *The Light of Grace: John Owen on the Authority of Scripture and Christian Faith*. Reformed Historical Theology 34. Göttingen, Germany: Vandenhoeck & Ruprecht, 2015.

Letham, Robert. "John Owen's Doctrine of the Trinity in Its Catholic Context." In *The Ashgate Research Companion to John Owen's Theology*, edited by Kelly M. Kapic and Mark Jones, 185–97. Ashgate Research Companions. New York: Routledge, 2015.

MacArthur, John. *Freedom from Sin*. John MacArthur's Bible Studies. Chicago: Moody Press, 1987.

Macleod, Donald. *The Person of Christ*. Contours of Christian Theology. Downers Grove, Ill.: InterVarsity Press, 1998.

McDonald, Suzanne. "Beholding the Glory of God in the Face of Jesus Christ: John Owen and the 'Reforming' of the Beatific Vision." In *The Ashgate Research Companion to John Owen's Theology*, edited by Kelly M. Kapic and Mark Jones, 141–58. Ashgate Research Companions. New York: Routledge, 2015.

———. "John Owen's *Discourse on the Holy Spirit*." In *The Oxford Handbook of Reformed Theology*, edited by Michael Allen and Scott R. Swain, 266–79. Oxford Handbooks. Oxford: Oxford University Press, 2020.

———. "The Pneumatology of the 'Lost' Image in John Owen." *Westminster Theological Journal* 71, no. 2 (Fall 2009): 323–35.

McGrath, Gavin J. *Grace and Duty in Puritan Spirituality*. Grove Spirituality Series 37. Cambridge: Grove Books, 1991.

McGraw, Ryan M. *A Heavenly Directory: Trinitarian Piety, Public Worship and a Reassessment of John Owen's Theology*. Reformed Historical Theology 29. Göttingen, Germany: Vandenhoeck & Ruprecht, 2014.

———. *John Owen: Trajectories in Reformed Orthodox Theology*. Cham, Switzerland: Springer International, 2017.

———. "Seeing Things Owen's Way: John Owen's Trinitarian Theology and Piety in Its Early-Modern Context." In *John Owen between Orthodoxy and Modernity*, edited by Willem van Vlastuin and Kelly M. Kapic, 189–204. Studies in Reformed Theology 39. Boston: Brill, 2019.

Mesimer, Brian A. "Habits and the Heart: Reclaiming Habituation's Place in Biblical Counseling." MA thesis, Reformed Theological Seminary, 2018.

———. "Rehabilitating Habituation." *Journal of Biblical Counseling* 34, no. 2 (2020): 53–79.

Muller, Richard A. *Dictionary of Latin and Greek Theological Terms: Drawn Principally from Protestant Scholastic Theology*. Second edition. Grand Rapids: Baker Academic, 2017.

Ortlund, Dane C. "'Created Over a Second Time' or 'Grace Restoring Nature'? Edwards and Bavinck on the Heart of Christian Salvation." *The Bavinck Review* 3 (2012): 9–29.

Owen, John. *Hebrews*. Edited by William H. Goold. 7 vols. Edinburgh: Banner of Truth, 1991.

———. *The Works of John Owen*. Edited by William H. Goold. 16 vols. Edinburgh: Banner of Truth, 1967.

Packer, J. I. *A Quest for Godliness: The Puritan Vision of the Christian Life*. Wheaton, Ill.: Crossway, 1990.

Page, Sydney. "Whose Ministry? A Re-Appraisal of Ephesians 4:12." *Novum Testamentum* 47, no. 1 (January 2005): 26–46.

Parker, Gregory W. "Reformation or Revolution? Herman Bavinck and Henri de Lubac on Nature and Grace." *Perichoresis* 15, no. 3 (October 2017): 81–95.

Payne, Jon D. *John Owen on the Lord's Supper*. Edinburgh: Banner of Truth, 2004.

Perkins, William. *The Works of William Perkins*, edited by Joel R. Beeke and Derek W. H. Thomas. Vol. 6, edited by Joel R. Beeke and Greg A. Salazar. Grand Rapids: Reformation Heritage Books, 2018.

————. *The Works of William Perkins*, edited by Joel R. Beeke and Derek W. H. Thomas. Vol. 10, edited by Joseph A. Pipa Jr. and J. Stephen Yuille. Grand Rapids: Reformation Heritage Books, 2020.

Pierre, Jeremy. *The Dynamic Heart in Daily Life: Connecting Christ to Human Experience*. Greensboro, N.C.: New Growth Press, 2016.

————. "Scripture Is Sufficient, but to Do What?" In *Scripture and Counseling: God's Word for Life in a Broken World*, edited by Bob Kellemen and Jeff Forrey, 94–108. Grand Rapids: Zondervan, 2014.

————. "'Trust in the Lord with All Your Heart': The Centrality of Faith in Christ to the Restoration of Human Functioning." PhD diss., The Southern Baptist Theological Seminary, 2010.

Pierre, Jeremy, and Deepak Reju. *The Pastor and Counseling: The Basics of Shepherding Members in Need*. Wheaton, Ill.: Crossway, 2015.

Pleizier, T. Theo J., and Maarten Wisse. "'As the Philosopher Says': Aristotle." In *Introduction to Reformed Scholasticism*, edited by Willem J. van Asselt, translated by Albert Gootjes, 26–44. Reformed Historical-Theological Studies. Grand Rapids: Reformation Heritage Books, 2011.

Powlison, David. *The Biblical Counseling Movement: History and Context*. Greensboro, N.C.: New Growth Press, 2010.

————. "A Biblical Counseling View." In *Psychology & Christianity: Five Views*, edited by Eric L. Johnson, 245–73. 2nd ed. Downers Grove, Ill.: IVP Academic, 2010.

————. "Calvinism and Contemporary Christian Counseling." In *The Practical Calvinist: An Introduction to the Presbyterian and Reformed Heritage*, edited by Peter A. Lillback, 495–503. Fearn, Scotland: Christian Focus, 2002.

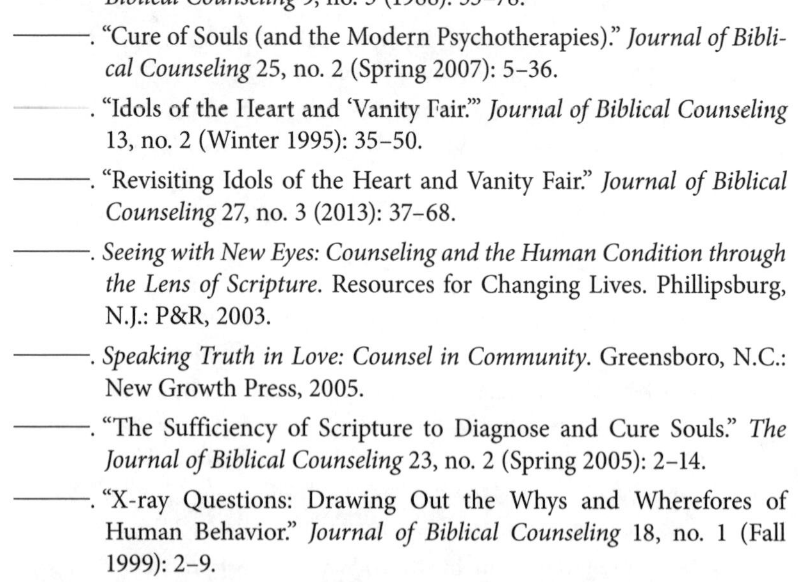

———. "Crucial Issues in Contemporary Biblical Counseling." *Journal of Biblical Counseling* 9, no. 3 (1988): 53–78.

———. "Cure of Souls (and the Modern Psychotherapies)." *Journal of Biblical Counseling* 25, no. 2 (Spring 2007): 5–36.

———. "Idols of the Heart and 'Vanity Fair.'" *Journal of Biblical Counseling* 13, no. 2 (Winter 1995): 35–50.

———. "Revisiting Idols of the Heart and Vanity Fair." *Journal of Biblical Counseling* 27, no. 3 (2013): 37–68.

———. *Seeing with New Eyes: Counseling and the Human Condition through the Lens of Scripture.* Resources for Changing Lives. Phillipsburg, N.J.: P&R, 2003.

———. *Speaking Truth in Love: Counsel in Community.* Greensboro, N.C.: New Growth Press, 2005.

———. "The Sufficiency of Scripture to Diagnose and Cure Souls." *The Journal of Biblical Counseling* 23, no. 2 (Spring 2005): 2–14.

———. "X-ray Questions: Drawing Out the Whys and Wherefores of Human Behavior." *Journal of Biblical Counseling* 18, no. 1 (Fall 1999): 2–9.

Prelock, Aaron R. "Disposition: An Approachable Ontology." *New Blackfriars* 103, no. 1108 (November 2022): 761–78.

———. "The Pastoral Disposition in the Thought of John Owen." PhD diss., VID Specialized University, 2020.

Rehnman, Sebastian. *Divine Discourse: The Theological Methodology of John Owen.* Texts and Studies in Reformation and Post-Reformation Thought. Grand Rapids: Baker Academic, 2002.

———. "Is the Narrative of Redemptive History Trichotomous or Dichotomous? A Problem for Federal Theology." *Dutch Review of Church History* 80, no. 3 (January 2000): 296–308.

Reinke, Tony. *12 Ways Your Phone Is Changing You.* Wheaton, Ill.: Crossway, 2017.

Renihan, Samuel D. *Deity and Decree.* Self-published, 2020.

———. *The Mystery of Christ, His Covenant, and His Kingdom.* Cape Coral, Fla.: Founders Press, 2019.

Sarles, Ken L. "The English Puritans: A Historical Paradigm of Biblical Counseling." In *Introduction to Biblical Counseling: A Basic Guide to the Principles and Practice of Counseling,* edited by John MacArthur, 23–37. Dallas: Word Books, 1994.

Saxton, David W. *God's Battle Plan for the Mind: The Puritan Practice of Biblical Meditation*. Grand Rapids: Reformation Heritage Books, 2015.

Schaff, Philip. *The Creeds of Christendom, with a History and Critical Notes*. Vol. 1, *The History of Creeds*. New York: Harper & Brothers, 1919.

Schwab, George M. "Critique of 'Habituation' as a Biblical Model of Change." *Journal of Biblical Counseling* 21, no. 2 (Winter 2003): 67–83.

Sibbes, Richard. *The Bruised Reed and Smoking Flax*. Edinburgh: Maclaren and Macniven, 1878.

Sire, James W. *Naming the Elephant: Worldview as a Concept*. 2nd ed. Downers Grove, Ill.: IVP Academic, 2015.

Smith, James K. A. *Cultural Liturgies*. 3 vols. Grand Rapids: Baker Academic, 2009–2017.

————. *You Are What You Love: The Spiritual Power of Habit*. Grand Rapids: Brazos Press, 2016.

Spence, Alan. *Incarnation and Inspiration: John Owen and the Coherence of Christology*. T & T Clark Theology. London: T & T Clark, 2007.

Sproul, R. C. *Are We Together?: A Protestant Analyzes Roman Catholicism*. Orlando, Fla.: Reformation Trust, 2012.

Stewart, Angus. "The Image of God in Man: A Reformed Reassessment (1)." *British Reformed Journal* 36 (Winter 2003): 22–31.

————. "The Image of God in Man: A Reformed Reassessment (2)." *British Reformed Journal* 37 (Spring 2003): 18–32.

————. "The Image of God in Man: A Reformed Reassessment (3)." *British Reformed Journal* 38 (Summer 2003): 21–34.

Tautges, Paul, and Steve Viars. "Sufficient for Life and Godliness." In *Scripture and Counseling: God's Word for Life in a Broken World*, edited by Bob Kellemen and Jeff Forrey, 47–61. Grand Rapids: Zondervan, 2014.

Thomas, Derek W. H. "John Owen and Spiritual-Mindedness: A Reflection on Reformed Spirituality." In *The Holy Spirit and Reformed Spirituality: A Tribute to Geoffrey Thomas*, edited by Joel R. Beeke and Derek W. H. Thomas, 127–37. Grand Rapids: Reformation Heritage Books, 2013.

Thomas, Geoffrey. *The Holy Spirit*. Grand Rapids: Reformation Heritage Books, 2011.

Toon, Peter. *God's Statesman: The Life and Work of John Owen*. Eugene, Ore.: Wipf and Stock, 2018.

Troxel, A. Craig. *With All Your Heart: Orienting Your Mind, Desires, and Will toward Christ.* Wheaton, Ill.: Crossway, 2020.

Trueman, Carl R. *The Claims of Truth: John Owen's Trinitarian Theology.* Carlisle, England: Paternoster Press, 1998.

———. *John Owen: Reformed Catholic, Renaissance Man.* Great Theologians. Aldershot, England: Ashgate, 2007.

———. "The Spirit and the Word Incarnate: John Owen's Trinitarian Christology." In *The Holy Spirit and Reformed Spirituality: A Tribute to Geoffrey Thomas*, edited by Joel R. Beeke and Derek W. H. Thomas, 29–38. Grand Rapids: Reformation Heritage Books, 2013.

Tweeddale, John W. "Living on Things Above: John Owen on Spiritual-Mindedness." In *The Beauty and Glory of Christian Living*, edited by Joel R. Beeke, 29–39. Grand Rapids: Reformation Heritage Books, 2014.

Veenhof, Jan. *Nature and Grace in Herman Bavinck.* Translated by Albert M. Wolters. Sioux Center, Iowa: Dordt College Press, 2006.

Viars, Steve, and Rob Green. "The Sufficiency of Scripture." In *Christ-Centered Biblical Counseling: Changing Lives with God's Changeless Truth*, edited by James MacDonald, Bob Kellemen, and Steve Viars, 89–105. Eugene, Ore.: Harvest House, 2013.

Vidu, Adonis. "Trinitarian Inseparable Operations and the Incarnation." *Journal of Analytic Theology* 4 (May 2016): 106–27.

Warfield, Benjamin B. "The Emotional Life of Our Lord." In *The Person and Work of Christ*, edited by Samuel G. Craig, 91–145. Philadelphia: P&R, 1950.

———. "The Human Development of Jesus." In *Selected Shorter Writings of Benjamin B. Warfield*, edited by John E. Meeter, 1:158–66. Phillipsburg, N.J.: P&R, 1980.

Warren, Tish Harrison. *Liturgy of the Ordinary: Sacred Practices in Everyday Life.* Downers Grove, Ill.: IVP Books, 2016.

Weaver, Noah J. "Grace Restores Nature: The Relationship of Nature and Grace in Christian Theology." *Puritan Reformed Journal* 9, no. 1 (January 2017): 65–83.

Welch, Edward. "How Theology Shapes Ministry: Jay Adams's View of the Flesh and an Alternative." *Journal of Biblical Counseling* 20, no. 3 (Spring 2002): 16–25.

Wellum, Stephen J. *God the Son Incarnate: The Doctrine of Christ.* Foundations of Evangelical Theology. Wheaton, Ill.: Crossway, 2016.

Westminster Assembly. *The Westminster Confession: The Confession of Faith, The Larger and Shorter Catechisms, The Directory for the Public Worship of God, with Associated Historical Documents.* Edinburgh: Banner of Truth, 2018.

Willis, E. David. *Calvin's Catholic Christology: The Function of the So-Called Extra Calvinisticum in Calvin's Theology.* Studies in Medieval and Reformation Thought 2, edited by Heiko A. Oberman. Leiden: Brill, 1967.

Wisse, Maarten, and Hugo Meijer. "Pneumatology: Tradition and Renewal." In *A Companion to Reformed Orthodoxy*, edited by Herman Selderhuis, 465–518. Brill's Companions to the Christian Tradition 40. Boston: Brill, 2013.

Wittman, Tyler R. "The End of the Incarnation: John Owen, Trinitarian Agency and Christology." *International Journal of Systematic Theology* 15, no. 3 (July 2013): 284–300.

Yuille, J. Stephen. *Puritan Spirituality: The Fear of God in the Affective Theology of George Swinnock.* Studies in Christian History and Thought. Eugene, Ore.: Wipf and Stock, 2008.

Index